"How vicious is the secular media's all-out assault on the Judeo-Christian underpinnings of America?

... It is ugly enough, and dishonest enough, and dangerous enough that a professed atheist has risen to Christianity's defense. One needn't agree with S. E. Cupp's views on religion (I don't) to admire her courage in writing *Losing Our Religion,* a terrific contribution to the much-needed national discussion."

—L. Brent Bozell III, founder and president, Media Research Center

"Knowing Americans' liberty is from God, not the government or the 'Groove Tube,' S. E. Cupp renders unto media what is media's: a reasoned, passionate, and precise skewering for its incessant campaign against people of faith."

—Rep. Thaddeus McCotter (R, MI)

"Using facts, intellect, wit, and charm, S. E. Cupp destroys the modern left's construct of Christian–as–Jerry Falwell clone. In *Losing Our Religion,* Cupp methodically proves how the mainstream media mocks, maligns, and marginalizes traditional values in the pursuit of creating a secular humanist politically correct hell on earth. And if you've been to Keith Olbermann's neighborhood recently, you'd know we're almost there."

—Andrew Breitbart

"Few people will do what S. E. Cupp does in *Losing Our Religion*— hold the liberal left and the liberal media accountable for the assault on our heritage and culture."

—Rep. Michele Bachmann (R, MN)

This title is also available as an ebook.

LOSING OUR RELIGION

WHY *the* LIBERAL MEDIA
WANT *to* TELL YOU
WHAT *to* THINK, WHERE *to* PRAY,
and HOW *to* LIVE

S. E. CUPP

THRESHOLD EDITIONS
NEW YORK   LONDON   TORONTO   SYDNEY

Threshold Editions
A Division of Simon & Schuster, Inc.
1230 Avenue of the Americas
New York, NY 10020

First Threshold Editions trade paperback edition April 2011

THRESHOLD EDITIONS and colophon are trademarks of Simon & Schuster, Inc.

For information about special discounts for bulk purchases,
please contact Simon & Schuster Special Sales at 1-866-506-1949
or business@simonandschuster.com.

The Simon & Schuster Speakers Bureau can bring authors to your live event. For more
information or to book an event contact the Simon & Schuster Speakers Bureau
at 1-866-248-3049 or visit our website at www.simonspeakers.com.

Designed by Aline C. Pace

Manufactured in the United States of America

10 9 8 7 6 5 4 3 2 1

ISBN 978-1-4391-7316-9
ISBN 978-1-4391-7644-3 (pbk)
ISBN 978-1-4391-7645-0 (ebook)

*This book is dedicated to all the men and women
serving in the military at home and overseas.
Thank you.*

Acknowledgments

Writing a book of this nature is simultaneously a lonely and communal process. I'd like first and foremost to thank my parents for their guidance, advice, support, and surprisingly adept editorial input.

A big hearty thanks also to my friends at Simon & Schuster: Mary Matalin, Louise Burke, Anthony Ziccardi, and particularly Abby Zidle, the best editor a girl could ask for. And thanks to my book agent, John Talbot, who's been a supportive (and hilarious) confidant.

Thanks to Governor Mike Huckabee, Newt Gingrich, Dinesh D'Souza, Martha Zoller, Kevin Madden, James T. Harris, and Kevin Williamson for their incredible contributions to this book.

Thanks to some brave and generous mentors who have been adventurous enough to do business with the likes of me: Sean Hannity, Tucker Carlson, Joshua Greenman, Greg Gutfeld, Bill Shulz, Andy Levy, Joshua McCarroll, Andrea Tantaros, Andrew Giangola, Howard Kurtz, Harvey Holmes, Chris Gonsalves, Chris Field, Mark Iwanicki, and Lynne Jordal Martin.

Thanks to family and friends who have lent me their constant support: the DePaolo family, the Miller family, the Cupp family, the Stanton family, the Payne family, and the Pincow family.

And thanks to my first religion teacher, Mrs. Hicks, who always indulged me in every wayward thought and presumptuous challenge I presented her with. I was a teenager then—please forgive me.

Contents

Foreword

Why on earth would I pen the foreword to a book written by a woman who is younger than some of my own children? Oh, did I mention it's a book about religion and the media but the book's author is not especially religious, and in fact could most charitably be called a "skeptic" when it comes to faith? We come not only from different generations, but from different worlds. So why would I bother?

The reason is simple—I like S. E. Cupp. I like her a lot. She is one of the smartest and most able communicators of reason and common sense in the country. She reaches a level of substance many writers twice and thrice her age only hope for, and she does it with style.

Losing Our Religion is a delightful read; it's sheer fun. She delivers the same sassy but classy perspective on some of today's most controversial issues in this book as she does on blogs, panels, and programs from college campuses to my own network, the Fox News Channel.

She does not rant and rave in a rabid "take no prisoners" approach, nor does she substitute volume for veracity and use hyperbole to thrash opponents in an entertaining but ineffective way. Instead, S. E. Cupp uses the sharp blade of careful research, thoughtful reasoning, and brilliant logic to dismember many of the sacred cows of today's liberalism and serve them up "well done" to the point of being charred. There's just enough spice in her stew to keep it interesting, flavorful, and appealing, but not so much as to make you reach for Pepcid when you've finished the read.

As a TV personality, S.E. has proven to be just provocative enough to keep it interesting, but doesn't slice and dice and create easy targets just to score on hapless leftists who don't see it coming. When she systematically exposes *Newsweek* for the embarrassingly diminished newsmagazine it has become, she cites example after example of how what was once a reliable read of political and cultural insight has become a bitter and laughable collection of left-wing literary lunacy. In her chapter about gay marriage, she undermines *NewsWEAK*'s religion writer Lisa Miller's fantasy about faith and the marriage issue by pointing out glaring examples of absurd conclusions and bias so blatant that it would make Maureen Dowd blush (if that were possible). I read the chapter on a plane and almost had to be restrained by the flight crew because I wanted to stand up and shout even though the "Fasten Seat Belt" sign was illuminated.

I recommend you fasten *your* seat belt as you read S.E.'s book, because she will rock your world with her chapter on evolution. With great skill and insight, she pushes back against the condescending contempt that the "swells" have bestowed upon the overwhelming majority of Americans who have the unmitigated gall to believe that the creation might in fact have a Creator. She doesn't get out a Bible and beat you over the head with it, but simply shows that some form of intelligent design is entirely plausible. Her goal is not to persuade the reader to adopt a particular point of view, but rather to recognize how glaringly dishonest it is for the minority to force dunce caps on those who hold to a view allowing for or adhering to the notion of creation involving a God. It will have churchgoers saying, "Amen, Praise the Lord, and Glory Hallelujah."

Even when discussing the very sensitive topic of abortion, S.E. brilliantly deconstructs the way the Left manipulates polling data as they cling to the notion that Americans as a whole think it's perfectly acceptable to terminate a life because it's inconvenient. She shows how "progressive" Democratic champions of abortion have been leading us on this grisly trail of disregard for humanity while showing more compassion for baby seals or crustaceans than for human infants. She even exposes an impressive list of Democratic officials who have "evolved" (or DE-volved) from staunch pro-lifers to the politically correct view of "choice" in the past sixty years.

The thoughtfully documented case *Losing Our Religion* makes for commonsense conservatism will irritate the daylights out of the elite establishment, including some Republicans who will squirm at the idea that we won't be a better party by abandoning core principles and imitating Democrats. But with bright, intellectual, and savvy young talent like S. E. Cupp, I am not so worried about the future of the Republican Party or the conservative movement. She can more than hold her own with the best of "them," and in a battle of wits, I would place my bet on her to win, not just to place or show.

While I don't pretend to be a prophet in biblical terms, I will make this prediction—you *are* going to like this book. And you're going to like S. E. Cupp as well. In fact, you're going to like her a lot.

Mike Huckabee

LOSING OUR RELIGION

INTRODUCTION:
THE REVOLUTION IS ALL AROUND YOU

Fidel Castro once said, "I began a revolution with eighty-two men. If I had to do it again, I'd do it with ten or fifteen and absolute faith. It does not matter how small you are if you have faith and plan of action."

Faith and plan of action: Neither is lacking in the revolution being waged here in America, right now, against you. Rest assured, the revolutionaries have an endless supply of faith and a detailed, comprehensive plan of action.

And that plan is unfolding in every American small town, and in every American big city, on the coasts and in the heartland, in schools and in libraries, on television and on the radio, in the halls of power and on the sidewalks of Main Street. It is everywhere, and it is not going away.

And now, with careful, covert nudges from the Obama administration, the revolution that began decades ago has gained unprecedented momentum. In a matter of just a few years, the revolution could be over, successfully won, and most of you will be left scratching your heads, wondering what just happened to everything you thought you knew and held sacred. Very soon, it will be too late.

This revolution is political, certainly. But it's more complicated than that. Like the revolutions of Castro and Mao Zedong and Stalin, this revolution is not just about power, it's also about knowledge. And, like most revolutions, this one makes particularly shrewd use of propaganda.

This revolution isn't led by the proletariat, or by the struggling and exploited masses held under the oppressive thumb of a power-hungry dictator. It's not led by the students or the workers or the bourgeoisie. Yet this revolution is, without a doubt, a class war.

This revolution does not require an army. It does not need guns or ammunition, bombs or missiles, surveillance or spy networks. It does not require its revolutionaries to dress in uniform, or to huddle in foxholes. Frankly, it doesn't even require them to leave their desks.

If this sounds ominous, it is. And it's much worse than you think.

This revolution, already in full throttle around the country, is being waged against you and me and every other American, and its goal is simple: to overthrow God, and silence Christian America for good.

If you think that has nothing to do with you, you're wrong. Whether you join the 90 percent of the country that believes or stand with the 10 percent of the country that does not is incidental. No matter what you believe, and how fervently you believe it, this particular war on God, just the latest in a string of them since the Enlightenment, is a war against *all* Americans—religious, atheist, and secular—not because of whom it targets, but because of who's behind it.

The revolutionaries are not in the White House, nor are they in the state house, though they often work in concert and toward similar goals. The revolutionaries are people you see and hear every day. They are people you trust. They are the people you rely on to tell you what to wear, what to buy, what to drive, what to watch, what to listen to, what to read, where to live, where to visit, where to eat, whom to like, whom to hate, whom to help, when to go outside, when to stay indoors, when to shop, when to save, what to think, what to believe.

The revolutionaries are in the media.

The people you trust to be fair, accurate, objective, and insightful, the so-called watchdogs of the state, protectors of truth, gatekeepers and guardians of freedom, are the very revolutionaries out to shame, mock, subvert, pervert, corrupt, debase, and extinguish your beliefs, the beliefs of the vast majority of Americans, and the values upon which this country was founded. They're doing the one thing they are never supposed to do: They're taking sides. For the great majority, this is problematic enough. But even for the minority—non-Christians and nonbelievers—this means that their guardians of truth are being dishonest, wholly subjective, and, frankly, un-American. Targeting faith is targeting Democracy, and that's something that should make every American deeply concerned for the future.

Poet Gil Scott-Heron said that "the revolution will not be televised." He was wrong. The revolution is not only on television, but on the radio, on the internet, in newspapers and magazines. It is being blasted over the airwaves, splashed across the front pages of every paper, screamed about online. The revolution to overthrow Christian America, to marginalize it to the fringes, to force it out of the mainstream to the far corners of the earth, is being led by reporters, writers, columnists, editors, pundits, producers, critics, and publishers all over the country—people who are, laughably and totally inaccurately, still referred to as the "mainstream media."

As Edmund Burke said after the French Revolution, gazing upon the press gallery of the House of Commons, "Yonder sits the Fourth

Estate, and they are more important than them all." He was only half right. The watchdogs need watchdogs of their own, as it turns out. Oscar Wilde knew this when he wrote "The Soul of Man Under Socialism" in 1891. "At the present moment, it really is the only estate. It has eaten up the other three. The Lords Temporal say nothing, the Lords Spiritual have nothing to say, and the House of Commons has nothing to say and says it. We are dominated by journalism."

Indeed, freedom of the press has morphed into power of the press. Assuring its freedom was originally born out of an urgency to protect these important watchdogs from the wrath of a controlling colonial government, giving it the power to criticize authority without retribution, to tell the truth without fear of imprisonment. Now, however, the press has become a political and ideological tool of oppression itself. Instead of watching the state, it is watching you. The press has become so politicized, so self-aware, and so power-hungry that the careful application of objectivity—or even opinion—is no longer the rule but the very rare exception. In short, these people can no longer be trusted.

Your news is filtered through an entirely subjective system of biases and prejudices that look not only to inform your views, but to guide them in one particular direction: left. But the liberalism of the press is only half the story. Less often discussed is its *secularism*, but in recent years the mainstream media has begun to reveal its particular antipathy for Christianity with more and more confidence.

Why does this matter? Because it puts democracy itself in the crosshairs in three very important ways. One, in targeting Christians the media is targeting the majority of Americans, which actually makes the attack all the more difficult to see and contain. Majorities make the mistake of feeling invincible by sheer volume, until one day, that majority wakes up and realizes that its entire way of life has changed while it was busy doing other things. The beauty of American democracy is that the minority is given a voice. The minority is protected by the legal system, special-interest groups, and especially by the media—and rightly so. But the majority, often considered generally satisfied and healthy by default, can go overlooked if it is not vigilant and proactive. What special-interest group is assigned to protect the majority? What's the majority version of the ACLU or the Anti-Defamation League? Who's looking out for hate crimes against 80 percent of the country? What watchdog organization is monitoring slander and libel against nearly everyone? Targeting the majority is nothing short of tyranny—the soft tyranny of minority bias.

Two, in unfairly targeting Christians and propagating untruths against them, the media has broken its promise to be fair and objective. Last, the opinion media, by spewing ugly invective against Christians, has forsaken the dignity, decency, and tolerance that once held our communities together—instead, it is driving them apart. All of this means that the mainstream press no longer deserves the privilege of controlling the conversation.

To address this threat I want to present five crucial tenets that form the backbone of our revolution against the mainstream media. These tenets make up a covenant—one that the mainstream media used to understand and respect. In the past decade we haven't become any less Christian (despite the media's insistence that we have) nor have we become any less democratic. So the media's decision to target Christian America is not a response to changing social mores. Rather, it is a deliberate effort to change them. The media isn't covering the story, it's creating it. By ignoring those tenets—indeed, by trampling on them—the media is telegraphing the following:

1. The Judeo-Christian values that form the basis of American democracy should be overthrown entirely—because a minuscule disgruntled minority finds them objectionable.
2. Religious tolerance is crucial to the success and health of any democracy—but not when it is applied to the vast majority.

3. A robust, fair, and objective press is better for freedom than a hostile, biased, and corrupt one—but not if being objective competes with the media's ideological impulses.

4. The spokespeople for our culture should commend good works, not mock them—unless those good works are being done by Christians.

5. Civility and decency are disposable commodities when the values of the citizenry compete with the secular values of the press.

And now the media has a willing accomplice in rewriting these crucial tenets of democracy.

After spending eight years railing against the Bush administration for Bush's Christianity, and, by proxy, against all Christians, the media abandoned any pretense of objectivity to help usher in a new ideological era under Barack Obama, who represented not only a chance for the kind of radical liberalism most of the media elite espouses, but also a chance for the kind of secularism it regularly promotes. Raised by atheists, uncomfortable with Christ, disconnected from evangelical America, and perceived as "too smart" to be "too religious," Obama offered an easy, convenient, anemic Christianity that was just what the liberal media wanted: totally opportunistic and entirely insincere.

Working in tandem, the Obama administration and the liberal media are strategically and surgically singling out American Christianity for extinction, and the very nature of this symbiotic relationship means that the two organisms take their cues from each other. Under Bush, the media was on its own. Under Obama, it has a willing accomplice in its distortion of the national discourse. With the president and his administration behind this vicious attack on faith, the media is being encouraged in unprecedented ways to target the values that built this country and continue to make it great.

The liberal media's portrayal of Christians as fanatics gave Obama the license to accuse them of bitterly clinging to religion. Likewise, Obama's decision to forgo a National Day of Prayer, cover up Jesus' name during a speech at Georgetown, and cancel a military flyover at "God and Country Day" gave the liberal media license to ignore, mock, and condescend to Christians in their columns, their commentary, and even in objective news reports themselves. In neither of these cases, however, does Obama or the liberal press that supports him represent mainstream opinion. The country is 80 percent Christian. That's not fringe. That's the majority.

Christians have been appropriately outraged by numerous offenses during Obama's short time in office, and by a political and cultural agenda that is clearly informed by socialist tenets. His nod to nonbelievers in his inaugural address, his continued confidence in the superiority of science over faith, his affinity for radical Marxist theology, all have conservative Christians worried. But Christians have been noticeably absent in their outrage at the media, which is frankly far more influential than any president could be alone.

The media is everywhere, after all—in school libraries, in classrooms, maybe in the elevators of your office building. It's on the televisions in airports and bars, on the radio in stores and taxis, on your computers and on your cell phones. Yet Christians, regularly the targets of a vitriolic and intolerant mainstream press, continue to watch MSNBC and CNN, continue to buy *Newsweek* and *Time* magazine, continue to subscribe to the *New York Times,* continue to click on the Huffington Post and Salon.com, somehow either able to separate these attacks from the news they are hoping to get, or maybe just unaware of them entirely. They are unaware because for so long they took it for granted that faith—the bedrock of American values—was protected and cherished. Not anymore.

One might say that Christian America has been practically complicit in this unraveling of the Judeo-Christian fabric of American democracy—or at the very least, complacent about it. The media attacks your churches, your towns, your values, your politics, your families, your livelihoods, your economic status, and your intelligence on a regular basis, and yet the outrage is reserved only for the media's rank liberalism. Liberalism and secularism may complement each other, but they are not the same. It's time Christian America woke up to the cold reality that the liberal media is waging war on you—and it's winning.

Its tactics are predictable and time-tested. Way back in 1784, Immanuel Kant, in response to the Reverend Johann Friedrich Zollner's question "What is Enlightenment?" wrote "Enlightenment is man's emergence from his self-incurred immaturity." This was Kant's condescending way of saying "reason is for smart people and religion is for idiots." Of course, Kant's views were shared by such luminaries as Karl Marx and the Marquis de Sade.

Today's Kants and Marxes and de Sades are far less eloquent, but they are still making a living by making fun of religious people. Every time Keith Olbermann calls pro-lifers "Christian jihadists," or Chris Matthews says Sarah Palin's faith isn't "normal," or Katie Couric calls Christian values "repugnant," or the *New York Times* says Christianity is "hypocritical," or Bill Maher says religion is a "neurological disorder," this should make Christians—and all Americans—really, really angry. Unlike the juggernaut that is Fox News, the ratings and circulations of liberal outlets are tanking, thanks to a wholehearted abandonment of objectivity during the 2008 presidential election. But if these media outlets are going to speak primarily to the secular and atheist elite fringes of American society, they should be marginalized to the fringes of the media as well. And instead they are marginalizing *you*, the majority.

The secularism and anti-Christian bias of the political left has been examined ad nauseam. But the media's explicit role in this power play has been largely ignored. Now more than ever, because the halls of power in Washington are smoothing the media's way, Christian America needs to get wise to this attack before Judeo-Christian values, which is to say *American* values, are relegated to a hush-hush subculture unable to operate in the open without fear of retribution and censorship.

This book is a first step toward that end. My intention here is to systematically expose the mainstream media's overt hostility toward Christian America, with a focus on the past decade and a specific eye toward just the last few years, in which I feel the rhetoric has grown infinitely bolder. This is not a survey of the history of media—it is ripped from the headlines, and current by design, to reflect the urgency of the media's disastrous state. Nor is it a sweeping historical account of religious or Christian persecution in America, which has been well documented. This project concentrates on American Christianity now, as it is portrayed in the press.

It is important to examine not just the big networks, or the biggest newspapers, or a handful of popular magazines. The media has evolved in such significant ways over the past decade that the threat of Christian marginalization has grown exponentially. Online magazines like Salon.com and the Huffington Post are important sources of news and opinion, both because of their ready accessibility and because of the perceived edginess of their content. They are speaking directly to the next generation in ways that the musty pages of the *Washington Post* or staid panel discussions of the McLaughlin Group cannot. Furthermore, these smaller outlets take their cues directly from the bigger ones, such as the *New York Times* and CNN and *Newsweek*. While we weren't looking, online magazines and even a number of bloggers became a significant part of the mainstream media, with the page hits, budgets, and influence to match. Reporters for online media have regular seats among the White House press corps. Their views may be fringe, but their impact is not.

I will address both news media (reporting) and opinion media (commentary). They serve different purposes, to be sure, and as such they are held to different standards. But to exempt columnists and commentators from scrutiny would be to ignore the fact that many try to wear both hats at once, and would suggest that it's okay for someone like MSNBC's Rachel Maddow to call you a terrorist and still be included under the all-encompassing and very forgiving "mainstream media" umbrella. Hers is not a mainstream view, and we should truthfully acknowledge as much.

This book is not, to be clear, an argument for censorship of any kind. As an opinion writer and commentator myself, I believe that censoring these ideas, painful though they are to read and hear, would do far more damage to democracy than airing them. But it is an attempt to redefine what counts as "mainstream." That a media outlet is well known, well funded, or really, really old doesn't mean it represents the mainstream anymore. Middle America is more accurately spoken for by the *Christian Examiner* than it is by the *New York Times,* yet we all still pretend that the *Times* represents good, thoughtful journalism, the kind Edward R. Murrow would be proud of.

Finally, a personal note in the interest of full disclosure. I am an atheist. I have been an atheist for fifteen years. And so my approach to this book insofar as it is a defense of Christianity is not one from within the structure but from outside of it. I'm not propping up a particular faith because it is my own, but instead because I believe in those five important tenets—that Judeo-Christian values, religious tolerance, an objective press, the benevolence of Christianity, and civility and decency make for a better American democracy.

These fundamental elements of our democracy are all in jeopardy. This issue is deeply important to me, and it should be important to you, whether you're Christian, Jewish, Muslim, Buddhist, atheist, humanist, or Wiccan. What matters is that we're all Americans, and we should all want to protect our singularly spectacular democracy. I'm hopeful that my defense of Christianity against a hostile media will be more effective *because* I'm a nonbeliever, and not in spite of it.

As for the revolution, well, it's already begun. We're now deep in the midst of the mainstream media's all-out assault on Christian America, Christian values, and Christian conservatism.

It's not too late. It wasn't all that long ago that the *New York Times* was urging the country to pray for the astronauts of the Apollo 13 mission on its front page. Or that KNBC was signing off its broadcast night after Johnny Carson and then the *Tomorrow* show with the sermonette "Let Us Pray" and the Navy Prayer. Or that *Time* magazine's examination of the "God is Dead" theological movement provoked an uproar among the nation's faithful.

But the situation is dire. When *Newsweek* devoted its 2009 Easter issue to a cover story announcing "The Decline and Fall of Christian America," only a small but vocal minority objected, despite the story's misleading statistics and analysis methods.

Mao Zedong said, "Revolution is not a dinner party, not an essay, nor a painting, nor a piece of embroidery; it cannot be advanced softly, gradually, carefully, considerately, respectfully, politely, plainly, and modestly."

The liberal media already knows this. It's advancing its own secular revolution against you loudly, quickly, haphazardly, viciously, impolitely, duplicitously, and openly.

What about your revolution? Remember, all it takes is faith and plan of action.

I

THOU SHALT NOT WORSHIP FALSE IDOLS (BUT *AMERICAN IDOL* IS FINE)

Worship is, in this country, both a public and a private act of devotion. While many Americans pray privately in their homes, around a dinner table, or before they go to bed, they also worship publicly, in church, at their places of business, on the athletic field, at their local soup kitchen, and, for many, every time they say the Pledge of Allegiance or sing the National Anthem.

But worship of any kind, private or public, gets religious America into serious hot water with the liberal media, which has come to mock and resent public displays of faith, or any acknowledgment of God or religion by the state. The mere suggestion that the country is in fact a Christian one is declared backward, dangerous, and heretical to the Constitution of the United States.

Christmas and Christian holidays, prayer, public references to biblical scripture, the Ten Commandments, "In God We Trust," one nation "under God," "God Bless America"—it's all now subject to ridicule and scrutiny by the liberal press, which has decided, without consulting the citizens of our country (80 percent of whom are Christian), that it's no longer seemly or appropriate to worship out loud. Their collective distaste for displays of Christian devotion has grown from mild to maniacal in less than a decade, despite the fact that the Christian population in the United States has grown from 159,514,000 to 173,402,000 between 2001 and 2008.[1]

To be clear, the liberal media has no problem with worship—as long as it's secular. The media worships a great many false idols in its daily broadcasts, front-page stories, news segments, and online features. The liberal media worships Hollywood and celebrity, breathlessly fawning over Angelina Jolie's every inconsequential gesticulation or Lindsay Lohan's less-than-shocking crimes and misdemeanors, or the latest castoff on the 147th *The Bachelor*. It worships its political demagogues, such as John F. Kennedy, Bill Clinton, Al Gore, and Barack Obama, and takes turns propping them up on pedestals so that you may worship them, too. It worships liberalism and all its causes célèbres, such as environmentalism, gay marriage, abortion, and, the ACLU's newest pet cause, jihadi rights. And, of course, it worships itself, with flashy correspondence dinners, magazine parties, self-satisfying award ceremonies, and giddy self-promotion. During the presidential election, CNN called itself "the best political team on television" as many as fifty times . . . in a single day.

But worship God? That's something else entirely. Not only has the liberal media seemingly stripped the word from its lexicon, but when it does bring it up it's to mock believers or champion the cause

---

1.   Barry A. Kosmin and Ariela Keysar, "American Religious Identification Survey (ARIS) 2008" (PDF). Hartford, Conn.: Trinity College, 2009.

of the angry atheist, who, the media promises us, represents the new majority opinion about God and faith—that faith should be banished to the far corners of the earth (Alaska would suffice) so that it is spoken of only in hushed tones in one's own bedroom. You know, like porn.

As a result of the liberal media's relentless efforts to shame God to a place on the dusty bottom shelf of modern American civilization, it seems that we now have a president who is taking direct cues from the media's vow of silence. And for that gift, the gift of God-omission, the liberal media rewards President Obama with positive coverage. Sure as the sun rises and sets, the cycle repeats.

OBAMA DEMOTES CHRISTIANITY, LIBERAL MEDIA REJOICES

Obama's first year in office was marked by the kinds of slaps to the faithful that we usually see only during an episode of *Real Time with Bill Maher*. But they were actually foreshadowed in a speech he gave in San Francisco on the campaign trail, in which he said, "You go into these small towns in Pennsylvania and, like a lot of small towns in the Midwest, the jobs have been gone now for twenty-five years and nothing's replaced them. And it's not surprising, then, they get bitter, they cling to guns or religion or antipathy to people who aren't like them or anti-immigrant sentiment or antitrade sentiment as a way to explain their frustrations."

The comment was shocking both for its sheer stupidity—how did that get past his campaign managers when he was going to the Pennsylvania primary just days later?—and for its alarming classism. Religious Americans bristled at the notion that tough economic times make them "cling" to anything, let alone their faith. And they took particular issue with the idea that "antipathy to people who aren't like them," "anti-immigrant sentiment," and "antitrade sentiment" were somehow equatable with religious devotion. At this moment, which Democratic challenger Hillary Clinton and Republican challenger John McCain both seized on readily, Obama seemed to reveal at best a lack of understanding of American faith, and at worst a real disdain for it. In short, he was in perfect lockstep with the liberal media.

So when he eventually became President Obama, the many continued indiscretions that would follow were swept quietly under the carpet by the liberal press, which saw in him a kindred secular spirit who wouldn't bore them with God references every other minute like the last guy did. "Finally," they sighed, "a president who is just as uncomfortable with public worship as we are."

And on the very day he was sworn in, Obama delivered another slight to religious America when he became the first president in the history of the United States to mention atheists, calling America a nation of, among other things, nonbelievers. He would, over the course of his first year, go on to regularly put nonbelievers on the same plane as the religious faithful. This isn't just an insult to believers. It should also be an insult to nonbelievers, who so militantly insist they are separate from those kooky God lovers, and intellectually superior to them. Lumping atheists into a group of so-called religious fanatics should be the last thing they want. But it's also an inaccurate comparison. Equating belief with nonbelief is equating apples and oranges. One implies a moral value system, the other is marked explicitly by the lack of one. That doesn't mean nonbelievers are immoral, of course, but it does mean they are structurally and intrinsically different entities. The president may as well acknowledge Beatles fans and dog lovers in the same breath if he's going to acknowledge nonbelievers, for they have as much to do with American values as atheism does.

For that inaugural nod, the country's self-avowed atheists—all 1.6 percent of them—rejoiced, and the liberal media was there to help them celebrate. Steven Waldman wrote of American atheists in the Huffington Post: "Not surprisingly, they greeted Obama's inaugural declaration with some surprise and joy." Waldman then quoted Ed Buckner of American Atheists as saying, "In his Inaugural Address today, President Barack Obama finally did what many before him should have done, rightly citing the great diversity of Americans as part of the nation's great strength and including 'non-believers' in that mix. His mother would have been proud, and so are we."[2]

Greg M. Epstein, Harvard University's humanist chaplain (yes, apparently that's a real post), similarly gushed in his *Washington Post* column, "I too was pleasantly surprised to see the President return, after a bit of wandering in recent months, to his previous practice of extending a rhetorical hand to my community in his oratory. As reiterated by my colleagues in the American Humanist Association's recent ad campaign, Obama is the proud product of 'parenting beyond belief'—his strong relationship with his Humanist mother S. Ann Dunham makes him living proof that family values without religion build character."[3]

It seemed that, despite Barack Obama's careful insistence during the campaign that he was a devoted Christian, with a simple mention of nonbelievers in his inaugural address atheists were ready to claim him as one of their own—he was living proof that being raised an atheist made him a better person!

And, in case anyone thinks the mention of atheists was a thoughtless or casual inclusion, David Axelrod, his senior adviser, admitted that Obama personally inserted the nonbeliever references into his inaugural speech.[4]

2. Steven Waldman, "Obama Touches the Untouchables: Non-Believers," Huffington Post, Jan. 20, 2009.
3. Greg M. Epstein, "Nonbelievers Are Believers Too," *Washington Post*, Jan. 23, 2009.
4. Laura Meckler, "Obama Walks Religious Tightrope Spanning Faithful, Nonbelievers," *Wall Street Journal*, March 24, 2009.

WAIT, WHERE DID JESUS GO?

The nonbeliever mention was just the beginning of Obama's courtship of the liberal press, notoriously averse to God-talk.

In April 2009, Obama gave a major address on the economy at Georgetown University, a private Catholic college in Washington, D.C. After the address it was discovered that the White House advance team had asked the school to remove or cover all religious imagery and signage, specifically a monogram symbolizing Jesus' name in Gaston Hall, where Obama spoke. The school did, in fact, cover the monogram with a piece of black-painted plywood.

The incident caused an uproar among Catholics, who denounced both the Obama administration for making such a demand and the school for conceding. Why did the president choose to speak at the Catholic school if he was going to insist on hiding its religious nature?

Bill Donohue, president of the Catholic League, criticized Obama for asking the school to "neuter itself." "No bishop who might speak at the White House would ever request that a crucifix be displayed behind him," he said.[5]

For America's Christians, it read as though Obama was uncomfortable with religion, or at the very least wished to dissociate himself from it. Religion scholars of all kinds dissected the moment, interpreting it as a fairly significant one in the president's first few months.

But, unsurprisingly, there were no mentions of the odd request in the *New York Times, Boston Globe,* CNN.com, *USA Today, L.A. Times,* or any other major newspaper or online news outlet. For the liberal media, it either didn't happen or didn't matter.

5. Foxnews.com, "Georgetown University Hid Religious Symbols at White House Request," April 16, 2009.

Newsweek did pick up the story online, but presumptuously assured readers it was no big deal in a short post called "Obama at Georgetown: WWJD?" "It's not that unusual a request," wrote an omniscient Holly Bailey in the article. "The White House usually prefers to have flags and a plain backdrop behind Obama when he speaks."[6]

The obvious response is, of course, then he shouldn't speak at an institution where religious imagery is literally nailed to the walls.

But besides that, it's simply untrue. When he spoke to the NAACP, he spoke in front of their insignia. When he gave a speech on the stimulus in Washington, D.C., he spoke in front of a U.S. Department of Energy sign. When he spoke in Ghana, he stood in front of a Ghanaian medallion and Kente cloths. All of this is entirely appropriate—the White House doesn't require every host venue to undergo an Extreme Home Makeover so that the president can speak there on camera.

So why the cover-up at Georgetown? This would become one of many instructive and revealing moments of Obama's first year that proved just how incomplete his understanding of American faith actually is. Presumably, he believed that the mere choice of Georgetown as a venue would make him appear comfortable with his Catholic constituents, and that covering its religious insignia would please his secular ones. Christian America didn't buy it. Unsurprisingly, the liberal media did.

Many liberal media outlets that covered his speech at Georgetown highlighted Obama's use of Christian allegory within the speech as proof that he could connect with the public through faith, entirely ignoring the fact that he had demanded all religious iconography be covered up or removed.

The *L.A. Times*, the *Boston Globe*, and NPR were just a few of the

---

6. Holly Bailey, "Obama at Georgetown: WWJD?" Newsweek.com, April 17, 2009.

outlets that covered the speech from this angle. The *Washington Post's* Dan Froomkin was positively glowing: "At the heart of a forceful speech delivered at Georgetown University, Obama placed powerful biblical imagery from Jesus's Sermon on the Mount, likening the boom-and-bust economy he inherited to a house built on sand and the future US economy he is working toward one built on a rock."[7]

In that one sentence we get Froomkin's vantage point—our economic woes were caused by George W. Bush, Obama's speech was brilliant, and his use of religious rhetoric to describe them means he is connecting with the common folk. After all, the opiate of the masses, when it is politically expedient and makes their guy look good, is just fine. This, despite eight years the media spent bemoaning every mention of God or the Bible by Bush. Who do they think they're kidding?

NATIONAL DAY OF . . . WHATEVER

In May, the president once again ruffled feathers when he decided not to attend the festivities on the National Day of Prayer, which is usually acknowledged with some fanfare by sitting presidents. He skipped a formal early morning service and did not attend a large Catholic prayer breakfast the next morning.

The snub was hardly insignificant. The National Day of Prayer was called by the first Continental Congress in 1775 when it asked the colonies to pray for the future of the nation. In 1952, President Truman signed a joint resolution by Congress declaring an annual national day of prayer, and in 1988 the law was amended by President Reagan to permanently set the day as the first Thursday of every May. Every year the president signs a proclamation encouraging all

---

7.   Dan Froomkin, "Obama Connects Most of the Dots," *Washington Post,* April 14, 2009.

Americans to pray. Since 1789 there have been 134 national calls to prayer by the president of the United States, and Gerald Ford and George H. W. Bush each signed two proclamations in one year in response to particularly challenging moments in history. Past presidents have celebrated in numerous ways, by attending religious services, with prayer breakfasts, and by giving speeches.

But when Obama decided to forgo the day entirely, the brushoff got very little national media coverage. There was nothing in *Newsweek*, nothing in the *Washington Post* by nonopinion columnists, and nothing in the *New York Times*.

CNN reported the story with carefully chosen words: "Obama Tones Down National Day of Prayer Observance."[8] The headline is, of course, misleading—he didn't merely tone it down, he skipped it altogether. His spokesperson Robert Gibbs said he would pray privately, which was naturally his right, but why does a public acknowledgment of the day preclude private acknowledgment—couldn't he do both? Out of respect for the religious majority, shouldn't he do both?

Other liberal news outlets, once again, chose to highlight another part of the story—that Obama would sign the proclamation that day. MSNBC's headline was "Obama Signs Day of Prayer Proclamation,"[9] and *USA Today* and others followed suit. For them, skipping the National Day of Prayer wasn't the lead story. Signing the proclamation was.

To be clear, signing the proclamation is no show of faith—it's required by law. Nonetheless, that very act was problematic for MSNBC's Rachel Maddow, who unleashed her wrath on the heretical moment on her May 7 show: "In a country founded in part so that

---

8. Kristi Keck, "Obama Tones Down National Day of Prayer Observance," CNN.com, May 6, 2009.

9. Associated Press, "Obama Signs Day of Prayer Proclamation," MSNBC.com, May 7, 2009.

religion would be a private matter for every citizen, in a country in which the government is constitutionally prohibited from endorsing any particular religious observation over any other, or even endorsing the idea of having a religion over not having a religion, having an official, legal National Day of Prayer in America has always been a little awkward. But religious forces have long been powerful here and have long sought to yoke the power of the state to particular forms of religious expression."[10]

In addition to sounding downright paranoid, Maddow also got a few things wrong. The country was certainly *not* founded "so that religion would be a private matter for every citizen." The country was founded on a principle of freedom *of* religion, not freedom *from* religion, and of course the Constitution's free-exercise clause states that Congress can't "prohibit the free exercise" of religious practice. It does not require the faithful to practice privately—in fact the Founding Fathers wrote the freedom of religion clauses as a direct rebellion against the persecution of believers. Quarantining worship to secret, closed-door meetings was the last thing they had in mind.

The National Day of Prayer *doesn't* endorse any particular religion, as Maddow suggests. It recognizes all religions and is strictly nondenominational. What it doesn't recognize is nonbelievers, that group of less than 2 percent who seemed so pleased to finally get a nod from a sitting president. But Maddow can rest easy—the National Day of Prayer doesn't mandate that atheists take to their knees. No prayer police will come to their houses in the dark of night and force them to use a rosary or read from the Koran. Really, what's the big deal?

And the National Day of Prayer, in existence since 1775, hasn't "always been a little awkward." It may be awkward for Maddow, but the majority of the country—a majority that is unequivocally religious—would disagree.

---

10.   Rachel Maddow, *The Rachel Maddow Show*, MSNBC, May 7, 2009.

As proof that the National Day of Prayer has no place in American politics, and that even the Founding Fathers thought so, Maddow borrowed a couple of Wikipedia passages suggesting that Thomas Jefferson and James Madison weren't big fans, and selectively quoted from them to make that assertion actually seem accurate. But she forgot to copy the other verses on the Wikipedia page, which relayed John Adams's views, Abraham Lincoln's views, and Benjamin Franklin's views, all of which were that the national call to prayer was, well, a pretty nice idea.

For the liberal media, Obama's prayer-day no-show was proof that he had either paid just the right amount of respect to America's religious population, or, at least for Maddow, a little too much. For the nation's believers, it was a significant slight.

And another was right behind it.

NO FLYOVER COUNTRY

In July 2009, for the first time in the forty-two-year history of the "God and Country Rally" in Idaho, the Pentagon denied a request for a military flyover. Held every year, the event honors the spiritual fabric of the country and the men and women who serve it, but this year, the first under the Obama administration, the rally was told it was too "Christian" to get a flyover. Rally director Patti Syme was shocked and disappointed, having had no problems in previous years. Local attendees to the annual rally were also confused—the event was non-denominational and the flyovers a long-standing American tradition.

Earlier in the year, incidentally, the Pentagon also stopped the practice of including a Bible quotation on the cover page of daily intelligence briefings it sends to the White House. But neither that nor the flyover denial got any play in the liberal media. There was nothing in the *New York Times, Newsweek,* the *Washington Post,*

MSNBC.com, CNN.com, the *Boston Globe*, ABCNews.com, *USA Today*, or any other major news outlet—except for Fox News.

But the Huffington Post did publish a column by Chris Rodda, the senior research director of something called the Military Religious Freedom Foundation, and, unrelatedly I'm sure, the author of "Liars for Jesus." For MRFF, which had already successfully campaigned to stop the Pentagon from sending Bibles to soldiers in Iraq, the move was finally the recognition that this special-interest group had been waiting for: "So, while those who seek to use the U.S. military to inseparably combine religion with patriotism might find the Pentagon's decision 'deeply troubling and disturbing' and will certainly get a lot of mileage out of this decision to spread the notion that the Obama administration is bent on 'crushing' religion, we at MRFF see it as a good sign that, under our new commander in chief, the Department of Defense might just finally be starting to obey its own regulations."[11]

The *New York Times* covered the MRFF's 2009 lawsuit against the military alleging that it forced religious practice on soldiers. The paper also covered MRFF's lawsuit against the Air Force, alleging a commander sent an email to his air personnel that directed them to an inspirational story on a Catholic website. And it covered MRFF's 2007 suit against the Defense Department on behalf of an atheist soldier who felt he was forced to attend prayer meetings. It seems the Military Religious Freedom Foundation has a direct line to the *New York Times*.

For the liberal media, God is out and atheism is most definitely in.

The so-called mainstream media's version of faith, which Obama seems to share, is essentially "Keep it to yourself, and we'll get along just fine." It's quite literally the "Don't Ask, Don't Tell" of the Obama

---

11.   Chris Rodda, "MRFF Congratulates Obama Administration and US Air Force for Doing the Right Thing," Huffington Post, July 6, 2009.

administration. That mantra is reflected in every adoring piece of press coverage Obama actually gets that deals with faith. The liberal media either praises him for his silence or exalts him for some pseudosecular act it claims is actually one of devotion. Case in point was *US News & World Report*'s 2009 list of the "10 Most Important Obama Faith Moments," compiled only one hundred days into office. The list was bewildering at best, and downright insulting at worst.

The lead-in to the list was *US News*'s dubious claim that "Barack Obama has embraced faith in a more visible way than any other president in recent memory." Apparently, for this magazine, just saying something makes it so. The list went as follows:

1. Rick Warren's Inauguration Day Invocation
2. Granting First TV Interview to Arabic Language Network
3. Reversing Mexico City Policy on Family Planning Providers Abroad
4. Opening Rallies With Prayer
5. Launching White House Office of Faith-Based and Neighborhood Partnerships
6. Convening a Faith Advisory Council
7. Joe Biden's Receiving Ashes on Ash Wednesday
8. Lifting Restrictions on Federally Funded Embryonic Stem Cell Research
9. Announcing Plans to Give Notre Dame's Commencement Address
10. Speaking to Muslim World From Turkey[12]

As any rational person could tell you, there isn't much on that list that constitutes a genuine "moment." And worse, almost every item is something George W. Bush did also—and was excoriated for. Bush gave interviews to Arabic-language networks, he spoke at universities,

---

12. Dan Gilgoff, "Ten Obama Faith Moments," *US News & World Report*, April 2009.

he opened rallies with prayers, he launched the office of faith-based initiatives (which Obama merely retained), and he spoke to the Muslim world from Turkey. Why when Obama does some of these things are they "important moments of faith" but when Bush did them they were either ignored or labeled problematic? The pandering, watered-down faith of liberals is okay, because it's politically useful to acknowledge 90 percent of the country. But the faith of conservatives—which most in the press fear is actually sincere—is just scary.

But more to the point, what do lifting restrictions on stem-cell use and subsidizing abortion abroad have to do with faith? Is *US News & World Report* suggesting that Obama's philosophy concerning right-to-life issues was informed by his religion and not his liberalism? If so, Obama would be the first to deny it, having always been clear that his faith is private, and doesn't color his politics. (I thought that was the reason the liberal media loved him so.)

But most ridiculous is the suggestion that, along with millions of other Catholics, Vice President Biden's going to church on Ash Wednesday was somehow an "important faith moment"—for Obama. It proves just how far *US News* had to stretch to get this list to ten. The bottom line is, the only important faith moments Obama has had are those that have deeply offended the faithful. It isn't likely we'll see that Top Ten in the liberal press any time soon.

AND THE ATHEISTS TAKE OVER THE EARTH

While the mainstream media may be uncomfortable with public displays of worship, it just adores public attacks on them.

Though the *New York Times* didn't report Obama's ducking the National Day of Prayer, it did cover a group trying to block it. The Freedom From Religion Foundation, the country's largest group of atheists and agnostics, filed a lawsuit seeking to bar an engraving of "In God We Trust" and the Pledge of Allegiance at the Capitol Visitor Center in Washington, as well as to ban the National Day of Prayer.[13] *USA Today* also covered it.[14] When a fringe group of atheists attacks religion, it's newsworthy, but when the president of the United States offends the faithful, it's ignored or celebrated.

USA Today reported on a similar incident, when a group of atheists and agnostics challenged the city of Warren, Michigan, for allowing a church to set up a prayer station at a city office.[15] And the *New York Times* hosted an online debate between a number of supposed scholars on whether roadside memorials that include crosses are unconstitutional after a number of atheists complained that they had to see religious imagery on the side of the highway from time to time, at sixty miles an hour.[16] That one-sixteenth of a second must be unbearable.

USA Today featured a story by the usually restrained Cathy Lynn Grossman questioning the relevance of saying "under God" in the Pledge of Allegiance in 2008. In it, she wrote that because the phrase wasn't added until 1954, we should drop it entirely. "When I read about civic battles today to add the name of God or a Ten Commandments to every public event or venue, I wonder: What is the desired effect to adding—or blocking—this? Do you have to say 'God' everywhere to know God? To develop good values?"[17]

Who's trying to add the name of God to every public event or venue? The better question is, Will removing "God" from every

13. Associated Press, "Group Seeks to Bar Religious Inscriptions," *New York Times*, July 15, 2009.

14. Lindsay Perna, "Atheists Sue to Stop 'In God We Trust' in Capitol Visitor's Center," *USA Today*, July 17, 2009.

15. Doug Stanglin, "Atheist Group Blasts 'Prayer Station' in City Building," *USA Today*, June 22, 2009.

16. "Should Roadside Memorials Be Banned?" *New York Times*, July 12, 2009.

17. Cathy Lynn Grossman, "The 'Greatest Generation' Didn't Pledge 'Under God,'" *USA Today*, Dec. 1, 2008.

public space and our national motto, anthem, and currency ever remove God from American consciousness? Or is it just an affront to a sweeping majority of the population geared to make a few feel more comfortable?

And then there was Michael Newdow, God's gift to the secular, liberal press. The *Sacramento Bee*, the *Seattle Times*, the *Tampa Tribune*, the Associated Press, the *Charlotte Observer*, the *Kansas City Star*, the *Sacramento Union*, *USA Today*, CNN, the *Oakland Tribune*, and many others all covered the atheist gadfly's fight to get the phrase "In God We Trust" off coins and currency and removed as our national motto in 2005 and 2006.

When he sued to get "under God" out of the Pledge of Allegiance, the *San Francisco Chronicle* was there, as was the *Boston Globe*, the *Philadelphia Inquirer*, *USA Today*, *Time* magazine, the *Orlando Sentinel*, the *Tampa Tribune*, CNN, *New York Newsday*, and dozens of others.

And when Newdow and a group of atheists wanted "so help me God" stricken from Barack Obama's inaugural oath, the *Miami Herald* was there. So were the *Brisbane Times*, the *Washington Post*, *Newsweek*, *USA Today*, the *Philadelphia Inquirer*, the *Los Angeles Times*, and more.

Newsweek's Lisa Miller, in fact, sided with Newdow, suggesting that saying "So help me God" might not be appropriate—since we don't know what our forefathers said at their inaugurations.

"We have no idea what most 19th-century presidents have said about God as they were sworn in because for most of American history there were no microphones and no recording devices. Legend has it that George Washington said 'So help me God' at his Inauguration, but new scholarship shows that this story may be as apocryphal as the one about the cherry tree."[18]

---

18.   Lisa Miller, "God and the Oath of Office," *Newsweek*, Jan. 10, 2009.

Well, so what? By that logic, we should have flown the original American flag, the one that recognized only thirteen colonies, at Obama's inauguration. And forbade minorities and women to attend. And we should have put the president in a wig, since we know Washington wore one. This kind of reasoning couldn't get any more arbitrary. Regardless, *Newsweek* wasn't there only to cover the story; it was there to promote it.

But Miller also thought Obama's inauguration would be the perfect opportunity to reach out to atheists in America. And why? Because we're fighting "religious fundamentalists abroad," and acting too God-crazy might make the terrorists angry. Seriously.

"Our new president might use his inauguration then to showcase the values that have made this country great: pluralism, moderation—and the separation of church and state. Though not as politically expedient, the better choice might be to pray in private."

Miller's suggestion that we should hide our religion from terrorists is alarming enough. Kowtowing to mass murderers so as not to tick them off is akin to negotiating with them, something the United States isn't supposed to do. But there's another flaw in her argument. If what makes this country great is pluralism, then the plurality of its faithful should be acknowledged and even celebrated, not watered down and shoved under the rug. Miller may be embarrassed by the American faithful. But the president shouldn't be. A presidential rejection of prayer is a presidential rejection of the majority, and therefore a presidential rejection of democracy itself.

It's not that these stories about random acts of atheist revolt aren't interesting, especially when an atheist's challenge makes it all the way to the Supreme Court, as Newdow's did. They should be covered. But why are one atheist's views legitimized by the press, while those of millions of Christians aren't? Why does Newdow offer "an important lesson in American history and public piety," as Miller suggests, while millions of Christians are somehow fanatical? Worse than being offensive, this is simply intellectually dishonest. The joke is that the maudlin pleas by outlets like *Newsweek* for pluralism and tolerance and inclusion inexplicably don't apply to the Christian majority. If American democracy gives its imprimatur to these pieties of equality, then they should work for all Americans, not just a few. A rising tide lifts all boats, as John F. Kennedy once said. But the media is going a step further. It isn't just selectively pushing tolerance for its own pet causes in secularism and liberalism—it's turning it against the majority, to paint Christian America as intolerant, fanatical, and oppressive. The media wants you to side with secularism, when it's not the role of the media to take sides or implore you to do the same. It's a breach of trust, and a failure of a supposedly honest press. Once again, the media is manipulating you.

THE TWELVE DAYS OF (INSERT NONDENOMINATIONAL HOLIDAY HERE)

The war against Christmas has been raging for years, with angry opponents and their liberal elected officials looking to rid the country of the sacred holiday once and for all. In 2004 and 2005 the culture war came to a fever pitch, with stories emerging across the country of protests against everything from Christmas plays and Christmas trees in town squares to the uttering of "Merry Christmas" at shopping malls. The liberal media alleged the war on Christmas was fabricated, entirely made up by right-wing nutjobs. When David Letterman interviewed Fox News's Bill O'Reilly about it on his late-night television show just after the 2005 holiday season, he told O'Reilly, "I just think that people like you are trying to make us think it's a threat. I don't believe you, I think you're making it up."[19]

---

19. David Letterman, *Late Show With David Letterman*, CBS, Jan. 3, 2006.

In the *New York Times*, Frank Rich likened the idea of a war on Christmas to the kind of trumped-up hysteria manufactured by Orson Welles's radio broadcast of the fictional *War of the Worlds*, calling it a "fake war on Christmas" drummed up by the shadowy, mustache-twisting conspiratorialists at Fox News in an effort to distract us all from the war in Iraq.[20] Talk about manufactured hysteria. . . .

And Salon.com's self-proclaimed secularist, Michelle Goldberg, continuing the theme of right-wing religious conspirators, said that the so-called war on Christmas was about more than just representation: "These fights are not about the right of values evangelicals to be heard. They are about their right to rule."[21] Goldberg, like most of the liberal press, likens evangelicals and Christians of every stripe to evil dictators, looking to take over the world one Christmas tree at a time.

In December 2005, conservative television personality and economist Ben Stein may have addressed the nonsense best when he laid out some of his views on the political correctness of the holiday season on the CBS *Sunday Morning Show*:

> *I am a Jew, and every single one of my ancestors was Jewish. And it does not bother me even a little bit when people call those beautiful lit up, bejeweled trees Christmas trees. I don't feel threatened. I don't feel discriminated against. That's what they are: Christmas trees. It doesn't bother me a bit when people say, "Merry Christmas" to me. I don't think they are slighting me or getting ready to put me in a ghetto.*
>
> *I don't like getting pushed around for being a Jew and I don't think Christians like getting pushed around for being Christians. I think people who believe in God are sick and tired of getting*

20. Frank Rich, "I Saw Jackie Mason Kissing Santa Claus," *New York Times*, Dec. 25, 2005.
21. Michelle Goldberg, "One Nation, Divisible," Salon.com, July 23, 2005.

pushed around, period. I have no idea where the concept came from that America is an explicitly atheist country. I can't find it in the Constitution and I don't like it being shoved down my throat.[22]

The majority of the country doesn't either. But the liberal media doesn't want you to know that.

When the town of Patchogue, New York, suddenly changed the name of its annual Christmas Boat Parade to the Holiday Boat Parade in 2008 at the request of a few offended residents, Grucci, the venerable fireworks company, pulled out of participating. Grucci vice president Philip Butler, a vocal opponent of the secularization of Christmas, said parade organizers were "using all the themes of Christmas and plagiarizing all those themes."[23]

Grucci has produced the fireworks displays at seven presidential inaugurations, the U.S. bicentennial, and three Olympics ceremonies. Their stand against the renaming of Christmas should have been a fairly well-covered story across the country. Yet Fox News and the *New York Post* were the only major media outlets to cover the Grucci boycott.

Though it may have totally ignored this story, during the lead-up to the 2008 presidential campaign the liberal media pounced readily on another one that, well, wasn't really a story at all.

In December 2007, former Arkansas governor Mike Huckabee released a campaign ad before the holidays to wish the country a Merry Christmas. In it, the Southern Baptist minister asked viewers if they were "about worn out of all the television commercials you've been seeing, mostly about politics." He stood in front of a Christmas

---

22. Ben Stein, CBS *Sunday Morning Show*, Dec. 19, 2005.
23. "New York Town's Parade Draws Fire for Dropping 'Christmas,'" Foxnews.com, Oct. 24, 2008.

tree in a red sweater with "Silent Night" playing in the background, and his message was simple and to the point: "Merry Christmas," from one Christian to another.

Yet, in something out of Conspiracy Theories for Dummies, the liberal press decided the intersection of what Huckabee told me was merely a bookshelf in his friend's house was a subliminal cross, meant to telegraph to the country an overtly Christian message—as if the Baptist minister wishing Christians a Merry Christmas was trying to hide a well-kept secret affinity for Jesus.

The idea that Huckabee was trying to channel Christ through a bookshelf is preposterous enough. But the liberal media's obsession with the nonstory was even worse.

USA Today, the *Boston Globe*, MSNBC, the *Chicago Sun-Times*, CBS News, *Time* magazine, NPR, and countless others ran with the story that there was some kind of hysterical national controversy over the commercial. While it was true that some Republicans criticized the ad, that was news only if you believe political campaigns are fought over tea and biscuits, and not in a boxing ring.

The *Washington Post*'s Joel Achenbach wrote of the contrived brouhaha that only the media seemed to be generating, "No Christmas ad has generated as much interest and controversy as the one from Huckabee, a kind of visual Hallmark card in which the candidate talks directly to the camera about celebrating 'the birth of Christ.' The spot incited much Internet buzz about whether it contains a subliminal image of a cross in the background." [24]

Wait, hold the phone—Governor Huckabee spoke "directly to the camera about celebrating 'the birth of Christ'"? Can he do that?! Notify the God squad and arrest that man!

ABC News also ran a story, one dripping with contempt for

---

24. Joel Achenbach, "Christmas Cheer, Campaigns an Awkward Mix for Iowa Voters," *Washington Post*, Dec. 24, 2007.

Huckabee. After the governor had huge and unexpected success in Iowa—despite the "controversial" ad—Tahman Bradley and Talal Al-Khatib wrote a story about the Republican candidate called "How the Grinch Stole Iowa."[25]

CNN's Anderson Cooper devoted an entire segment to the flap, complete with dueling guests, on his *360 Degrees* program on December 17. Huckabee's Merry Christmas ad was—no joke—his lead story.

"Tonight Mike Huckabee, out in front in Iowa, releases a new ad wishing voters a Merry Christmas and controversy erupts over his bringing Christ into it. We're digging deeper on that and keeping them honest on what's driving his surging campaign."[26]

Digging deeper on what? Keeping who honest? Was Cooper suggesting some shadowy cabal of stealth Christians or ninja altar boys were secretly "driving his surging campaign"? When did CNN's silver-haired anchor become a conspiracy theorist?

And Salon.com got in on the action, dispatching liberal-in-chief Glenn Greenwald to pen something pithy about the whole unbelievable thing. Referring to the "GOP establishment," he writes: "On a more festive and Christmas-appropriate note, one of the most joyous aspects of this holiday is that people who devote every day, all year long, to spewing unbridled anger, resentment, hostility and palpable hatred towards an ever-expanding roster of Enemies—immigrants, liberals, Muslims, war opponents, treasonous journalists—put all that aside for part of a day and publicly show everyone that they realize what is truly important, who they really are."[27]

Even *Rolling Stone* had something to say about it, and (sort of) commended Huckabee's response to all the undeserved commotion.

---

25.   Tahman Bradley and Talal Al-Khatib, "How the Grinch Stole Iowa," ABCNews.com, Dec. 19, 2007.

26.   Anderson Cooper, *Anderson Cooper 360 Degrees,* CNN, Dec. 17, 2007.

27.   Glenn Greenwald, "Political Christmas Wishes," Salon.com, Dec. 25, 2007.

In making light of the situation, and subtly ridiculing the conspiracies surrounding his simple ad, Huckabee said, "I will confess this: If you play the spot backwards it says 'Paul is dead. Paul is dead.'"

For that nod to the Beatles, *Rolling Stone*'s Tim Dickinson wrote, "I gotta give the Huckster credit. When's the last time we saw a member of the religious right who was fluent enough in the touchstones of the 60's left to pull off [a Beatles reference]? Seriously. Here he is with a vote-for-me-and-baby-Jesus ad . . . and Huckabee defuses the tension he's created with a joke about the White Album? As if to say, how much of a Jesus freak can I be if I also know how to play 'Jesus is Just Alright'?"[28]

Besides the condescending assumptions by Dickinson that Huckabee and other Christians must be out-of-touch "Jesus freaks," it's likely the "Huckster" took this as a compliment. Anyone who knows him can attest he's got a well-developed sense of humor. You know, for a Jesus freak. (He told me that he found the whole thing hilarious.) But let's not tell him that the title of Dickinson's piece was "The Evil Genius of Mike Huckabee."

Huckabee's instinct to brush off the attacks against him and Christian America by the left-wing media is a good one, and probably what keeps him sane. And Ben Stein's effort to make sense of all the preposterous political correctness around public worship is also an attempt to politely deal with an aggressive attack machine that seems hell-bent on putting the faithful in their place—which is in the closet.

In 2009, the war on Christmas raged anew. Atheists in Illinois and Arkansas fought to get their beliefs positioned next to those of the faithful in the state capitols. In Springfield, Illinois, the Freedom From Religion Foundation erected its winter solstice display next to a Christian nativity scene, a Jewish menorah, and a bizarre display by the ACLU. The declaration read:

---

28. Tim Dickinson, "The Evil Genius of Mike Huckabee," *Rolling Stone,* Dec. 19, 2007.

At this season of the winter solstice, may reason prevail. There are no gods, no devils, no angels, no heaven or hell. There is only our natural world. Religion is but myth and superstition that hardens hearts and enslaves minds.

It was also joined by a comment from the Friends of Festivus, a group celebrating the fictional holiday invented by a *Seinfeld* character more than a decade ago. Nice. A federal judge also allowed the Arkansas Society of Freethinkers to display a four-sided sign honoring the winter solstice and famous atheists throughout time. The states complied, of course, because they wanted to avoid a "controversy." Let's examine how much sense that makes. Bowing to the whims of a tiny minority—how many Festivus adherents can there really be?—so as to avoid a "controversy" with 90 percent of the country who believe in God is in fact begging for a controversy. And they got one. Christians from all over the country rightly complained that propping up the aggressive anti-God attacks of a select few on one of the world's holiest of days is not "inclusion." It's un-American. Christmas and Hannukah have nothing to do with atheism, so acknowledging it in a holiday display is not only incongruous, it's an implicit and wholly unnecessary assault on the faithful. But the media didn't see it that way—countless liberal outlets asked what all the fuss was about. Fox News covered the war on Christmas, while MSNBC, CNN, and the rest told their viewers it didn't really exist.

I am a nonbeliever. Yet I easily identify with both Huckabee and Stein in wanting to get to the bottom of this marginalization of the faithful. I don't need to feel "represented" in my beliefs, nor do I need the president to publicly and officially "recognize" them. But here's the bottom line: If atheists are so opposed to public displays of worship, why the heck are they so pleased when they get a public shout-out?

In 2009, a Sonoma, California, man fought to get an angel removed from atop Christmas trees in government buildings, arguing that it was "very offensive to agnostics, atheists, and those who believe in separation of church and state to be subjected to this by their government."[29] Very offensive? What exactly were nonbelievers being subjected to? The state can acknowledge religious America without breaking the boundary between church and state—and it does so all the time. Christmas is a national holiday, for one. Federal employees are given the day off. President Obama acknowledged the Muslim feast of Ramadan with an official state dinner. The White House celebrates Christmas and prominently displays its own Christmas tree. Acknowledging the importance of religion—with a Christmas tree, a National Day of Prayer, or a God and Country military flyover—isn't subjecting nonbelievers to anything. No one is forcing them to participate, or even agree.

Public worship isn't an affront to secular America. It's a celebration of both individual faith and the values upon which this country was founded. The media's attack on those values is a threat to everyone because it means those within the press are now comfortable taking the liberty to demean and suppress any and all values—it might be the National Day of Prayer or Christmas today, but who's to say it won't be the values *you* or your grandchildren hold most sacred tomorrow? If the media can so brazenly go after the majority, why wouldn't it eventually go after the minority?

Indeed, Christians will *become* the minority if, in the interest of avoiding a "controversy," so many willingly succumb to the media's assaults. The secular Left is embracing the controversy, and they're winning, while religious America is fleeing from it, and losing. If Christians think that there's no real danger in letting the mainstream media take regular potshots at them, they're dead wrong. The media is giving a massive microphone to the anti-Christian extremists

---

29. Jesse McKinley, "In Reversal, Stars Adorn Trees Again," *New York Times,* Dec. 24, 2009.

in the explicit hope that they succeed. Christians, if they care about their way of life, should fight back against the tyrannical media with as much vitriol and aggression as the godless Left is fighting them with.

Pretty soon the war won't be over Nativity scenes and Christmas trees in the town square—it will be over Nativity scenes and Christmas trees in their own homes. Does that sound paranoid? What's to stop the secular Left from ridding *all* of America of religious acts of devotion? They are already telling us what kinds of lightbulbs to use in our homes. They're telling us we can't smoke in our own homes. They're regulating our water and our fast food and our soda consumption. And all with the help of an eager leftist press that is telling you in newspapers, on the radio, over the internet, and on television that you're a bad person if you neglect the environment, eat McDonald's, smoke too much, or drive a pickup truck. The liberal secular press is already attacking your values. Attacking your God is implied. If you follow the media's assault on Christianity to its logical conclusion, the fight to preserve Christian values and public worship will be over when there's nothing left to preserve.

II

THOU SHALT HATE PROP 8

In November 2008, a controversial ballot proposition was passed in California, changing the state constitution to read, "Only marriage between a man and a woman is valid or recognized in California," delivering a huge blow to gay marriage activists who thought they had this one in the bag.

Their optimism was somewhat understandable. California has become a reliably liberal state. It has voted for a Democratic president every election year since 1992. In 2008, the state voted for Barack Obama 61 percent to John McCain's 37 percent, and raised over $15 million in campaign financing, 97 percent of which went to Obama. San Francisco, home to that famous intersection of Haight and Ashbury streets, alone raised nearly $2 million, with Los Angeles and Berkeley not far behind.

But as is often the case in liberal circles, many forget that a state is not only its cities. California is not just San Francisco, Los Angeles, and Berkeley, that stalwart trifecta of liberal elitism. There is more to California than the Hollywood Hills, Malibu, and its liberal colleges—a whole lot more.

California is also Republican strongholds like Stockton, Bakersfield, Fresno, Modesto, and Orange County. In fact, of California's fifty-eight counties, only eighteen voted for climate change commando Al Gore in the 2000 presidential election. And only twenty-two counties voted for John Kerry in 2004. Thirty counties voted for Obama in 2008.

If you think of California only as Tinseltown and UC Berkeley, you'd probably assume that God fled the state in the 1960s, when the only popular objects of worship were marijuana, black light posters, and Bob Dylan, and has yet to make his return. But not so. The state has nearly 2 million evangelical Christians, and 10 million Roman Catholics, the largest population of any state. It also has more than 750,000 Mormons, second only to Utah. Sixty-two percent of the state's residents report they are "absolutely certain" of a belief in God, according to a Pew Research Center survey in 2008.[1]

But you'll forgive gay marriage activists, and their surrogates in the liberal media and Hollywood, for assuming their fight against Prop 8 was an easy win. After all, to hear them tell it, the whole country now firmly believes that gays have the unequivocal right to get married, and those who don't are Bible-thumping hicks from the middle of the country—who don't count anyway. Much like every other social debate over a litmus-test liberal piety, the issue has been resolved, simply because the liberal media says so. Get on board, opponents, because the country is officially moving on without you.

---

1. Duke Helfand, "Survey Shows Californians Less Religious Than Rest of Nation," *Los Angeles Times*, June 24, 2008.

GAY MARRIAGE IS HERE TO STAY

It's true, acceptance of homosexuality has gained momentum in recent decades, thanks to some heady normalization by popular culture, the rightful success of gay activists at forging distinctions between the stigma of the AIDS virus and homosexual culture, and the courage of more and more public figures coming out of the closet. Fifty years ago, the idea of a television show like *Will & Grace* or *The L Word* living comfortably in the mainstream alongside *I Love Lucy* or *The Honeymooners* would have been a long shot, to say the least.

But acceptance of gay marriage—both the idea of it and its ambiguous constitutionality—has yet to soar to the stratospheric heights that the liberal media routinely claims, even if some of those opposed to gay marriage support civil unions or domestic partnerships.

In December 2008, *Newsweek* declared "A Gay Marriage Surge" was sweeping the nation. The evidence? A poll, conducted conveniently by *Newsweek* itself, that found 55 percent of respondents favored legally sanctioned unions for gay couples. Of course, the same poll found that only 39 percent supported actual marriage rights. Obviously, *Newsweek* plays it a little fast and loose with the word "surge."[2] Interestingly, in the same story, it offered some "unrelated" data: "On another note, the Newsweek Poll surveyed attitudes toward President-elect Barack Obama. Consistent with other recent surveys, it found broad public approval of his transition (72 percent) and of his cabinet picks (also 72 percent)."

Conflating support for gay marriage with support for Barack Obama is, needless to say, a shamelessly obvious attempt at painting a larger picture: If you don't approve of gay marriage, you probably

---

2. Arian Campo-Flores, "A Gay Marriage Surge," *Newsweek,* Dec. 5, 2008.

don't approve of Barack Obama, and you, therefore, are officially part of the fringe minority.

Reuters also proclaimed a victory for gay rights, when it cited a Quinnipiac poll in June 2009, declaring, "New Yorkers Supportive of Gay Marriage."[3] But were they? Well, not if you actually read the polling data. When asked a vague question about the issue, 51 percent of New Yorkers said they supported a law giving same-sex couples the right to get married. But in another more specific question, respondents were given three options to choose from: Same-sex couples should be allowed to marry; they should be allowed to form civil unions; or there should be no legal recognition. Only 46 percent of New York State voters said same-sex couples should be allowed to marry, and 27 percent said they should be able to form civil unions. Is the support of 46 percent of a population really "support"? If so, it's tepid at best.

This is no recent trend bolstered by a young, new Democrat in the White House. When the Senate defeated the Marriage Protection Amendment in 2006, the story was front-page news for the liberal media, which decisively declared that America no longer cared about protecting marriage. But as James C. Dobson, founder and chairman of Focus on the Family Action, pointed out, when Alabama became the twentieth state to support traditional marriage—and by a whopping 81 to 19 percent—there wasn't a single reference to it in the *New York Times* or *Washington Post,* and virtually no mentions in any other national papers.[4]

And even some in the media admit to widespread bias on coverage of the gay marriage debate. *Washington Post* media critic Howard Kurtz wrote in 2004, "ALL of the press was being way too sympathetic

---

3. Reuters, "New Yorkers Supportive of Gay Marriage: Poll," July 23, 2009.
4. James C. Dobson, "Media Provides Cover for Assault on Traditional Marriage," CNN.com, Oct. 20, 2006.

to the gay marriage side, given that there are many, many Americans who don't support that issue."[5]

Washington Post ombudsman Michael Getler agreed: "Critics who say the paper has had few, if any, features portraying opponents of this social change in a positive or even neutral light have a point. The overall picture, it seems to me, could use more balance."[6]

And so did *Boston Globe* ombud Christine Chinlund, who wrote in 2003 of opponents of gay marriage: "One need not agree with them to think that their views need to be reflected, probed and understood as part of the essential coverage of this historic shift."[7]

That's some serious soul searching, and rare admission of guilt in the liberal media. Of course, it's the job of an ombudsman to address such issues. But it's not merely about covering both sides of the story. It's about good reporting. Sometimes writing about hot-button issues means making predictions about their larger implications, tying them to other issues, and digging for the stories that no one is writing.

To that end, the *Chicago Tribune's* ombudsman, Donald Wycliff, said of the gay marriage issue, "Where we run into trouble is in discerning the stories that haven't yet been written, or even conceived."[8]

While the liberal media is busy promoting its stance on gay marriage, it is ignoring (in some cases, knowingly) important issues that may concern the very groups they are trying to protect. If they're not going to be objective reporters, but advocacy journalists, they should be honest and diligent advocates at least. As Julie Hollar made clear in *Fairness and Accuracy in Reporting,* issues like domestic abuse in gay relationships, the problems that children of gay couples face, divorce

---

5. Howard Kurtz, WashingtonPost.com, June 26, 2004.
6. Michael Getler, *Washington Post,* March 21, 2004.
7. Michael Getler, *Washington Post,* March 21, 2004.
8. Donald Wycliff, *Chicago Tribune,* July 8, 2004.

rates, the effects of gay marriage on heterosexual marriage, or the impact of gay marriage on taxes simply aren't being investigated.[9]

PROP 8 AND *NEWSWEEK* MAKE
STRANGE BEDFELLOWS

Though the liberal media's had a tricky time with gay marriage for years, the controversy over California's Prop 8 put the issue in a white-hot national spotlight, and it seemed that any shaky commitment to objectivity that once existed was summarily tossed out the window. And no one was more "on board" with the gay marriage activists, and against its opponents, than *Newsweek,* which for a few short months in 2008 became an unabashed megaphone for the cause.

In October 2008, David J. Jefferson, a *Newsweek* editor, broke the fourth wall of media theater to write about his own personal experience as a gay man and wondered aloud if his previously certified marriage would be affected by a Yes vote on Prop 8. "Will My Marriage Last?" he asked, and then took several conspicuous swipes at religious opposition. "The Proposition 8 team is preying on parents' fears that their children can somehow be 'turned' gay if they encounter gay people or learn anything about the 'homosexual lifestyle' (a phrase used by the religious right that is code for 'burn in hell')."[10]

He characterized the opposition as either categorically "religious" or "homophobic," which the liberal media routinely alleges are one and the same, but fails to acknowledge that many, including even some gay men and women, oppose a federal amendment that changes the definition of marriage, because they feel it should be left to the

---

9.   Julie Hollar, "Media's Gay Marriage Consensus," *Fairness and Accuracy in Reporting,* Sep./Oct. 2004.

10.   David J. Jefferson, "Will My Marriage Last?" *Newsweek,* Oct. 30, 2008.

states. Many feel the government shouldn't be ruling on such private domestic issues as marriage at all. There are also those who oppose marriage, but believe that domestic partnerships and civil unions should afford gay couples the same rights as heterosexual couples. And there are those who like gay folks just fine, but for whom "marriage" has religious significance. Of course there is little or no room for nuance on this issue. You are either in favor (and thus, an enlightened, compassionate human) or opposed (and thus, a savage creature from the Paleolithic period—or an evangelical Christian).

Never mind that the seeming patron saint of His and His towels, Barack Obama, also does not support the legalization of gay marriage—or at least he says he doesn't. The liberal media gleefully positioned Obama as a sympathetic ally to the cause, and he may yet be, but thus far he's done little to overturn the Defense of Marriage Act (DOMA) or advance gay rights.

Maybe the media didn't know about Obama's views on gay marriage when he was running for president. Well, all it had to do was look. As early as 2004, while running for the Senate, he said during WBBM-AM's *At Issue,* "I'm a Christian. And so, although I try not to have my religious beliefs dominate or determine my political views on this issue, I do believe that tradition and my religious beliefs say that marriage is something sanctified between a man and a woman."[11]

Vice President Joe Biden made a similar statement on *The Ellen DeGeneres Show* in 2008: "[Neither] Barack Obama nor I support redefining from a civil side what constitutes marriage." And he walked the same line during his debate with Sarah Palin.

So did Secretary of State Hillary Clinton, whose husband signed DOMA into law in 1996, when she told the *New York Daily News:* "Marriage has got historic, religious and moral content that goes back

---

11.   Nicole Ziegler Dizon, "Obama Opposes Gay Marriage," *Chicago Tribune,* Sep. 24, 2004.

to the beginning of time, and I think a marriage is as a marriage always has been, between a man and a woman."

Also against gay marriage are John Edwards, John Kerry, Harry
Reid, Bill Richardson, and Rick Warren, Obama's choice of pastor for
his inaugural invocation, to name a few.

No matter for *Newsweek,* though. This was a battle between the
Left and the Right, the secular and the religious. In Jefferson's piece,
he argued not only that gay marriage should be universally accepted,
but that our public schools should teach our children all about it.
"Many parents have no problem with their children being taught about
the existence of gay couples, since the purpose of an education is—
presumably—to learn about subjects with which one is unfamiliar."

In the rest of his piece, which read more like a "What I Did on
My Summer Vacation" essay than anything resembling news or insight, he went on to describe his wedding in excruciating detail, from
the cake to the decor to the officiant, the dancing, the ring bearer and
flower girl, the songs, the readings, his friends in attendance, and all
the rest. It was three interminable pages about his big day.

Not only does it seem an obvious conflict of interest to allow
a magazine editor to inject himself into a political issue in his own
magazine, but more offensively, when is someone else's wedding ever
that interesting? Unless you're marrying a royal, no one cares what
song you chose for the first dance. But for *Newsweek,* this was feature-
story material, and they had a guy on the inside.

Jefferson wrote yet another piece just two weeks later, titled "How
Getting Married Made Me an Activist." (To be clear, wearing both
an impartial editor's hat and that of an activist simultaneously is no
small feat, and one that requires a singular dexterity and presump-
tion.) Before the story itself, an omniscient *Newsweek* editor intro-
duced the topic to mitigate any ambiguity left by the title: "This
Newsweek editor's wedding has put him in the middle of the culture
wars. Now, as he and his spouse wait to see if their marriage is valid,

they wonder if history will be on their side." In case there was any doubt, now *Newsweek* itself was entering the debate.

But the assertion that Jefferson had just ended up in "the middle of the culture wars" is an unfathomable insult to the intelligence of its readers. Jefferson wasn't merely plucked from his *Newsweek* office and dropped into the middle of a national controversy. He thrust himself into it with reckless abandon by choosing to write about himself, as opposed to covering the issue through someone else's eyes. And he did so with the giddy imprimatur of his magazine. This is akin to a national newspaper allowing its health reporter to cover the health-care debate by writing about her ailing grandmother. Personal anec-dote, for *Newsweek*, was as good as reportage.

In this second piece, there was—unbelievably—more wedding description, but also a warning to Mormons, who had spent an es-timated $15 million to help pass Prop 8, that they would now find themselves on the receiving end of angry gay protests. "That's made the Mormon church a prime target as the gay community does its Prop 8 postmortem," he wrote. "Some activists are calling for the IRS to revoke the church's tax-exempt status; others have suggested boy-cotting companies with Mormon executives who supported the ban and getting Hollywood types to pull out of the Sundance Film Fes-tival in Park City, Utah." Look out, Mormons—gay America is ready to take you down. And *Newsweek* just published their blueprint.

And Jefferson was right. Gay activists vandalized Mormon tem-ples and buildings in California and Utah and sent threatening letters and packages containing white powder to Mormon and Knights of Columbus centers. How many stories on the violence against Mor-mons and Catholics were featured in the *New York Times* or *News-week*? Zero. Not one.[12]

---

12. Eric Gorski, "Anger Over Gay Marriage Vote Directed At Mormons," *USA Today*, Nov. 13, 2008.

But another important question is, would *Newsweek* have published an article titled "Why I Think Gay Marriage Is Unconstitutional" by one of its editors? Would any *Newsweek* editor ever write
such a thing? The answer to both questions is undoubtedly, No.

But the worst was yet to come. A slew of sugary online packages
helped to match images with their central story line. A photo mon-
tage called "A Changing Tide" showed gay couples in passionate lip
locks, embraces, and various states of protest.

A *Newsweek* video probed, "Is Gay the New Black?" comparing
the protests over Prop 8 to the civil rights movement.

And then ... the big one. After California voted in favor of passing Prop 8, banning same-sex marriages, *Newsweek* published a cover
story by its religion editor, Lisa Miller, titled "The Religious Case for
Gay Marriage." In it, Miller cherry-picked from scripture quotations
that she felt affirmed the gay rights position, the argument being, of
course, that the main opponents of gay marriage are Christian literalists who cite the Bible as support for traditional marriage. It was
sloppy, and incredibly offensive to Christians, who thought she was
bastardizing their most sacred text.

Among her arguments: The Bible actually advocates bachelor-
hood, because Christ was "emphatically unmarried." Furthermore,
"The apostle Paul (also single) regarded marriage as an act of last
resort for those unable to contain their animal lust."[13] Her evidence?
A passage in which Paul says, "It is better to marry than to burn
with passion," which anyone who's seen a single episode of *Desperate
Housewives* knows means, better to marry than to be promiscuous.
But this, Miller, insists, is "one of the most lukewarm endorsements
of a treasured institution ever uttered."

Another argument: The condemnation of homosexuality in the
Bible isn't really serious. "The Bible does condemn gay male sex in

---

13.   Lisa Miller, "The Religious Case for Gay Marriage," *Newsweek,* Dec. 6, 2008.

a handful of passages . . . but these are throwaway lines in a peculiar text given over to codes for living in the ancient Jewish world. . . ."

Yet another argument: The references to homosexuality in the Bible, overt as they may seem, don't mean what we think they mean, and people who are smarter than any Bible-thumping hick from Kansas have discovered their real implications. "Paul was tough on homosexuality," she writes, "though recently progressive scholars have argued that his condemnation of men who 'were inflamed with lust for one another' (which he calls 'a perversion') is really a critique of the worst kind of wickedness: self-delusion, violence, promiscuity and debauchery." Right.

And finally, stories about male friendships in the Bible are actually explicit endorsements of homosexuality. "Gay men like to point to the story of passionate King David and his friend Jonathan, with whom he was 'one spirit' and whom he 'loved as he loved himself.' Here, the Bible praises enduring love between men. What Jonathan and David did or did not do in privacy is perhaps best left to history and our own imaginations."

Tony Perkins, president of the Family Research Council, called Miller's piece a "joy ride," and wrote in the *Washington Update,* "As with most joy rides, few beyond the driver find it entertaining. The public is endangered and the vehicle is almost always devalued in the process. This ride is no exception. *Newsweek*'s credibility is severely damaged by Miller's reckless treatment of scripture."[14]

It's easy to point out the problems in applying scripture to our modern lives, especially if the person doing the pointing doesn't view the Bible as a sacred text to begin with. But blurting out random and baseless interpretations of Christians' (and Jews') most important beliefs is reckless, irresponsible, and sheer conjecture, like me saying "Thou shalt not steal" was likely just a typo, and imploring the world

---

14. Tony Perkins, *Washington Update,* Dec. 9, 2008.

to throw away its irons because what God really meant was, "Thou shalt not steam."

Furthermore, while Miller is right that some opponents of gay marriage use the Bible as a reference point, it's clear that most do not. A CBS News poll released in April 2009 found that 34 percent of Republicans think same-sex couples should be allowed to form civil unions (incidentally, 24 percent of Democrats think they shouldn't be legally recognized at all). Twenty-five percent of white evangelicals are in favor of civil unions.

If that's true, then it's simply counterintuitive that all those Republicans and all those evangelicals oppose gay marriage because the Bible is against it, but favor civil unions because Christ never explicitly mentions them. More likely is their belief that marriage is a sacred tradition, but homosexual couples should be recognized by law as partners and afforded the same rights as heterosexual couples. Painting the opposition to gay marriage as biblical literalists, though, makes calling them crazy and backward much easier.

Scores of angry letters poured in to *Newsweek*, many questioning why it allowed a piece that brazenly distorted one biblical verse after another to make a political argument for a piece of state legislation. Miller hardly backed away. In fact, she accepted an invitation to appear as a guest on the gay advocacy group Human Rights Campaign's XM Sirius Radio show, aptly titled *The Agenda, with Joe Solmonese*. The HRC jubilantly declared the piece a triumph, saying it debunked "popular myths about the Bible's stance on marriage," and urging proponents to email *Newsweek* editor Jon Meacham in support.

And then, on December 9, just three days later, a *Newsweek* web-only piece reported on the post–Prop 8 protests, much as the rest of the media did—with unbridled enthusiasm.

"Since voters approved the initiative on Nov. 4, taking away same-sex marriage rights granted by the courts only a few months earlier, the gay community nationwide has mobilized in a way not seen since those harrowing days of the '80s. Protests have erupted outside Mormon temples across the country, which spent some $20 million lobbying for the ban. Residents have flocked to local protests. And as the reality sunk in that four anti-gay state measures had passed on election day, more than a million people rallied at their local City Halls in a coordinated day of demonstrations."[15]

IF A PROTEST HAPPENS IN A FOREST . . .

Indeed, the protests gave the liberal media yet another opportunity to convince the country that, despite what happened in California, gay marriage was coming, whether it liked it or not. Their alacrity was fairly predictable, though. The liberal media, after all, loves a good protest.

Last year, the *New York Times* wrote at least thirteen stories about the demonstrations against Prop 8. Not thirteen stories about the gay marriage ruling in general—just about the protests surrounding it. Thirteen stories in less than two months.

It also featured two dozen stories on Gay Pride celebrations around the world in June and July 2009. The *Washington Post* published a number of pieces on Gay Pride as well, not the least of which was one on the front page of its Weekend section. In it, writer Ellen McCarthy predicted a favorable turnout in dramatic fashion: "This year, this weekend, there will be 200,000. Or more."[16]

Or less. When the Media Research Center reported that only thirty thousand showed up, the *Washington Post* did not correct its estimate.

But how many stories did the *New York Times* feature on the Tea

---

15. Jessica Bennett, *Newsweek*, Web Exclusive, Dec. 9, 2008.
16. Ellen McCarthy, "Proud Voices," *Washington Post*, June 13, 2008.

Party protests of 2009, which brought out more than a million dem-
onstrators, according to WorldNetDaily, in cities around the country?
One. It's like the whole thing never happened.

Because the protests—which were nonpartisan, and for lower
taxes, smaller government, and fiscal responsibility—were successfully portrayed by the liberal media as a "Republican cause," and everyone knows that "Republican" is just a proxy for the religious right,
they were either mocked or ignored.

The *New York Times'* single news story on the protests, by Liz
Robbins, was hardly objective. "All of these tax day parties seemed
less about revolution and more about group therapy. At least with the
more widely known protests against government spending, people attending the rallies were dressed patriotically and held signs expressing
their anger, but offering no solutions."[17] And in it, she was sure to
mention that one protest, in Houston, featured some antiabortion activists. These were the words of a reporter, mind you—someone whose
job is to report on the scene in an objective and unbiased way, like the
play-by-play announcer at a baseball game. Instead, Robbins was the
color man, unabashedly offering her own opinion and insight.

But the *Times* did include a scathing column by Paul Krugman
about the protests—before they even happened—and their irrelevance. "Republicans have become embarrassing to watch. And it
doesn't feel right to make fun of crazy people. Better, perhaps, to focus on the real policy debates, which are all among Democrats." He
called the protesters "clueless," "bad for the country," and the "subject
of considerable mockery, and rightly so."[18] And *Newsweek*'s Howard
Fineman wrote that the GOP was effectively dead, and no tea party
could revive it.[19]

---

17. Liz Robbins, "Tax Day Is Met with Tea Parties," *New York Times,* April 15, 2009.

18. Paul Krugman, "Tea Parties Forever," *New York Times,* April 12, 2009.

19. Howard Fineman, "The GOP Ground Game," *Newsweek,* April 18, 2009.

And on MSNBC's April 10th *Countdown*, with fill-in host David Shuster—who followed his colleague Rachel Maddow's public display of maturity by calling them "teabagging parties," something CNN's Anderson Cooper also echoed—*Newsweek*'s senior editor Daniel Gross said he didn't think the president should pay attention to the rest of the country's squabbles. "To get bogged down with a— you know, what seems to be a fringe group of people throwing consumer products into the lakes and rivers of this nation doesn't seem to be worthy of his attention."[20]

It's hard to ignore the imbalance in the liberal media where their favorite pet causes—like gay marriage—are concerned. Pitting gay rights against so-called biblical literalists makes the debate an easy one to showcase on MSNBC, in the *New York Times*, or in *Newsweek*, but the ploy is utterly transparent.

GAY RIGHTS ACTIVISTS WANT YOU TO BE MORE TOLERANT—YES, SERIOUSLY

The generous support lent to Prop 8 by the liberal media seems to have given many on the airwaves, in television, and in the blogosphere license to ratchet up the dialogue against Christians who oppose gay marriage. The irony of a group that is asking for more tolerance using the media to inflict a horrendous assault on its opposition is palpable.

In 2009, when Miss California, Carrie Prejean, was put in the awkward position of having to explain her position on gay marriage to a nationally televised audience, her convictions—the same as the president's, vice president's, and secretary of state's—were rewarded with an onslaught of hateful invective by the liberal media.

---

20. MSNBC, *Countdown with Keith Olbermann*, April 10, 2009.

Gossip blogger Perez Hilton, who is openly gay and champions the gay marriage cause, has become one of her most vocal opponents. After the Miss USA competition, at which he was a judge and the very one who posed the question, he posted a video blog denouncing her with the kind of language so-called rights activists generally try to avoid: "She gave the worst answer in pageant history. She got booed. I think that was the first time in Miss USA ever that a contestant has been booed. She lost not because she doesn't believe in gay marriage. Miss California lost because she's a dumb bitch."[21]

He's used that word to describe her numerous times. When she was fired by the pageant, his headline read "Dumb Bitch Reacts to Being Fired."[22] He has also called her the "c"-word. But Perez Hilton, whose real name is Mario Lavandeira, has become an uneasy spokesperson for gay rights. He has famously feuded with activists who didn't think his campaign to "out" gay celebrities publicly was particularly kind or tolerant. And in 2009, he got in trouble again with gay America for calling Black Eyed Peas frontman Will I. Am a "faggot" during a fight outside a nightclub in Toronto. For that, he was met with scores of angry emails and letters from the gay readers who were once his mainstay, calling him a hypocrite, especially in light of the fact that he had earlier waged an all-out war on another actor, Isaiah Washington, for using the same derogatory term. He wrote an impassioned mea culpa on his website and insisted he'd never been a spokesperson for gay rights. Well, not anymore he isn't.

But for those who say that Perez Hilton is safely relegated to the confines of the online, left-wing fringe, the so-called mainstream media would beg to differ. The liberal press routinely uses him as

21. Perez Hilton, Perezhilton.com, April 20, 2009.
22. Perez Hilton, Perezhilton.com, June 11, 2009.

its go-to guy on all things gay. As Japhy Grant's Salon.com article explained, he's been featured by the Associated Press, the *Guardian*, *Ocean Drive*, *GO*, the *Los Angeles Times*, *Details*, *Paper*, the *New York Post*, *Hispanic* magazine, the *New York Times*, MTV, *Good Morning America*, and countless others.[23] As Grant put it, "What does it say about the mainstream press that it has adopted him?"

And in a hilarious moment of unintended levity, Grant also quotes Lavandeira as saying, "In my own way, subserviently, I am trying to make the world a better place."

And other, more prominent and purportedly "mainstream" voices seemed to take up his smear campaign against Prejean. MSNBC's Keith Olbermann featured her in one of his "WTF Moments," on May 12, 2009: "It's not that she's wrong on the issue, though she is. It's about her. It's about the amazing, holier-than-thou know-it-allism that she has exuded from the moment she was asked [the question]."[24]

Holier-than-thou? Know-it-allism? She answered a question she never expected to be asked honestly and some might say even hesitantly. What she said was hardly offensive, but it certainly wasn't what she was "supposed" to say if she wanted to win the favor of Hollywood or the liberal press. "No offense to anyone out there, but that's how I was raised and that's how I think it should be—between a man and a woman."

She even said, "No offense!" But for Olbermann, the idea of anyone, especially a Christian beauty queen, clinging to traditional views on marriage is patently absurd. He ridicules a point she made in an interview after the competition, in which she says she felt, in that moment, tempted to back away from her beliefs, but that God gave her the strength to give an honest opinion.

---

23. Japhy Grant, "Perez Hilton's Gay Witch Hunt," Salon.com, Dec. 15, 2006.
24. Keith Olbermann, MSNBC's *Countdown with Keith Olbermann*, May 12, 2009.

"God and Satan battling it out for the future of freedom of speech inside the head of Saint Carrie of La Jolla!" Olbermann cackled.

Bill Maher also didn't think much of Prejean's views, or the rest of the country's, for that matter. On CNN's *Reliable Sources,* Howard Kurtz asked him what he objected to.

"Well, I thought her answer—not the answer at the pageant, but later, when she said, 'Satan was trying to tempt me with that,' I think that says a lot about our country because, you know, here's a person who believes in Satan, as does, I would guess, 60, 70, 80 percent of this country. This dumb, dumb, country believes in demons and some creature with horns and a tail and a pitchfork who's going to make you burn in a mythical place if you don't believe in an imaginary friend. That's really the root problem of it, isn't it?" [25]

For ideologues like Olbermann and Maher, for whom religion is the country's worst attribute, it's not that she opposed gay marriage. It's that she dared do so from a place of faith. In that same interview, Maher couldn't resist a swipe at Prejean by way of another famous believer: "Let's see . . . she's extremely Christian, she's kind of hot, and she's dumb. Looks like the Republicans have a new vice presidential candidate."

But if Keith Olbermann, Perez Hilton, and Bill Maher can be considered "opinion-makers," and are thus exempt from any rules of ethical journalism, what about a popular evening news anchor—like Katie Couric? Surely someone of her unimpeachable stature would resist an opportunity to attack gay marriage opponents like Prejean.

Well, not if you happened to be at Princeton University's Class Day for graduating seniors in June 2009. The CBS anchor addressed the graduating class with an earnest message: "Don't be a hater. Princeton has taught you to think critically, to approach things with a healthy dose of skepticism. And that's a good thing, as Martha Stew-

25. CNN, *Reliable Sources,* May 24, 2009.

art would say. But you really must guard against the cynicism and nastiness that are so pervasive today, particularly on the internet. Rise above the collegial nastiness and instead . . . celebrate excellence." [26]

But "Do as I say, and not as I do" was apparently Katie's other message, because she jumped at the opportunity to slam Prejean for her opposition to gay marriage. "A Latina has just been nominated to the Supreme Court . . . only the third woman in history. And I heard she was graduated summa cum laude from a little school in New Jersey. Hillary Clinton was the first serious female presidential candidate and made 18 million cracks in the ultimate glass ceiling. And then, of course, there's Carrie Prejean, Miss California. No one has done more to motivate gay rights activists since Anita Bryant. (Your parents know who she is.)"

Likening Prejean to Bryant was not a compliment. Bryant, a Christian conservative, led a successful campaign in Miami to repeal a gay rights ordinance, prompting gay rights activists to boycott oranges and orange juice. Bryant became an enemy of the state for gay America, and it appears Katie Couric believes Prejean should meet a similar fate.

In a lecture to graduating seniors on the perils of "nastiness," she also took a shot at—who else?—Sarah Palin. "Coming here was a real no-brainer! After all, I can see New Jersey from my house!"

And despite warning the audience of the particular nastiness that resides on the internet, Couric promptly posted her remarks online on the Huffington Post.

Carrie Prejean is an awkward spokesperson for traditional marriage, given the scandals that have followed her. And, frankly, the conservative media is to blame for holding her up as one. They were right to seize the moment and defend her response at the pageant, but she has hardly been an unimpeachable role model. But what other choice

---

26. Katie Couric, "My Speech to Princeton's Class of 2009," Huffington Post, June 1, 2009.

did they have? Who else is speaking up for traditional marriage, besides right-wing pundits and religious leaders? The citizenry needs its own voice, and for a few weeks, Carrie Prejean was theirs.

Soon, though, the liberal media got some new red meat to sink its teeth into, thanks to another post–Prop 8 pop culture moment.

When Kris Allen, an affable, good-looking Christian singer, won *American Idol* over his eccentric and theatrical competitor Adam Lambert, who was rumored to be gay, the liberal media blamed—you guessed it—homophobic Christians. Lambert had been a favorite of gay activists like Perez Hilton, and of Hollywood. When he lost—inexplicably—there were even rumblings that the "election" was fixed somehow, to keep Lambert from the title.

Never mind that Lambert was inconsistent, or that Allen was a favorite among texting-addicted teenage girls, a big chunk of the *American Idol* voting contingent. None of that mattered—the liberal media fell back on the only explanation it ever offers when its anointed protégés lose: blame the backward, intolerant Christian masses.

The *American Idol* "upset" prompted *Newsweek*'s Ramin Setoodeh to offer this searing analysis: "Whoa. So it's really true: Kris Allen is the new American Idol. Really? Seriously?" [27]

His shock was mitigated by what he considered an obvious explanation for the loss: "You could say . . . that religion is an irrelevant criterion for judging a singing competition. But the fact remains that *Idol* is one of TV's most family-friendly shows, and it draws a large number of Christian viewers. Kris Allen had the edge here."

The *Examiner*'s gay and lesbian issues point man, Kelvin Lynch, likewise explained it. "Kris is practically a poster boy for heterosexual, white-bread Christianity, while Adam is an in-your-face Jewish gay

---

27. Ramin Setoodeh, "American Idol—And the Winner Is . . ." Newsweek.com, May 21, 2009.

man. That could very well have played a significant role in the final voting among red state voters with texting capability."[28]

And Elliot Olshansky wrote in the *New York Daily News:* "Going into the finale, there was talk of 'red state-blue state' politics at work, with Lambert's painted fingernails, 'guyliner,' and uncertain sexuality against Allen's down-home, churchgoing sensibilities. Given the current political climate, that matchup appeared to favor Lambert, but a number of blue-state types may be 'too cool' for *Idol*'s mass appeal, and unlikely to vote."[29]

To be clear, Adam Lambert never said he was gay during the show. He didn't run onstage draped in a rainbow flag, screaming, "Death to the breeders," celebrating Satanism. So what was it the liberal media thought Christian America objected to? Nail polish? Makeup? Hair products? Have you seen the guys in popular Christian rock groups? They don't exactly look like the Vienna Boys' Choir.

The suggestion that Christian viewers not only correctly interpreted Lambert's guyliner as code for "gay" rather than theatrical effect, but then decided gay men have no business in, um, show business, is hysterical, paranoid, and incredibly bigoted. Middle America has long accepted the holy union that is gay man plus chorus. Who do you think makes up audiences at Broadway shows like *Phantom of the Opera, Guys and Dolls,* and *The Lion King*? It's the Smiths from Topeka, Kansas. It's not Keith Olbermann and Bill Maher.

But the whole thing was a setup from the get-go. Liberal Hollywood threw its weight behind Lambert early on. Adam was a sure thing for them, but only because they wanted him to be. His performances were criticized by the judges more than once. But it's not like these *Idol* arbiters based their convictions on statistics or polls. Singer Katy Perry

28. Kelvin Lynch, "Kris Allen Was American Idol—Did Religion Play a Role?" Examiner.com, May 20, 2009.

29. Elliot Olshansky, "How Adam Lambert Didn't Win American Idol—Anatomy of Kris Allen's Surprising Win," *New York Daily News,* May 21, 2009.

put his name on her cape during a performance—and the *Daily News* claimed this was actually evidence that he was supposed to win.

With few and obscure exceptions, Christians didn't launch the attack campaign against Adam Lambert that the liberal media launched against Christians. And to his credit, Lambert—who did eventually admit to being gay after the show had finished—was gracious, generous, and dignified in defeat, refusing to join in the hysteria fanned by the liberal media around him. For him, like the rest of the country, it was simple—voters simply liked Kris Allen more.

American Idol thus went the way of the Miss USA pageant and other onetime innocuous entertainment vehicles—it had been politicized. Not by intolerant Christians, but by an intolerant liberal media that could offer no other explanation for dissent than the lunacy of fringe believers.

Christians are often casualties of the liberal media's myopia, its unwavering commitment to its own causes, and its refusal to see the bigger picture. In 2009, religion writer Jonathan Merritt wrote in *USA Today*'s *On Religion* column, "Evangelical opposition to anything even remotely concerning 'the homosexual agenda' has often been vitriolic and unbalanced by a message of love for our gay neighbors. Thus, it is understandable that people have incredibly negative perceptions of Christians."[30] So, intolerance of gay men and women is not understandable, but intolerance of Christians is? And the Christians were asking for it?

Furthermore, he wrote, gay men and women "often suffer as societal pariahs at the hands of misinformed Christians who believe that gays have chosen their sexual orientation."

All of this is true—some evangelical Christians have been overtly hostile to gays, and many gay men and women have suffered due to their intolerance. But if the liberal media could step outside its bubble

---

30.   Jonathan Merritt, "An Evangelical's Plea: 'Love the Sinner,'" *USA Today*, April 20, 2009.

once in a while, it might see that more and more, it's Christians who are on the receiving end of a firing squad. It's Christians who aren't tolerated. And the very folks who are shedding light on intolerance toward gays are the ones inflicting their vitriol on Christians.

When you consider that the majority of the country believes that marriage should be between a man and a woman, and that many of those opposed to gay marriage are willing to support civil unions, then the gay marriage issue isn't about Christians' forcing their beliefs on the minority, it's about the minority forcing their beliefs on Christians. And the media is more than happy to back their cause.

Is calling Carrie Prejean a bitch, a "c"-word, or "Saint Carrie of La Jolla" really any better than calling someone a faggot? In the interest of civility and decency, shouldn't the mainstream media rise above the hateful rhetoric of bigots instead of joining in? But here again, as always, the media eagerly forsakes its commitment to truth and objectivity to promote its own biases and liberal ideology. How is that doing you a service? Even if you agree with MSNBC or the *New York Times* about gay marriage, or anything else, the point of journalism isn't to reaffirm your own beliefs—it's to report the news. And in the case of opinion journalists like Keith Olbermann, you are being twice disserviced: once when he gives you only half the story, and again when he attacks Christian America, not on the merits of their positions, but simply because they are Christian. That isn't an opinion—that's just bigotry. And it's the very accusation Olbermann and the rest of the liberal press levies against Christian America. While the media complains that Christians are intolerant, narrow-minded, judgmental, and terrible people for raising objections to gay marriage out of one side of its mouth, it hurls insults and hate-filled invectives against them out of the other. The hypocrisy is so thick you could mop it up. Why would you trust someone who lies to you, openly judges you, and regularly mocks you?

III

THOU SHALT WORSHIP PROFITS, NOT PROPHETS

A Christian community is called the "Catholic Jonestown." Jesus-loving cartoon vegetables go on a murderous rampage. A scripture-quoting superhero is akin to "child abuse."

When Christianity markets its messages to mainstream America, the liberal media launches into attack mode to slander and smear those efforts as gratuitous, exploitative, profiteering, or merely hilarious. The examples above are some of the characterizations the press uses to worry, frighten, and outrage their readers and viewers over Christianity's evil plot to convert consumers, one Bibleman action figure at a time.

It's ironic, considering that Western culture has long appreciated the power of the almighty dollar. Success, in America in particular, is often defined by box-office figures, net worth, annual earnings, and a place on the vaunted Fortune 500 list. As proud capitalists, we have little problem with making money, even when it's on the back of some morally just and supposedly incorruptible ideological cause. Great and noble ideas, we say, can also be profitable.

Take, for example, ecoconsumerism and the so-called greening of America. Adherents of the cause—determined to eat healthier, live longer, and clean up the planet—are undeterred by the fact that it is also a billion-dollar business that has made a lot of people very wealthy. Nor does it matter much that the ecosolutions these liberal activists are pushing aren't always good for the consumer's wallet or his health—or that of the planet. Glossy magazines, entertainment shows, and even the mainstream press fawns over just how "green" its celebrity gods are, and even gushes over how much money they shell out to do it. "Halle Berry spent sixty thousand dollars to turn her three baby nurseries green—isn't she a saint for making the planet cleaner one organic baby wipe at a time?"

Al Gore has made millions pimping a green agenda, and the Left has beatified him for it, regardless of whether science has actually proved him right. The popular grocery totes made from cotton or canvas being sold at trendy stores around the country actually require more water and energy to produce than plastic ones. But sales in that industry shot up 1000 percent in 2008.

And then there's the organic food craze, largely propagated by liberal anticorporate activists who want to shame you into buying four-dollar tomatoes and seven-dollar toilet paper. Never mind that a 2009 study by the London School of Hygiene & Tropical Medicine, published in the *American Journal of Clinical Nutrition,* found that organic food has no nutritional or health benefits over ordinary food. Researchers said that "consumers were paying higher prices for organic food because of its perceived health benefits, creating a global organic market worth an estimated $48 billion in 2007."[1]

Even Hollywood makes money by promoting the industry not just as an entertainment vehicle, but as a moral imperative and philanthropic cause. Movie studios, producers, directors, screenwriters, actors, musicians, and artists regularly insist that, in addition to entertaining people, their work betters communities and educates people, and therefore the country needs to invest heavily in the arts and in art and music education. As the National Endowment for the Arts likes to say, "A great country deserves great art."

The idea that any of these "causes"—ecoconsumerism, the arts, or dozens of others—remains totally untainted by either money or politics is patently absurd. Why is it okay to call the godless and billion-dollar business of climate change a "moral imperative," but promoting the Christian cause through business is a moral corruption? In yet another effort to target Christians as evil fanatics, the liberal media regularly slams them as unholy marketeers who care more about their profits than their prophets.

FILM AT ELEVEN! CHRISTIAN BUSINESSES ARE REALLY, REALLY WEIRD

The liberal media routinely paints Christian business ventures or Christian products as problematic, unseemly, and somehow silly, simply for delivering to consumers the religious or spiritual experiences they want. Marketing to special-interest groups is just fine when it's secular—marketing to women, African-Americans, Hispanics, gays, and lesbians is either altruistically servicing the needs of under-

---

1. Reuters, "Organic Food Is No Healthier, Study Finds," July 29, 2009.

represented minorities or just good business. But marketing to Christians is exploitation and ugly profiteering.

ABC News' Dan Harris filed a report for *World News Tonight* in 2006 that asked very theatrically if Christian business owners were "spreading or exploiting their faith?"[2]

As is customary in the liberal press, stories of this nature usually make use of some cutesy, condescending wordplay to bring home just how funny all this faith business really is. Harris's was no exception. "At Irene Trammell's Christian fitness club in California," Harris says, "you can work your thighs while you proselytize."

There was also this clever bon mot: "Mark Gadow's Christian Faith Driving School in Maryland gives new meaning to the old bumper sticker 'Jesus is My Co-Pilot.'"

Hilarious.

But Harris's real message in this report was the shocking news that—get ready for it—in business, some people may be less than honest. "Buyer Should Still Beware," the feature warns. "While Christian businesses say they give to charity and treat their customers according to biblical principles, there are some hucksters out there."

Never mind the fact that consumers can fall victim to swindles in all types of business in every corner of the earth. Worse was that Harris's claims of Christian swindling went totally unsubstantiated. He offered not a single shred of evidence of any evil Christian hucksters out to take you for a ride. He didn't interview a single person about an alleged experience of being taken by a Christian businessman. He gave us no records of fraud or corruption in Christian businesses. But none of that nonreporting stopped him from sounding the alarm.

---

2. Dan Harris, "Christian Businesses Making a Profit While Saving Souls," ABC News, Jan. 13, 2006.

And there were more alarms to come. "There are those who believe Christian businesses exploit religion to get customers," says Harris. And who were these people? Well, he talks only to one—not a Christian businesswoman or a Christian customer, or the head of the local small business association, but instead the liberal media's go-to authority, the college professor.

" 'I'm not sure Jesus Christ would have done that,' said Boston College professor Alan Wolfe, who studies religion in public life. He says Christian businesses both hurt democracy—because they segregate people—and are bad for Christianity. 'Because their Christianity requires that they go out and save the souls of other people—people not like themselves,' Wolfe said."

With one quick sound bite from Wolfe—who is, incidentally, a onetime Marxist scholar, author of *The Future of Liberalism,* and former adviser to President Clinton—we learn that Christian businesses like fitness clubs and driving schools do no less damage to the country than destroy the whole of democracy. And you thought you were just working out.

And, somehow, because Christianity requires its followers to encourage others to believe with them, Christians who do just this are, for Harris and Wolfe, bad for Christianity. The circular logic notwithstanding, one wonders just how well this religion professor really understands American Christians.

When the revered Baptist preacher Billy Graham held a three-day revival at Flushing Meadows Corona Park in 2005, which brought tens of thousands of worshipers to Queens, New York, to hear him speak, the moment was a good opportunity for some in the liberal press to poke a little fun at the event and the "kind of people" who went to it.

Stephen Miller, of the now-defunct libertarian paper the *New*

York Sun, set up the colorful mise-en-scène by employing the wildly popular aforementioned technique of using religious wordplay. You know, because the story's about God and stuff. Here are some of the sillier examples.

"It was those millions, the emblazoned-T-shirt Christians thirsting for salvation, who were Rev. Graham's focus this weekend. They were thirsting for water too, and the amounts available showed that the seamless garment could apply as much to Rev. Graham's organizational team as to Christ's tunic."

TRANSLATION: It was hot that day, but event staffers had plenty of water on hand.

"Audience members, many attending from out of state, wandered the grounds in large numbers hours before scheduled events kicked off, forming lines for refreshments at the Lemon Ice King of Corona and Corn King that were nearly as long as the lines they formed for the King of Kings later."

TRANSLATION: There were a lot of people there.

"Banks of water fountains had been constructed, and public-address announcements urged celebrants to keep themselves fully hydrated during the sweltering afternoons. Hundreds of portable toilets in banks of between 40 and 50 were located strategically, and in what must count as something of a secular miracle, there was rarely a line."

TRANSLATION: Going to the bathroom didn't take that long.

Elizabeth Spiers of Salon.com decided on a similar approach when she covered the three-day event, which she respectfully called "a spiritual three-ring circus." She found the whole thing, she makes very clear, ripe for mockery. In her essay she gives the bulk of her attention not to Graham's words or messages, but to the merchandising and marketing at the event, which she decided was "pandering to New Yorkers" as well as "pandering to the kids of today." At most concerts and sporting events, entertaining attendees and selling merchandise and refreshments don't merit a four-paragraph description in a literary feature, but at the Graham event they were notable as "an odd hodgepodge of elements."

"As with most affairs where money changes hands, there appeared to be a fringe market around the Graham enterprise. In between sessions, attendees were encouraged to buy books from the Crusade bookstore including a coffee-table volume that offered a photographic history of Graham's various crusades throughout the years. Signage for Snapple was everywhere and the concession stands served only Pepsi, lending unwitting credence to any conspiracy theories about the inherent evil of Coca-Cola. There was also the occasional middle-aged woman with a cooler offering black-market bottles of Poland Spring water at the cut-rate price of 'One dollar, one dollar!' But for a gathering of this size with absolutely no drunks and the world's only immaculate portable toilets, the program officials and cops on hand appeared to consider the sales a tolerable infraction."[3]

Wait, hold the phone—they had Snapple, Pepsi, and water there? Those people *are* bizarre!

Wow, Spiers really makes you feel like you're there, doesn't she? You get the impression that the only reason Salon sent her to the Billy Graham revival was explicitly to make fun of it. You're not meant to learn anything about the event from pieces like this, except that Elizabeth Spiers found it really, really weird. Is that reporting? Is that even useful or interesting commentary? Seems cheap, catty, and puerile to me. But that's the state of the liberal media today—Christians represent nothing more than a sensational opportunity for classist, elitist snark. A more interesting angle might have been a discussion of Graham's message, or an examination of what attendees were hoping

3. Elizabeth Spiers, "A Spiritual Three-Ring Circus," Salon.com, June 27, 2005.

to find there. Why are so many people looking to connect through Christ today? What accounts for Billy Graham's continued popularity through the decades? Even a lighter look at the event could be interesting without sounding wholly uninformed about the world in which Spiers lives. The problem with this continual "otherizing" of Christians—making them sound alien and fringe—is that it makes the media appear not only hostile but uneducated. Accepting Spier's account of the Billy Graham revival is accepting her worldview that Christianity isn't mainstream—which it is.

THIS JUST IN: CHRISTIANS WILL CONVERT YOU WITH SONG AND DANCE!

In recent years, a number of Christian businesses and Christian products in particular have caught the skeptical secular eyes of the liberal media. And to read about them you'd think they represented the second coming of, well, something really, really scary.

One was the opening of a new theme park in Orlando called the Holy Land Experience, a biblically themed edutainment center featuring re-creations of a Jerusalem street market, the Wilderness Tabernacle, the Qumran caves where the Dead Sea Scrolls were found, the garden tomb where Jesus' body was laid to rest, and the world's largest indoor model of Jerusalem, circa A.D. 66. There are song-and-dance shows, a daily reenactment of the Passion, classes, guest lectures, and church services, and the most recent addition is the Scriptorium, which houses the world-renowned Van Kampen Collection of manuscripts, scrolls, and other religious artifacts, and other objects from the Eberhard Nestlé library. As is to be expected, there are myriad food, drink, and shopping options, like lunch at the Oasis Palms Café or coffee at the Sycamore Tree, and the Shofar Shop or Old Scroll Shop for souvenirs.

To most people in mainstream America it sounds a lot like any other theme park or museum. And as a destination it makes a lot of sense—most families try to find vacations that speak to their interests, whether they're water sports, shopping, culture, hiking, golf, or in this case, faith.

But to the liberal media, the conflation of Christianity and good, old-fashioned family fun is cause for confusion, skepticism, and, yes, some more well-timed mockery.

In San Francisco, where "serious" culture is a head shop on Ashbury Street, Neva Chonin had an absolute ball with the Holy Land Experience in the *San Francisco Chronicle.* "Me, I figure the Holy Land Experience is almost grand enough to qualify as the Second Coming. Almost. It could be so much more. Where are Job's Wild Ride, Noah's Splash Mountain, Gomorrah Land, the Crown of Thorns Ring Toss, the Calvary Sculpture Garden, the Cast-the-First-Stone Kissing Booth and the Seven Holes of the Cross mini-golf course? Guaranteed draws, all of them."[4]

But most in the media are far less creative than she is. Most just really want you to know how weird and "unusual" the park is.

The *Tennessean* writes, "The park stages daily re-enactments of the Crucifixion and the Resurrection—heavy fare for the average tourist. But those who seek it out tend not to be your average tourists."[5] How's that? Those who seek out a trip to the Holy Land Experience tend to be Christians, presumably—who represent 80 percent of the country—so actually, they probably are simply "your average tourists."

MSNBC picked up an AP story in which the park is described as equally strange. The setup was nearly identical—because, as everyone

---

4. Neva Chonin, "Welcome to Florida's Biblical Theme Park," *San Francisco Chronicle,* Jan. 15, 2006.

5. Jennifer Brooks, "Two Bible Parks? It's Possible," *Tennessean,* June 16, 2008.

in the news business knows, if it bleeds, it leads: "Jesus Christ is crucified and resurrected here six days a week. Snarling Roman soldiers
whip and drag him, and somber audience members watch. Some quietly weep at a pageant bloody and cruel. It is the grand finale at the
Holy Land Experience, and not the attraction most tourists envision
in an Orlando vacation."[6]

And Joan Branham performed the same one-two punch—insulting both the whole idea of the park and its visitors simultaneously—in
a *Newsweek* column called "The Crucifixion and Ice Cream": "Amid
cell phones ringing, video cams rolling and ice cream melting under
the Florida sun, a blood-spattered Jesus stumbles through the crowd
on his way to Golgotha, where nasty Roman soldiers strip him, nail
him to the cross and crucify him—while perspiring tourists look on
in Bermuda shorts. After the resurrection sequence, visitors applaud
and line up for a photo op, not with Mickey or Minnie, but a disciple
or bloody-handed yet friendly centurion. Welcome to Orlando's most
unusual theme park, the Holy Land Experience."[7]

Of course Branham's account is not really meant to tell you
anything about the park; it's meant to horrify you. The thought of
"perspiring tourists . . . in Bermuda shorts" watching a Passion play—
something millions of Americans do in churches every Lent—is
supposed to send shivers down your spine. Meanwhile, the live entertainment at Universal Studios, which includes a gruesome Horror
Makeup Show, Beetlejuice's Graveyard Revue, and the bug-and-
testicle-eating extravaganza that is Fear Factor Live, is no competition for "Orlando's most unusual theme park."

Time magazine's Michael Kinsley took a similar tack in a fear-
laced jeremiad against the Holy Land Experience's subliminal intent

---

6. Associated Press, "Florida Theme Park Recreates Crucifixion," MSNBC.com, Aug. 8, 2007.
7. Joan Branham, "The Crucifixion and Ice Cream," *Newsweek*, May 23, 2008.

to convert unsuspecting parkgoers, likening Christians to communists and cults: "[The] marketing strategy does not inspire confidence. It is a comic-book variation on the classic conversion strategy used by proselytizers of all sorts, from cults like the Moonies to communists in their heyday to sects within Judaism that recruit among Jewish tourists in Israel. You befriend your targets when their guard is down, disguising your true intent; then you gradually draw them over to your side."[8]

The park doesn't likely draw too many Muslims, Buddhists, Hindus, Taoists, or atheists, but if they do stumble on the Holy Land Experience during their Orlando vacations, Kinsley can probably rest assured that the "Crystal Living Waters" fountain and light show isn't going to convert them. But this hits on an important question. The secular liberal press has made its opinion of Christianity very clear—it's a joke, a fraud, a fringe belief, and a prehistoric relic from the Dark Ages. So why all the paranoia? Why are writers like Kinsley so afraid of a Christian amusement park? Or a Christian gym? Or a popular evangelist? Their fear, and the disproportional attention they give to spreading it, give them away—they're not as worried about the spread of Christianity as much as they're terrified that you're not. Their anxiety is an implicit acknowledgment of their minority status as secularists, even as they insist to you, the reader and viewer, that they represent the majority. And an intellectually superior one, at that.

Another story that threw the liberal media into a tailspin revolved around Tom Monaghan, the founder of Domino's Pizza and a devout Catholic philanthropist. When word got out that he wanted to create a town in Collier County, Florida, called Ave Maria, which would

---

8. Michael Kinsley, "Don't Want to Convert? Just Say No," *Time*, Feb. 19, 2001.

conserve rural agriculture and natural resources, center on a Catholic
university, and foster Catholic values and business practices, the media was aghast.

The town, still in development, has a cathedral, a golf course and
tennis club, a hospital, a school, and the kinds of business every other
town in America has—grocery store, coffee shop, bookstore—and
was intended to be a place where Christian values would be preserved
and protected. Monaghan wanted to limit the sale of pornography
and contraceptive devices, but was later forced by the ever-watchful
ACLU to promise he wouldn't break any laws to ensure that. The
town was never planned to exclude or prohibit non-Christians from
entering it or in fact living there if they wanted.

But for the liberal media, it was downright subversive.

Salon.com's Lori Leibovich wrote a piece called "Large Pie, No
Abortion," in which she said, "The town, about 25 miles east of Na-
ples, is being built around Ave Maria University, the first Catholic
University to open in the U.S. in 40 years. It will be set on 5,000 acres
with a 'European-inspired' town center and a 'massive' church that
will sport a 65-foot crucifix, the largest one in the nation. Who knew
there could one day be a town creepier than Disney's Celebration?"[9]

Indeed, town squares and church crosses are pretty creepy.

"Still, the idea of a religiously governed town in the U.S. makes
me profoundly uncomfortable." She goes on to quote another frequent Salon contributor and abortion activist, Frances Kissling,
who likened the concept to Islamic fundamentalism. "This is un-
American," said Kissling. "I don't think in a democratic society you
can have a legally organized township that will seek to have any kind
of public service whatsoever and try to restrict the constitutional
rights of citizens."

9.   Lori Leibovich, "Large Pie, No Abortion," Salon.com, March 2, 2006.

Leibovich also took issue with Monaghan's vision of a community that espouses Christian values. (Someone should tell her to avoid all the states between New York and California.) "But," she concluded, "if Ave Maria comes to be, at least it will likely offer 24-hour pizza delivery."

The first language of the secular liberal media has always been smug condescension. More than that, though, Kissling's decision that a town like Ave Maria is "un-American," and Leibovich's approval of it, are preposterous, and even dangerous. First, no one is herding unwitting Protestants, Hasids, or atheists from neighboring towns into Ave Maria and forcing them to live within Catholic guidelines. Living there is a choice, presumably made by folks who *want* to live Christian values and share those values with their neighbors. And it's their constitutional right to do so. There is no difference between prohibiting a Catholic in Boston from practicing Catholicism and prohibiting a bunch of them from practicing it in Ave Maria. Who is Ave Maria hurting? That Kissling and Leibovich find this town so threatening says more about them than it does about Monaghan or any of the people who want to live there.

In the *New York Times* the concern wasn't so much about the town, but about the university it was organized around. Reporter Tamar Lewin was fearful of just how Christian the school would be. Kind of Christian is okay—but really, really Christian is, you know, scary. "Ave Maria will be far more conservative than most of the nation's 235 Catholic colleges and universities. While it will be independent of the church, as the major Catholic universities are, it will have no coed dorms and no gay-support groups. Although attending Mass will not be required, Mr. Monaghan says he expects most students to go regularly.... Highly regarded institutions like Georgetown, Notre Dame and Boston College balance their quest for first-rate scholarship from a diverse faculty and a diverse student body against their commitment to a strong religious identity."[10]

Ave Maria University, she worried, would not. Even though students who didn't want to get their college education in such a conservative environment probably just wouldn't go there, it seems the mere existence of such a place proved too troubling for the *New York Times* and its purportedly objective reporter.

Katie Couric, high priestess of the secular liberal media elite, was equally concerned about "diversity" and "tolerance." (Ironically, calls for diversity and tolerance by the liberal press never seem to extend to Christianity.) On NBC, which slapped the words "Catholic Town USA" onto the segment, Couric said to Monaghan that some people may think Catholic values "wholesome, but in other ways, I think people will see this community as eschewing diversity and promoting intolerance."[11] Again, for Couric, the mantra seems to be "Do as I say, not as I do."

And she pushed Monaghan even further: "But do you think the tenets of the community might result in de facto segregation as a result of some of the beliefs that are being espoused by the majority of residents there?"

De facto segregation—sounds scary, right? But what, exactly, did she mean? Was she suggesting that the community's promotion of Christian values would probably attract only people who wanted to live similarly Christian values? If that's the case, how is Monaghan's Ave Maria different from the nation's many Hasidic communities? Or Hispanic enclaves? Or, for that matter, retirement communities? Best of all, how is it different from San Francisco or Cambridge, Massachusetts, where throngs of like-minded

10. Tamar Lewin, "A Catholic College, A Billionaire's Idea, Will Rise in Florida," *New York Times*, Feb. 10, 2003.

11. L. Brent Bozell, "There Go Those 'Controversial Catholics' Again," Media Research Center, www.mrc.org, March 8, 2006.

liberals migrate every year to surround themselves with "their kind of people"?

She ended the segment in her own inimitably adorable way: "Well, we'll probably be following this story, because I know the ACLU is too."

On another network, Martin Bashir interviewed Monaghan on ABC's *Nightline,* and was similarly foreboding: "Not everyone is delighted at the prospect of a town so avowedly Catholic, especially those concerned with civil liberties. You know that it's been described as a Catholic Jonestown, a kind of Catholic Iran, where individual rights and liberties are curtailed."[12]

So, you remember Jonestown, right? The People's Temple commune founded by Jim Jones, who later persuaded 907 people, many of them children, to drink cyanide, in the largest mass suicide in history? Yeah, Ave Maria is going to be just like that.

Echoing Ms. Couric, Bashir also asked if Ave Maria would be "welcoming to unbelievers."

To read and listen to the liberal media, you'd think Ave Maria was something out of *Children of the Corn,* and Tom Monaghan, who once owned the Detroit Tigers, was David Koresh. I was curious about Ave Maria, so I actually went there, which is something most of its critics can't say. It was noteworthy only for its ordinariness. It was a small, quiet community with a few gated subdivisions, a golf course, a bright and cheery town square, and a beautiful Frank Lloyd Wright–inspired cathedral. I went to Mass, had an egg and cheese sandwich and an iced coffee at the local lunch spot, and looked at the golf carts for sale in one of the store windows. I bought a Jesus doll in the local toy store for the daughter of a friend. People were friendly and

---

12. Brent Baker, "ABC's *Nightline* Regurgitates Attack on 'Catholic Jonestown,'" Media Research Center, www.mrc.org, Aug. 9, 2007.

polite. And yet somehow, this non-Christian made it out alive to tell the tale.

HIDE YOUR CHILDREN: THE
CUCUMBERS ARE COMING

When Christian marketing reaches out to children, the media gets even more hysterical. Christian toys, games, cartoons, action figures, kids' books, and movies, which offer parents an opportunity to filter the kinds of influences their kids are subjected to by secular outlets, are likened to Cold War propaganda vehicles out to corrupt and convert your children into an army of Christian soldiers. MTV and VH1 are fine parental substitutes, apparently, but a Christian cartoon is religious indoctrination.

Veggie Tales was and still is a wildly popular animated children's television series, featuring the trials and tribulations of Bob the Tomato and Larry the Cucumber. Creators Phil Vischer and Mike Nawrocki infused the cartoons with subtle Christian morality themes and lessons from the Bible, a plus for Christian families looking to find something meaningful on television. Not unlike *SpongeBob* or *Dora the Explorer,* the show spawned books, music, and merchandise, as well as a live touring show and full-length feature films.

In 2008, *Veggie Tales* debuted its second movie, *The Pirates Who Don't Do Anything,* and, totally unprompted, some critics were quick to "reassure" parents that they didn't have to worry—the movie wasn't too religious. *Boston Globe* movie reviewer Ty Burr felt it important to point out to fear-stricken moms and dads—in the title of the review no less—that "They Don't Do Anything But Entertain." He also reassured them that " 'The Pirates Who Don't Do Anything' is notably secular—well, there's a speech by the king toward the end that might metaphorically refer to a Higher Power, but it'd take a theologian to pluck it out."[13]

Whew, what a relief, right?

The *New York Times*'s Neil Genzlinger went the opposite direction, warning parents at the outset that *Veggie Tales* is no ordinary kids' cartoon.

The headline for Genzlinger's review is "For Values-Based Produce, a Heroic Seafaring Quest." And his very first sentence? "You don't have to go far into the press material for 'The Pirates Who Don't Do Anything' before you hit the phrase 'faith-and-values-based property.' It is used to describe this and earlier offerings from the Veggie Tales franchise."[14]

But then, in a bizarre reversal, or maybe even total abandonment of what seems like his main thesis—after all, it's in both the title and the lead—after warning us twice that *Veggie Tales* is "values-based," he writes, "but the 'faith' component of this rather ordinary film for children doesn't make itself readily apparent."

And he never develops the "values-based" thread any further. The review simply and matter-of-factly goes on to say it's an unspectacular movie that he didn't find particularly funny or clever, but that kids will probably enjoy. So if the "values-based" components of the film weren't even noticeable, and he's not going to tell us where they're subliminally tucked away, then why bother mentioning them in the first place? It's an arbitrary, but entirely calculated decision by Genzlinger to direct your attention to the fact that this seemingly secular (and therefore benign) kids' movie is actually (dun, Dun, DUN) "values-based."

---

13. Ty Burr, "They Don't Do Anything But Entertain," *Boston Globe*, Jan. 12, 2008.
14. Neil Genzlinger, "For Values-Based Produce, A Heroic Seafaring Quest," *New York Times*, Jan. 11, 2008.

Even when the religion's ostensibly invisible, Christians can't win.

In 2006, NBC began airing *Veggie Tales* episodes with permission from the series' creators, but with one very notable exception—all the God and religion references were taken out. Most noticeable to fans was that NBC dropped the program's signature sign-off message: "Remember, kids, God made you special and he loves you very much." Parents, Christian advocacy groups, and conservative media watchdogs were outraged. Media Research Center's L. Brent Bozell said, "NBC has taken the very essence of 'Veggie Tales' and ripped it out. It's like 'Gunsmoke' without the guns, or 'Monday Night Football' without the football."[15]

Meanwhile, NBC simply said the show was edited to meet "network broadcast standards." Alan Wurtzel, the NBC executive who oversees those standards, put it another way: "We are not a religious broadcaster."[16] And NBC spokeswoman Rebecca Marks said, "Our goal is to reach as broad an audience as possible with these positive messages while being careful not to advocate any one religious point of view."[17]

Which one religious point of view did NBC think they'd advocate by including "God made you special and he loves you very much" at the end of each show? That could have referred to any one of the three major faiths, as well as countless other religions. Their response, in short, was a total copout—it wasn't the appearance of advocating one religion that bothered NBC, it was the appearance of advocating

---

15.   L. Brent Bozell, "NBC Slices and Dices 'Veggie Tales,'" Media Research Center, www.mrc.org, Sep. 8, 2006.

16.   Edward Wyatt, "Conservatives Want More Religion in One NBC Show, and Less in Another," *New York Times*, Sep. 23, 2006.

17.   Nadine Johnson-Barthel, "Religious Messages Sliced From 'Veggie Tales,'" *Milwaukee Journal Sentinel*, Nov. 20, 2006.

any religion. And in that case, NBC shouldn't have aired the show at all, especially since it didn't even consult with show creators beforehand to let them know their Christian cartoon was now an entirely secular endeavor.

As the Media Research Center's Bozell wrote on his website, "This is one of those moments where you understand that networks like NBC are only talking an empty talk and walking an empty walk when it comes to the First Amendment. . . . They have told parents concerned about their smutty programs . . . that if they're offended, they have a remote control as an option. Change the channel. Block it out. But when it comes to religious programming—programming that doesn't even mention Jesus Christ—just watch the hypocrisy. Instead of telling viewers to just change the channel if they don't like it, or put in a V-chip for Bible verses, they demand to producers that all that outdated old-time religion has to be shredded before broadcast."

NBC's Wurtzel seemed to admit as much: "Clearly the show has religious themes. It puts forth some very specific religious values. We had to make a decision about where it went further than we considered appropriate."

NBC's standards are very high, indeed. That very same year the network planned to air a taped concert by Madonna, during which she sings while mounted on a cross, wearing a crown of thorns, imitating the crucifixion. First the network said it would air the concert in its entirety, defending the concert moment as entertainment. Then, when the letters poured in from outraged Christians who considered the move by Madonna blasphemous and tasteless, the network said it would consider editing certain parts of the concert. The final decision was to cut away during the "Live to Tell" performance and show different camera angles while she was on the cross.

Earlier, NBC had also defended its 2004 broadcast of the Golden

Globes, in which U2 front man Bono blurted out the f-word, as a "free-speech issue." It's a battle they had no problem fighting when it was the f-word, a prime-time broadcast, and a popular liberal singer-activist, but one they obviously didn't want to fight when it was the g-word, a Saturday morning broadcast, and a couple of cartoon vegetables.

As is the case with most Christian cultural products, *Veggie Tales* has been either dismissed, criticized, or totally censored by the liberal media. When this anti-Christian meme is taken up so wholeheartedly by the media, it's only a matter of time before it becomes mainstream within the popular culture.

Another popular children's show, *Bibleman,* got similar treatment by the liberal press during its long run on television. The evangelical superhero who encouraged kids to have a personal relationship with Jesus was scorned, ridiculed, and harassed by the secular media for his overtly Christian messages, as were Trinity Broadcasting Network for airing it and Christian America for watching it.

But one review stands above the rest, and that was Carl Strock's 2008 column in the *Schenectady Daily Gazette.* The headline read, "It's Bibleman! But Is This Child Abuse?"[18] Some highlights from his condemnation, which is more condescending than it is accusatory:

> *Correspondents of the Christian persuasion frequently urge me to visit a church, apparently in the belief that I will be won over and will give up my skeptical ways. Not to appear recalcitrant, I finally accepted. On Friday evening I attended Grace Fellowship, located in a somewhat down-at-the-heels strip mall in Latham. I admit my motivation was not entirely worshipful. In part I*

---

18. Carl Strock, "It's Bibleman! But Is This Child Abuse?" *Schenectady Daily Gazette,* April 13, 2008.

wanted to evaluate the proposition put forth by Richard Dawkins, prominent British biologist and atheist, that the religious indoctrination of children is a form of abuse as pernicious as sexual abuse.

It wouldn't be fair to call the show childish, since it was after all aimed at children, but still it was pretty lame, with Bibleman whacking various villains with his light saber while forcefully shouting, "No weapon used against you will defeat you! Isaiah 54–17!" which sounded like football signals. Or, "We set our eyes not on what we see but on what we can't see! 2 Corinthians, 4–18!" Whack, whack.

The only time I personally felt any sympathy was when one of the villains responded, "You are so self-righteous." "Go, Lothar," I almost said out loud. But of course Lothar got obliterated like all the "enemies."

Does it constitute child abuse to lead children in the way of religion? ... For the prosecution, I note that at the end of the show, again with his mask off, [Bibleman] preached to the children present that they could have "a new beginning and a fresh start" by coming forward and pledging themselves to Jesus. ... Now, is it abusive of impressionable young minds to tell them they have sinned and need a fresh start? To tell them there is an invisible man up in the sky who has an "awesome plan" for them? To instruct them that evil can be combatted with random quotations from ancient lore? I prayerfully contemplate these questions and do not arrive at a satisfactory answer.

It seems an obvious question, but why is it always the self-proclaimed nonbelievers who trot off sanctimoniously, armed with their double Ph.D.'s in cynicism and derision, determined to expose the brash irrationality and uncultured underbelly of American

Christianity to the sophisticated upperclasses of the liberal secular aristocracy, and end up doing it with all the couth and urbanity of Howard Stern?

To answer Strock's question, no—it's not child abuse. Raising children religious—or telling them "there is an invisible man up in the sky"—is no more abusive than telling them that they're going to die alone, most likely from some terminal and painful disease like stomach cancer or dementia, after which they'll rot in the ground, where countless generations of maggots will feed on their decaying flesh. Both constitute a choice for parents to make. And if Strock could find it within himself to visit other frightening places where the rest of the country hangs out, he'd realize that most parents choose the invisible man up in the sky to flesh-eating maggots.

But the larger point is, writers like the smarter-than-thou Strock aren't really examining the merits of Christian doctrine—whether or not supernatural end-of-life explanations have a psychological effect on children, for example. They are attacking Christian values by way of cheap mockery and condescension, which is neither a journalistic tool of reportage or opining, nor an academic method of investigation, regardless of how smugly they insist it is. But if you like your think pieces with a heavy dose of intellectually flimsy ridicule, you will have endless options in the liberal press.

CHRISTIANS READ?! SOMETHING FISHY'S GOING ON HERE

Another arena in which the marketing of Christianity gets sidelined and mocked is Christian publishing, responsible for massive successes like Rick Warren's *The Purpose Driven Life*, the eschatology novels in Tim LaHaye and Jerry B. Jenkins's *Left Behind* series, and the Joel Osteen empire, all of which are routinely dismissed by the liberal media as somehow less cultured and less serious than so-called mainstream titles.

Rick Warren's book, in particular, which sat on the *New York Times* best-seller list for one of the longest periods in history, and yet was never reviewed by the newspaper, has confounded and amused the liberal media for years for its simple messages and straightforward evangelism.

The *Washington Post* tried very hard to wrap its head around the unfathomable success of *The Purpose Driven Life*, in a 2004 report on the "unexpected" success of Christian publishing ventures.

Staff writers Linton Weeks and Alan Cooperman wrote, "Unabashedly religious, the book is being read and studied by millions of people in and out of churches across the country. Readers are buying extra copies at churches and in bookstores and passing them along to friends. As a crossover bestseller, flying off the shelves in both the Christian and mainstream markets, it is a modern marketing miracle."[19]

"A modern marketing miracle"? It's hard to tell if Weeks and Cooperman are being serious or cute, since Christianity is so often discussed in such terms, without real attention to accuracy or tone, but is the success of Warren's book really any more "miraculous" than, say, the success of the Bible? Alas, there is nothing more implausible to the liberal media than the idea that Americans are supremely religious, most likely Christian, and thus really enjoy experiencing their faith in a variety of ways, which include—gasp!—reading.

In an attempt to prove to you that Rick Warren is not really a pious or devout spiritual leader who sincerely wants the best for your purpose-driven life, but rather that he's a manipulative marketeer

---

19. Linton Weeks and Alan Cooperman, "Faith, Moving Mountains of Books," *Washington Post*, Feb. 22, 2004.

wrapping his radical evangelism in innocuous-sounding touchy-feely-isms, the *Washington Post* journos go on to neatly describe the book as such: "It is a Christ-centered book. It is a book about God. It is filled with Scripture and it is preachy."

Finally, they leave us with a curious thought to ponder . . . curious because it makes little sense: "Using the pulpit to market ideas is as old as Moses. But Warren is taking it to a new level. His ingenious system raises some questions: What else can be sold to such a captive, captivated audience? And who else might take advantage of the opportunity?"

I'm not really sure what Weeks and Cooperman are implying here, but it sounds fairly ominous. They seem to suggest that "captive" Christians in particular are dumb enough to fall for anything, so Rick Warren or some other conniving Christian profiteer will surely craft another clever marketing scheme to wrest even more of their hard-earned greenbacks from out of their cookie jars and mattresses. On the other hand, maybe Christians just like to read about their faith. Crazy, but true.

The *New York Times* had an equally difficult time buying the idea that Christian America really reads. For reporter Rachel Donadio, the success of *The Purpose Driven Life* couldn't be the result of a massive Christian audience—it could be due only to the wiles of scheming marketers.

"It's unclear whether the stellar sales of 'The Purpose Driven Life' and other religious titles speak to a newfound spiritual thirst in the culture—portending a third Great Awakening, as Warren argues—or are more indicative of great marketing."[20]

The popular *Left Behind* series of books was also framed using this kind of schematic. Echoing the usual treatment given to

---

20. Rachel Donadio, "Faith-Based Publishing," *New York Times*, Nov. 28, 2004.

the Holy Land Experience—choosing shock value over thoughtful analysis—the *New York Times* wrote that the series was "based on Dr. LaHaye's literal, bloody interpretation of the Book of Revelation." And again, the *Times* just couldn't understand its popularity: "[It] has become one of the biggest surprise hits in American popular culture."[21]

Why so surprising? LaHaye and Jenkins write about something that matters a great deal to a great many people, in a colorful and captivating way. Why is it any more surprising than the success of romance novels or chick flicks, considering more than half the population is women?

Unsurprisingly, *Newsweek* wasn't any better. One piece asked of books like *Left Behind,* "Sure, they sell. But are they serious?" And *Newsweek*'s self-proclaimed "religion guru," Kenneth L. Woodward, had this to say: "Sociologists tell us that the United States is experiencing a religious revival—a third 'great awakening' echoing those of the 18th and 19th centuries. But if the best-seller lists are any guide, the revival looks more like a collective leaving of the senses."[22]

Yes, Middle America—he's making fun of you.

Christian events, vacations, books, television shows—they're all fodder to the liberal press, which would much rather make fun of Christian America than understand it. The marketing of various Christian experiences to the public, whether it's a fitness club or a way of life in Collier County, Florida, is seen as bizarre, dangerous, or hilarious to the liberal secular elite, which still can't understand what all this God business is really about. The fact that the liberal media always finds the popularity and success of Christian cultural projects so

21. David Kirkpatrick, "In 12th Book of Best-Selling Series, Jesus Returns," *New York Times,* March 29, 2004.

22. Kenneth L. Woodward, "Platitudes or Prophecy?" *Newsweek,* Aug. 27, 2001.

"surprising" is more than just a little revealing. If they were any more out of touch with mainstream America they'd be France.

But it also speaks to something more sinister. Yes, people in the mainstream media have become a bunch of schoolyard bullies, taunting America's Christians for sport. But make no mistake, they are also trying to marginalize Christianity. The liberalism that pervades the mainstream press requires them to—because the fixed and demanding morality of Judeo-Christian values means their moral relativism, where just about anything goes, is in jeopardy. To ensure they will not be judged for their decisions or behavior—by God, by the faithful, by their next-door neighbors—and that their lives will continue to be consequence free, the liberal ideologues in the mainstream media want to convince you that Christian morality is out. It's stupid, it's weird, it's backward, it's even a little funny. Instead they will peddle another kind of judgment, one predicated on intellectual superiority, elitist classism, and a philosophy of meaningless and arbitrary causes du jour—environmentalism being the most obvious. By disguising these sanctimonious decisions to buy organic baby food or drive a hybrid car as a moral code, they think they have set up an equal system of comparison. And theirs, they assure you, is better than yours. It's not merely Christianity that is under siege—it is American values themselves.

And why? Because American values—the ones set forth not just by the Founding Fathers but by the Bible—are really, really hard! The Ten Commandments ask a lot of their adherents. But more than being a list of dos and don'ts, Christian values require reflection, good works, generosity of spirit and mind, and most of all, the acknowledgment that you are not the center of the world. The danger of secularism, especially the brand being peddled by the mainstream media and the American Left, is that it asks nothing of you. And that absence of moral imperatives leaves an opening for anyone—the eco-nuts, PETA, Hollywood, and most dangerously, the State—to fill it with their own moral imperatives (and make a ton of money doing it, incidentally). Meat is murder, they'll tell you, but abortion isn't. Science is god, but God is junk science. Vegetarianism and evolution aren't value systems, but the secular press sure spends a lot of time trying to convince you they are. Real value systems are simply too much work.

IV

THOU SHALT EVOLVE

According to a 2009 Gallup poll, only 39 percent of Americans believe in Darwin's theory of evolution. The rest believe that God created humans as described in Genesis, or guided human evolution over a longer period of time. Or they have no opinion at all—not exactly a ringing endorsement of Charles Darwin's chef d'oeuvre, *On the Origin of Species*.

In February 2009, the liberal media celebrated what would have been Darwin's two-hundredth birthday with an onslaught of lengthy op-eds lauding his insight, intellect, and contributions to science, not the least of which was his theory of evolution. While Darwin's work was inarguably important, and there's certainly nothing wrong with honoring the world's most influential thinkers, the liberal media routinely uses him as the unimpeachable antithesis to religious America.

He represents science while believers represent faith. He represents reason; believers, emotion. He represents fact, where believers represent a mere hunch. For liberals, Darwin is the antidote to Jesus, quite literally the Anti Christ, and those who criticize his theory of evolution are part of a backward and still-evolving fringe minority of Bible-thumpers and rednecks.

Except, of course, that they are not a minority.

For all the liberal grandstanding about America's growing more and more secular by the minute, this poll hardly represents a recent shift. Gallup has been covering this issue for decades, and in every study—in 1982, 1993, 1997, and 1999—Americans' belief in creationism has never drawn less than 44 percent.[1]

But that doesn't stop the media from declaring evolution's truth. CNN covered Darwin's birthday with predictable imbalance. "The evidence for evolution is overwhelming. We can see it all around us," declared one scientist in their report.[2] And though CNN acknowledged critics of the theory, Azadeh Ansari confidently proclaimed, "But most of Darwin's theories are now accepted as a foundation of biological science."

The New York Times was similarly matter-of-fact. Nicholas Wade wrote, "Not only was Darwin correct on the central premises of his theory, but in several other still open issues his views also seem quite likely to prevail."[3]

The counterarguments to evolution, such as creationism and its younger cousin, intelligent design, have faced enormous backlash from the liberal press, which takes turns either attacking or mocking their proponents as fanatics and idiots. Joy Behar, The View's liberal philosopher of stand-up, even had the considerable bad taste to say

---

1. David Quammen, "Was Darwin Wrong?" National Geographic, Nov. 2004.

2. Azadeh Ansari, "Darwin Still Making Waves, 200 Years Later," CNN.com, Feb. 12, 2009.

3. Nicholas Wade, "Darwin's Evolving Genius," New York Times, Feb. 9, 2009.

that teaching creationism to children is a form of child abuse. Better put those bedtime Bible stories away, parents, or Joy Behar will have you arrested.

But the debate over the legitimacy of evolution isn't really about a battle between fact and fiction. It's about Christianity, and the liberal media's attempt to eradicate it from all corners of society. For the Left, God has no place anywhere in 2010, least of all in science, and therefore any opposing theories to evolution have no place in our schools (or, absurdly for Behar, in our churches or homes). Jesus has officially left the building.

The media has adopted a slew of clever techniques to convince average Americans that anything other than Darwin's theory of evolution is simply hogwash, and by extension, so is Christianity. But under closer scrutiny, its methods—which look more like the tricks of slick salesmen than anything science would ever endorse—are fraught with holes.

EVOLUTION IS TIME-HONORED

The media asserts that the theory of evolution has withstood the so-called test of time. It's been around for ages, battered by the rigors of the scientific method, and tried over and over again successfully in the court of public opinion. Quite simply, it's survived so long that it has become conventional wisdom.

In a 2004 article in *Wired,* the author's opinion of creationism was less than thinly veiled by its title, "The Crusade Against Evolution." In it, Evan Ratliff writes, "In science, not all theories are equal. Those that survive decades—centuries—of scientific scrutiny end up in classrooms, and those that don't are discarded."[4] For Ratliff,

---

4. Evan Ratliff, "The Crusade Against Evolution," *Wired,* Oct. 2004.

questioning Darwin is nothing less than an affront to common sense and decency. And despite the fact that scrutiny and healthy debate form the basis of scientific inquiry itself, any attempt to re-examine evolution is, well, preposterous. "This is an issue, of course, that was supposed to have been settled long ago." So put away your microscopes and hang up your lab coats, Christians. This one's been put to bed.

National Geographic's David Quammen also offered evolution's supposed durability as proof of its validity, and used Darwin himself to do it. "This is how science is supposed to work. Ideas come and go, but the fittest survive."[5]

But evolution has hardly "survived." Darwin's theory was met with overwhelming skepticism when it first debuted, both from religious authorities who called him a heretic, and from a general public that was unwilling to consider his radical new idea. And more than sixty years after *On the Origin of Species* was published in 1859, Darwin had done little to convince the American public, when in 1925 the Scopes trial found in favor of teaching creationism in schools.

In fact, it wasn't until 1968 that the Supreme Court struck down laws banning the teaching of evolution in public schools, not because Americans had fully embraced it and had thrown their Bibles away, but because it violated the establishment clause of the First Amendment. Bringing evolution into the classroom did not mean the spontaneous abandonment of religion; it simply meant Darwin's theory could be taught alongside it.

But it wasn't until the 1980s that the Supreme Court ruled against teaching creationism and evolution together and kicked creationism out for good. That's just thirty years that U.S. public schools have been teaching only evolution in biology classes. To put it another

5. David Quammen, "Was Darwin Wrong?" *National Geographic*, Nov. 2004.

way, the decade that gave us Pac-Man, Bon Jovi, and Gary Coleman is the same one that declared evolution the only appropriate explanation for human existence. The personal computer, CNN, and Michael Jackson's *Thriller* album are all older than the federal acceptance of evolution in American education. Since when does three decades make something unimpeachably "time-honored"?

Furthermore, what does the theory's age have to do with anything? The Bible is centuries old, after all, and no one on the Left is arguing for its credibility. Likewise, creation stories like the one in the Bible have been around since the dawn of time, not just a mere 150 years. Even British philosopher William Paley's theory of intelligent design dates back to 1802, some fifty years before Darwin's *On the Origin of Species*.

And what does longevity have to do with acceptance? As the polls suggest, evolution hasn't fully caught on in the United States, despite its lengthy 150-year existence. Even in Britain, Darwin's homeland, a "Rescuing Darwin" survey showed that half of the 2,060 people questioned were either strongly opposed to his theory or confused about it. Longevity proves nothing—slavery was once a time-honored institution, documented as far back as 1760 B.C. and considered the bedrock of nearly every ancient civilization. But we've since rejected it. Is it possible we've evolved past Darwin?

The idea that evolution is so widely accepted that it's become convention is both inaccurate and illogical. In the *National Geographic* story from 2004, Quammen contradicts himself in pursuit of a convincing argument for evolutionary theory. He writes that other well-known, widely accepted scientific theories—gravity, continental drift, relativity, the earth's orbit around the sun—constitute explanations that have "been confirmed to such a degree, by observation and experiment, that knowledgeable experts accept it as fact. And the rest of us generally agree. We plug our televisions into little wall sockets, measure a year by the length of the earth's orbit, and in many other ways live our lives based on the trusted reality of those theories."

Evolution, he admits, has not met a similar fate. The reason Americans haven't embraced Darwin, according to Quammen? "Honest confusion and ignorance." (He also blames scriptural literalists and creation activists, but mostly it's just good old-fashioned stupidity.)

"Many people have never taken a biology course that dealt with evolution nor read a book in which the theory was lucidly explained. Sure, we've all heard of Charles Darwin, and of a vague, somber notion about struggle and survival that sometimes goes by the catchall label 'Darwinism.' But the main sources of information from which most Americans have drawn their awareness of this subject, it seems, are haphazard ones at best: cultural osmosis, newspaper and magazine references, half-baked nature documentaries on the tube, and hearsay."

And here's where his argument falls apart. First, as previously discussed, evolution has been taught exclusively in biology classes for thirty years. So, most American adults have in fact "taken a biology course that dealt with evolution." But more important—and more obvious—how does our stupidity explain the fact that we've, as he asserted, embraced the other equally confusing scientific theories? Most people have never taken a quantum physics class, and most people have never seen an atom, but most believe they exist. No human actually witnessed Pangaea breaking apart into seven continents 250 million years ago, but that idea seems to have caught on. You may not understand, exactly, how the contestants of *American Idol* get from Hollywood to your TV set, but you trust that they'll be there when you turn it on.

It's illogical that sheer American stupidity is behind our unwillingness to buy into evolution, and the notion is contradicted even by those who assert it. It's simply another disguised attack against religious belief. The liberal media often equates stupidity with faith—Bill Maher has said, "Faith means making a virtue out of not thinking. It's nothing to brag about."[6] So suggesting that evolution is complicated, but has the unwavering imprimatur of the scientific community, is another way of saying faith and science are incompatible and believers are on the losing side of the argument. This says nothing of the fact that faith is also complicated, and presumes that the decision to believe is really just blind ignorance. But those who have problems with evolution aren't too stupid to get it. They've simply made a decision to believe something else.

Would we accept the media's routinely telling us that Jews or Muslims are stupid? Would we accept the media's telling us atheists are stupid? The liberal press insists that we pay intellectual respect to the values of other major religions and to those of nonbelievers, and rightly so. We argue about secularism on the basis of its constitutionality, not on its philosophical merits. Since 9/11, we have vigorously deconstructed the values of Islam so as to carefully distinguish between radical fundamentalist terrorists and mainstream Muslims with the intellectual focus of a surgeon's scalpel. Why does the media, then, take a jagged-edged hatchet to the intellectual arguments for Christianity?

EVOLUTION IS, LIKE, TOTALLY FAMOUS

In addition to the trope that Darwin's been time-tested, the liberal media also uses another trick to reinforce his supremacy: He's a huge celebrity.

---

6. Bill Maher, *Religulous*.

Everyone knows the Left is celebrity obsessed, and the liberal press is no exception. If you happen to espouse the politics with which the media agrees, your celebrity is a plus, a positive attribute. (See Barack Obama, Bill Clinton, Hillary Clinton, and the Kennedys, all of whom wear their celebrity proudly, with encouragement from their friends at MSNBC and the *New York Times*.) But if your politics are in conflict, your celebrity is of course a detriment, an unbecoming pandering to the square states. These folks are routinely described as fame-hungry "media whores." It doesn't help if you're openly Christian. (See Mike Huckabee, who was mocked endlessly for his star turn as a television talk show host, and Sarah Palin, for whom becoming a "national figure" meant she was selling out, and whose rise in popularity meant she was chasing the spotlight.)

So in the battle against the religious right over evolution, it's no wonder the liberal media likes to prop up Darwin as a celebrity and pin down those who dare to criticize him as the opposite of celebrity: Middle America. Darwin is essentially the Tom Hanks of science—as A-list as it gets. Never mind, of course, that there is no "celebrity" bigger than Jesus, and no book more famous than the Bible.

In *Religulous,* the hour-long atheism infomercial by Bill Maher, he visits the Creation Museum and the Holy Land Experience, two entertainment and learning centers for people of faith. There are classes and exhibits, films and tours, and rides and games for children. For Maher, learning about faith is moronic and a waste of time, creation stories are bogus—"People will make up any story and cling to it," he says—and scientists all agree on the specifics of evolution, which is categorically untrue. But the idea that creationism would get its own museum, for Maher, deserves endless ridicule. He'd undoubtedly have no difficulty accepting the Rock 'n' Roll Hall of Fame, Madame Tussaud's Wax Museum, the Hollywood Walk of Fame, or any other institution that celebrates, well, celebrity.

The *New York Times* celebrated Darwin's two-hundredth birthday with myriad examinations of his life, and with one feature in a section in which Darwin probably would never have suspected he'd end up: the Style section. In a kooky conflation of evolutionary biology and, well, total fabulosity, the *Times'* women's spring fashion magazine presented readers with an array of sexy shoes, asserting that the ones you'd wear coincide somehow with your own views on evolution. It was called "Survival of the Hippest," and, yes, it was very scientific.

If you chose the Christian Louboutin sandal flats, it meant you believe in "Darwin's original theory of natural selection: Nature edits out the least fit."

If you chose Christian Dior's fertility fetish heels, it meant you believe in "Darwin's theory revised to include sexual selection: Looking good can trump staying alive."

If you chose Alexander McQueen's sports wrap, it meant you believe in "modified sexual selection based on physical fitness: That which doesn't kill you shows that you're healthy."

Of course there was no option to choose a shoe that represented a belief in creationism or intelligent design—but those Bible-thumping hicks probably couldn't afford them anyway. According to the feature, "One look at your feet and every hot geek knows which branch or twig of Darwinism you favor."[7] Evolution, for the *New York Times*, was, like, totally fashion-forward, and those who believe in it can dress like true fashionistas.

On the other hand, the Dover, Pennsylvania, school board that challenged the teaching of evolution as the only possible explanation for human development were not celebrities, but the case enjoyed national media attention thanks to a liberal media eager for yet another

---

7. Lynn Phillips, "Survival of the Hippest," *New York Times Women's Fashion Spring Magazine*, 2009.

opportunity to paint Christian America as hopelessly uncool, out of touch, and in fact, outright dangerous.

Tammy Kitzmiller v. *Dover Area School District* was the first case brought in federal court against a public school district's teaching intelligent design as an alternative to evolution. When the school board mandated that a disclaimer to evolution lessons be read before class, stating that evolution was just a theory, that others existed, and that literature to that nature was available upon request, eleven parents of students in the school district sued, under the gleeful representation of the ACLU and various other activist groups.

It was a bench trial—meaning no jury—before Judge John Jones, a conservative appointed by George W. Bush, that lasted from September to November 2005. After months of testimony by scientists on both sides of the debate, Jones ruled in favor of the parents, asserting that because intelligent design was too close to creationism to teach in school, requiring teachers to read the disclaimer about the gaps in evolutionary theory was unconstitutional. The decision banned intelligent design from being taught in the district's public schools.

The trial, by all accounts, was fair. The media's coverage of it was not. *Time* magazine actually entered the debate, naming Judge Jones one of the one hundred most influential people of the year. It called proponents of intelligent design "unpolished local activists who make rash religious statements that don't hold up in court. (Supporters of the Darwin disclaimer in Dover, Pennsylvania, have publicly proclaimed the country a Christian nation.)" Of course, they were right, by anyone's statistical interpretation. The country is nearly 80 percent Christian, regardless of the rightly imposed division of church and state. Their point was that a majority of parents in Dover and elsewhere are Christian, and thus had a jury trial occurred, the results might have been different.

The *Time* article goes on to characterize intelligent design proponents as hicks, pointing out that proponents of intelligent design like school board member Connie Morris, from another case in Kansas, represent "the sparsely populated western half of Kansas." In case calling them "unpolished local activists" wasn't clear enough, *Time* wants you to know these guys are country bumpkins from the middle of nowhere.

A Nova public television special called "Judgement Day: Intelligent Design on Trial" recounted the events in Dover with an alarming liberal bias, as did most major media outlets.

In the special, the narrator describes Dover as a quiet, rural place, with dozens of churches and only one high school, painting a picture of life between the coasts, overrun by Christian fanaticism. In categorizing creationists, the narrator explains that they "reject much of modern science in favor of a literal reading of the Bible." If one had never met someone who believes in creationism, one might think from this documentary that they're a bunch of Luddites who refuse to use telephones and hair dryers, when in fact many modern scientists have found a way to reconcile their faith with a pursuit of science. Furthermore, to say that creationists reject "much of modern science" is absurdly overstating.

And representatives of both groups—Darwinists and creationists—agree that science and faith are not mutually exclusive. In 2008, Archbishop Gianfranco Ravasi, a Vatican official, said that "evolutionary theory is not incompatible a priori with the teaching of the Catholic Church, with the message of the Bible and theology, and in actual fact it was never condemned."

Dr. Francis Collins, the director of the Human Genome Project and author of *The Language of God: A Scientist Presents Evidence for Belief,* said, "As a believer, I see DNA, the information molecule of all living things, as God's language, and the elegance and complexity of our own bodies and the rest of nature as a reflection of God's plan."[8] But the idea that some scientists believe in God, and some Christians accept science, is inconvenient for the devout Darwinists in the liberal press.

The television special went on, "They believe God created everything fully formed. Including humans. In just six days." Even if we ignore the fairly judgmental "just" in that last sentence, the charge also fails to acknowledge that not all creationists are biblical literalists, and many believe that while God created the earth and everything on it, this probably didn't happen "in just six days." And it said that mainstream religions have made peace with evolution, but creationists reject Darwinism, positioning creationists as outside the mainstream, which flies in the face of decades of polling. But the media is not interested in reporting these nuances—they are simply out to marginalize Christianity so that it appears as fringe and frightening as possible. Acknowledging that creationism isn't necessarily incompatible with evolution, or that many creationists are entirely willing to interpret the account of creation in the Bible, would be to acknowledge that creationists and Darwinists can probably speak a common language on the beginning of time. And that means that Christians aren't really that scary after all.

But worst of all, the television special devoted considerable time and attention to the treatment of the evolution proponents, and of the judge, by so-called religious extremists, alleging that the plaintiffs and Jones were the recipients of death threats and vandalism. The charges are true—they were. So were the defendants on the intelligent design side of the trial, but Nova doesn't mention this.

While the mainstream media covered the attacks on Judge Jones and the plaintiffs with alacrity, no one bothered to show the other

8.   Dr. Francis Collins, "Collins: Why This Scientist Believes in God," CNN.com, April 6, 2007.

side. When I talked to two of the defendants in the case, they didn't mince words about how they think they were unfairly portrayed. Heather Geesey, a Dover school board member who was called as a witness for the defense, said, "Yes, our side was reported with bias. I realized early on how they twisted [defendants] Bill Buckingham and Alan Bonsell's words, so I never said anything. I still don't think people understand everything that really happened."

And not surprisingly, they were on the receiving end of death threats as well. "I got email from all over the world. I couldn't believe that these professors who are supposed to be educated people would take time to send me emails that would say things like, 'I hope you burn in hell.' I also got emails trying to convert me. And I loved the emails asking if I thought we should also teach students about the flying spaghetti monster in science class."

Bill Buckingham, another school board member who testified in the trial, was forced to move due to the hostile reaction to his position, which was simply that evolution should be balanced with something else in school, like intelligent design or creationism.

BELIEVING IN EVOLUTION MAKES US LOOK GOOD

Not only is evolution really old and really famous, it also, apparently, makes us look a lot better to the rest of the world, which has long been a preoccupation of the Left and the liberal media. "Looking bad" is really the only mortal sin liberals recognize, and of course the promise of "restoring America's image" around the world drove all of them to vote for Barack Obama in 2008. Under George W. Bush, of course, we'd become incredibly unpopular, and liberals wanted to be liked again, by Europe, Russia, Saudi Arabia, Pakistan, Syria, Iran, North Korea, and everyone else.

So it's no wonder the liberal media is desperate to convince average Americans that evolution is the only acceptable explanation for
human development. They love to incite fear in the general population
and among lawmakers that teaching the controversy over evolution
will make us look stupid in the international scientific theater—in
places like China, for example. *Time* magazine's Claudia Wallis wrote
that President Bush's endorsement of teaching both evolution and
its alternative theories in public schools showed our weakness to the
scientific community. Developments in cloning by South Korea, she
said, were proof that "the U.S. is losing its edge."

She quotes Gerry Wheeler, executive director of the National Science Teachers Association, as saying of Bush's comments, "It sends a
signal to other countries because they're rushing to gain scientific and
technological leadership while we're getting distracted with a pseu-
doscience issue. If I were China, I'd be happy." What this hysteria fails
to acknowledge, of course, is that China doesn't allow a public debate
on religion. It barely allows a public debate on anything. It controls
its population by infanticide, executes its own bureaucrats, and jails
its journalists. It may be advancing in the sciences, but communist
China lives in the dark ages where human rights and democracy are
concerned. Further, concerns over what South Korea thinks of the
United States are nothing more than breathless paranoia. For the
secular left, though, which is eternally seeking the approval of secular
Europe, any debate over creation theory is an embarrassment.

And embarrassing religious America into getting on board is not
beneath the liberal media. By insisting that religion makes you look
stupid, it tries desperately to pressure believers into switching sides.
A *New York Times* editorial tried to suggest that Louisiana governor
Bobby Jindal, if he wants to appear smart and credible, will chuck his
silly Christian views out the window and nip any talk of adding creationism to biology classes in the bud. "As a biology major at Brown
University, Mr. Jindal must know that evolution is the unchallenged

central organizing principle for modern biology." So shame on you, Bobby Jindal, if you don't agree.

For *Wired*'s Evan Ratliff, teaching creationism means the possible end of civilization, and at the worst possible time. "In an era when the government is pouring billions into biology, and when stem cells and genetically modified food are front-page news, spending even a small part of the curriculum on bogus criticisms of evolution is arguably more detrimental now than any time in history." The idea that teaching the controversy is a waste of valuable time and resources, that it contradicts the national agenda of progress in science (and the absolute that is evolution), and could potentially challenge the way science is applied to everything, is fearmongering at its worst.

And moreover, as Joy Behar had suggested on *The View*, teaching creationism is bad for our youth. Echoing her sentiments, a *New York Times* editorial declared, "In school districts foolish enough to head down this path, the students will likely emerge with a shakier understanding of science." So in effect, the argument here is that by increasing debate on a controversial subject, providing students with more information, instead of withholding it, and acknowledging a theory that more than half the country believes in, we will make our kids dumber? This is the same group that wants to teach students about every form of contraception under the sun—except abstinence, the one that always works. It is ironically the kind of knowledge-guarding, secrecy, and paranoia that most cults exhibit. You don't talk about God in schools the way you didn't talk about child molestation in Jonestown. Religion is the bogeyman of the cult that is liberalism.

EVOLUTION IS LEGIT

And more than being old, famous, and face-saving, evolution for the liberal media is simply more credible than religion, to no one's surprise. Creationism, intelligent design, or any other theory of human existence is religious mumbo jumbo, the kind of stuff we abandoned during the Enlightenment. Except, of course, that we haven't.

The fact that half the country prefers the Bible's explanation to Darwin's does not deter the liberal media from discrediting Christianity at every turn. If a noted scientist suggested aliens are responsible for human development, he would earn easier acceptance than anyone who believes God played a role.

The author of *Wired*'s "Crusade Against Evolution," Evan Ratliff, characterizes intelligent design as Godspeak dressed up as science. For him, the theory's proponents want to "simply co-opt the vocabulary of science and redirect it to a public trying to reconcile what appear to be two contradictory scientific views. By appealing to a sense of fairness, ID finds a place at the political table, and by merely entering the debate it can claim victory."

And he doesn't hide his contempt. In the piece he calls evolution-backers "two scientists," but intelligent design proponents are merely "two representatives," despite the fact that one is Stephen Meyer, a professor at Palm Beach Atlantic University, and the other is Jonathan Wells, a biologist with a Ph.D. in molecular and cell biology from UC Berkeley. The article goes on to point out, though, with a smug "I told you so," that Wells is also a follower of Sun Myung Moon, and said that praying convinced him he should devote his life to exposing the holes in Darwin's theory.

Never mind that, as Ratliff admits, Darwin himself likely heard the call from above to study evolution. He studied to become a clergyman, and though he eventually denounced Christianity, he never became an atheist, preferring to think of his god as simply some unseen higher power. While Wells's call to scientific inquiry is crazy, for Darwin's we are eternally indebted. We are grateful Darwin abandoned religious pursuits, and, as *National Geographic* wrote, he "joined that round-the-world voyage aboard the *Beagle* instead of becoming a country parson." For the liberal media, there is no higher calling than that which seeks to destroy religion.

In the *Pittsburgh Tribune,* Edward Humes covered the evolution debate with shrewd objectivity. "There are really two theories of evolution. There is the genuine scientific theory and there is the talk-radio pretend version, designed not to enlighten but to deceive and enrage." He called intelligent design proponents purveyors of an "awful and pervasive straw-man image of evolution that pundits harp about in books and editorials, and, yes, on talk radio, and this cartoon version really is stupid." He neglects to check his own straw-man image of creationism, of course, which sets it up as some manufactured modern phenomenon delivered unto us by the overlords of the AM dial. Sorry, religious America. No room for you at this inn.

In *Wired*'s account, Case Western Reserve University physicist Lawrence Krauss says that those who question evolution are, well, crazy. "What these people want is for there to be a debate. They argue, 'People have different opinions, we should present those opinions in school.' That is nonsense. Some people have opinions that the Holocaust never happened, but we don't teach that in history."

He's right, we don't. Because it's a conspiracy theory. We don't teach other conspiracy theories in school either, like whether we actually landed on the moon, or whether aliens landed in Roswell. It's arguable that history books of the future won't teach Rosie O'Donnell's conspiracy theory that the government caused 9/11. But the belief that God is responsible for creating the universe, and every creature in it, is not a conspiracy theory. It's not a fringe worldview when half the American population believes it. It is, quite simply, the majority opinion.

That doesn't stop people like MSNBC's Chris Matthews, though, from likening creation theory to a fringe belief, and believers to crazy conspiracists. On a May 5, 2009, *Hardball* broadcast in which he interviewed Congressman Mike Pence, he asserted that Republicans don't want to address climate change because their religion makes them antiscience. "There are people that really are against science in your party who really do question not just the science behind the climate change but the science behind evolutionary fact, that we were taught—you and I—in our biology books. They don't accept the scientific method. They believe in belief itself." The self-proclaimed Catholic also went on, "There are people on your side of the argument who believe that all the prehistoric bones we've discovered in this world, all the dinosaur bones and all that stuff was somehow planted there by liberal scientists to make the case against the Bible."

Moreover, he tried to pressure Pence into agreeing with his strawman argument: "I think you believe in evolution but you're afraid to say so because your conservative constituency might find that offensive. You don't believe that, you don't, you don't take a fundamentalist view of, of the seven days of creation do you?" Pence was too smart, and likely too offended, to take the bait.

The liberal media's sweeping crusade against Christianity hinges on an ability to condescend to the faithful, to paint them as "extreme," and to quarantine them in far-right, backwoods, out-of-touch camps that they will contend are no longer relevant. Acknowledging nuanced points of view—say, for example, that theism and science are not mutually exclusive, and that other theories can accommodate both Darwin and the Bible—is not convenient or marketable. And the attack on Christianity is coming from all sides, bolstered and promoted by a willing accomplice in the media itself.

Academics tell us science is good, religion is evil. Global warming is a fact, the Old Testament is fiction. Morality is relative, but liberalism is fixed. The masses are stupid, the educated are enlightened. We know all this because the liberal media is right beside the academics, the celebrities, and liberal elected officials, broadcasting their agenda, running alarmist stories about clandestine Christians. Like the one *Newsweek* ran about Sarah Palin, in which Jonathan Alter wrote, "She thinks global warming is a hoax and backs the teaching of creationism in public schools."[9] This, despite Palin's clear answer to the evolution question in her interview with Katie Couric, who asked, "Do you believe evolution should be taught as an accepted scientific principle or as one of several theories?"

Palin answered, "Oh, I think it should be taught as an accepted principle. And, as you know, I say that also as the daughter of a school teacher, a science teacher, who has really instilled in me a respect for science. It should be taught in our schools. And I won't deny that I see the hand of God in this beautiful creation that is Earth. But that is not part of the state policy or a local curriculum in a school district. Science should be taught in science class."[10]

The pursuit of scientific explanations for human existence or anything else is, of course, the cornerstone of modern civilization. But, as noted earlier, many scientists agree that faith and science are not incompatible, and some intelligent design proponents believe in evolution, but claim God was ultimately its architect. Further, many atheists, like me, who put more faith in evolution than any other explanation, are more than willing to admit that they don't know how life began, even if we're unwilling to accept that God did it. The animosity toward those who would, though, undermines the very fabric of America's insistence that religion is a protected institution, and believers like our Founding Fathers and every president

9.   Jonathan Alter, *Newsweek*, Aug. 29, 2008.
10.   CBS News interview with Katie Couric, Sep. 30, 2008.

we've ever elected should have the right to practice their beliefs, pass them on to their children, and avoid the humiliation and harassment that previous generations and other countries have levied against them.

The push by the liberal media to eradicate belief from every public space by insisting that religion is silly and science is superior ignores the fact that for many Christians, faith is inextricable. Just because a Christian sits enclosed within the four walls of a science classroom doesn't mean God isn't in that room with him or her. It isn't the role of the state—and it certainly isn't the role of the media—to tell Christians to check their religion at the classroom door.

The media's continual propping up of science (and its attack on Christianity) raises another issue. Just how unimpeachable is science? Ever since the Enlightenment, liberal secularists have been insisting that God is the enemy of science and reason, that religion is ideological and science is fundamental. When President Obama took a jab at President Bush in his inaugural address, claiming he wanted to "restore science to its rightful place," this was the distinction he was making. But in 2009, as global warming activists started packing their bags for a sanctimonious (and utterly fruitless, it would prove) climate summit in Copenhagen, it was discovered that some scientists at the University of East Anglia in Britain had been fudging the numbers on global warming for years, in an effort to ratchet up the anxiety over climate change. Alas, the ideology of the Far Left had corrupted science, but much of the mainstream media either buried the story or insisted it wasn't as bad as it looked. If President Obama really wants to restore science—and it's in need of restoration—he should insist that the ideology of the Far Left has no more place in it than the ideology of the Far Right. But we won't hold our breath.

The point is, science has become increasingly politicized, and the liberal media's go-to elected official to speak on its behalf is Charles Darwin. He's a smart guy, to be sure. But he'll never replace God.

The liberal media is not interested in acknowledging our nation as a deeply religious one. It is interested only in destroying it. Evolution has become a favorite weapon in its arsenal, and Christians are squarely in the crosshairs.

V

THOU SHALT WORSHIP AT THE ALTAR OF THE MULTIPLEX

Hollywood recognizes no other gods but those of the almighty box office—the overlords of the summer blockbuster, and the Holy Trinity that is domestic gross, foreign gross, and the DVD release. Its church? The multiplex. Its altar? The ticket counter. Its hagiography reveals a vaunted list of revered and record-setting saints with appropriately serious-sounding names: *The Dark Knight, Star Wars,* and *Shrek the Third.* And one word, above all others, can bring Hollywood to its knees in a swoon of religious ecstasy: "trilogy."

So when Hollywood finds itself in the uncomfortable position of confronting actual religion, things can get pretty ugly. Though religion in film has often meant box-office gold, the God onscreen is direct competition for the gods behind the movie studios, and the goddesses who walk the red carpet. It's an awkward tête-à-tête that plays out every time a film deals with religion, and the liberal media furiously gets to work penning bizarre screenplays of its own about the imagined battle between God and the gods of Grauman's Chinese Theater.

It was not always thus. When Cecil B. DeMille's final film, *The Ten Commandments*, debuted in 1956, it was hailed as a masterpiece. It was nominated for seven Academy Awards and won one, for Best Visual Effects, which may carry a little less weight now that the secret behind Moses' parting of the Red Sea has been revealed: running film footage of water being poured into U-shaped tanks in reverse.

Nonetheless, the film was critically acclaimed, wildly popular, and a financial juggernaut. *The Ten Commandments* was the number-one moneymaker of 1957, earning a net profit of $18.5 million. Adjusted for inflation, it is the fifth-highest-grossing movie of all time in the United States and Canada, and held the record as the highest-grossing religious film until *The Passion of the Christ* in 2004.[1] Others followed dutifully in its footsteps. *Ben-Hur*, for one, won a record eleven Academy Awards.

But as the secular Left grew more and more uncomfortable with overt religiousness in popular culture, and more and more hostile toward the religious Right it claimed was supporting it, movies that celebrated popular religious themes became a frequent target of the liberal media, which in recent years has launched a full-throated campaign against the films it deemed "too Christian."

It's not just Christian America's God or their values that are regularly excoriated by the liberal press—it's even their movies. If you aren't worried that the secular Left is trying to destroy Christianity, watch how it recently handled the release of two important movies.

---

1. BoxOfficeMojo.com.

IN A WORLD . . . WHERE TALKING LIONS AND POLAR BEARS ROAM THE EARTH . . .

When word that the beloved children's books by C. S. Lewis, *The Chronicles of Narnia*, would be turned into a film series, the liberal press took turns discussing just how difficult they would be to market to mainstream audiences, given the Christian undertones of the books.

In 2005, before the first film, *The Lion, the Witch and the Wardrobe*, debuted, the *New York Times* ran a series of stories expressing collective skepticism about the saleability of Christian allegory at the theaters.

Jeff Leeds, in a story titled "Marketing of 'Narnia' Presents Challenge," contended that the Walt Disney Company's decision to release two soundtracks for the film—one a compilation of religious songs, the other a secular collection—wasn't in fact a brilliant marketing ploy, but a "tricky" battle plan. "Disney's tricky marketing strategy for 'Narnia'—which includes aggressively courting Christian fans who can relate to the story's biblical allegory while trying not to disaffect secular fans—is particularly tricky when it comes to music."[2]

To be clear, that's "tricky" twice in one sentence. "It seems like a huge gamble," fretted one magazine editor Leeds interviewed.

A follow-up piece by Charles McGrath in November again worried that a screen adaptation of the wildly popular children's books would meet a chilly reception at the box office, because, unlike the *Harry Potter* and *Lord of the Rings* series, the *Narnia* books were, problematically for the *Times*, religious. This, despite the fact that

---

2. Jeff Leeds, "Marketing of 'Narnia' Presents Challenge," *New York Times*, Oct. 12, 2005.

Christians make up 80 percent of the country's population, and the books are classics beloved by generations of children. Because the liberal media is uncomfortable with religion, well, so, too, must be moviegoers.

McGrath wrote, "Like the Rowling and Tolkien books, Lewis's evoke a richly imagined parallel universe, but they differ in including a frankly religious element: not just an undercurrent of all-purpose, feel-good religiosity but a rigorous substratum of no-nonsense, orthodox Christianity. If you read between the lines—and sometimes right there in them—these stories are all about death and resurrection, salvation and damnation."[3]

But there was more. For McGrath, the series wasn't just hard to market because of its overt Christian themes, it was literarily worse for them: "If the series is read in what is now the canonical order, [they] unmistakably spell out the theological dimensions of the story, but if you're not forewarned, it is perfectly possible to read most of the other volumes without a clue that anything more is going on than meets the eye. Actually, the books are better when read without the subtext. Aslan, for example, is much more thrilling and mysterious if you think of him as a superhero lion, not as Jesus in a Bert Lahr suit."

Narnia was good news for Disney if it was trying to reach Christian audiences, McGrath argued, and bad news if it hoped to compete for the kinds of fans who went to see *Lord of the Rings* and *Pirates of the Caribbean*, audiences that the *Times* decided simply weren't interested in Christian allegories. "If it is too upfront about the religious references . . . that could be toxic at the box office."

Joining the *New York Times* in its breathless anxiety was *Entertainment Weekly*, for which the early endorsement of Focus on the

---

3.   Charles McGrath, "The Narnia Skirmishes," *New York Times*, Nov. 13, 2005.

Family, which it lambasted as "the controversial conservative group led by Dr. James Dobson that's known for a staunch anti–gay marriage platform," posed a huge potential problem for *Narnia* at the box office.

"Sure, the prospect of 2 million ticket buyers is alluring. But is the endorsement of a potentially polarizing political/religious interest group worth it? Aggressively publicized thumbs-ups from groups like FOF could turn off secular audiences."[4]

So how did it do? *The Chronicles of Narnia: The Lion, the Witch and the Wardrobe* held the number-one or number-two spot at the box office for six straight weeks, grossed $745,011,272 worldwide, and had the second-largest domestic gross in 2005, behind only *Star Wars: Revenge of the Sith*. It is currently number thirty-two on the list of all-time top-grossing films, ahead of three of the *Harry Potter* films, according to MovieWeb.com.

When the movie proved a huge commercial success, seemingly against all odds, the liberal media turned to other tactics to marginalize the movie. The mainstream press dished out largely lukewarm reviews that ranged from scathing—MSNBC's John Hartl called it a "Lord of the Rings wannabe"[5]—to reluctantly complimentary. *Newsweek* offered up, among the film's only pluses, "It's faithful to the novel, and only as religious as you want it to be."[6]

The liberal media wasn't above attacking C. S. Lewis himself, a long-dead author, in its critiques of the Disney movie based on his book. The press used the film as an opportunity to paint him simultaneously as a blind believer, Christ's all-time best publicist, and a disturbed and conflicted sinner.

---

4. Michelle Kung, " 'Chronicles of Narnia' Gets a Conservative Endorsement," *Entertainment Weekly*, Oct. 21, 2005.

5. John Hartl, " 'Narnia' is a 'Lord of the Rings' Wannabe," MSNBC.com, Dec. 9, 2005.

6. Jeff Giles, "Next Stop Narnia," *Newsweek*, Nov. 7, 2005.

And the *New Yorker* piled on in an exceedingly long account of Lewis's tortured life by Adam Gopnik, published, not coincidentally, just a week before the film hit theaters. "Lewis developed and craved what even his Christian biographer, Jacobs, calls 'mildly sadomas-ochistic fantasies'; in letters to a (homosexual) friend, he named the women he'd like to spank, and for a time signed his private letters 'Philomastix'—'whip-lover.' A bright and sensitive British boy turned by public-school sadism into a warped, morbid, stammering sexual pervert."[7]

Gopnik goes on to question Lewis's faith—and the validity of belief in God in general: "A startling thing in Lewis's letters to other believers is how much energy and practical advice is dispensed about how to keep your belief going: they are constantly writing to each other about the state of their beliefs, as chronic sinus sufferers might write to each other about the state of their noses. Keep your belief going, no matter what it takes—the thought not occurring that a belief that needs this much work to believe in isn't really a belief but a very strong desire to believe."

And in case there was any ambiguity about Gopnik's distaste for Lewis, he offers that his best-selling books would have been better if, well, they didn't insist on talking about God so much.

The emotional power of the book, as every sensitive child has known, diminishes as the religious part intensifies. The most explicitly religious part of his myth is the most strenuously, and the least successfully, allegorized. Aslan the lion, the Christ symbol, who has exasperated generations of freethinking parents and delighted generations of worried Anglicans, is, after all, a very weird symbol for that famous carpenter's son—not just an un-Christian but in many ways an anti-Christian figure. In the final Narnia

---

7.   Adam Gopnik, "Prisoner of Narnia," *New Yorker,* Nov. 21, 2005.

book, "The Last Battle," the effort to key the fantasy to the Bibli-
cal themes of the Apocalypse is genuinely creepy, with an Aslan
Antichrist. The best of the books are the ones, like 'The Horse and
His Boy,' where the allegory is at a minimum and the images just
flow.

But just a few years later the liberal media would have a direct
answer to C. S. Lewis's *Narnia* films that would help it put Christianity right where it likes it best: at odds with secularism, in the kind of
battles that are usually fought by hand-wringing existential theorists
like Jean-Paul Sartre.

Philip Pullman's fantasy trilogy *His Dark Materials* is the anti-
Narnia. Pullman, one of Britain's most outspoken atheists, admits
he wrote the children's series explicitly as a means of denouncing
organized religion. "I'm trying to undermine the basis of Christian
belief,"[8] he once said in an interview, and he has described *The Chronicles of Narnia* as religious propaganda. He has also said, "If there is a
God, and he is as the Christians describe him, then he deserves to be
put down and rebelled against."[9]

In short, he was everything the liberal media loves in a man.

So when the first book in the trilogy, *The Golden Compass,* was to
become a movie, it's no surprise that the liberal press decided that the
film version of *this* children's allegory—a decidedly anti-Christian
one in which God is killed and the Church is overthrown—was going to become a blockbuster, come hell or high water.

In the run-up to the movie, the *New York Times* wrote no less than
five stories on the making of *The Golden Compass,* which starred
Nicole Kidman as an evil emissary of the "Magisterium," named,

8. Alona Wartofsky, "The Last Word," *Washington Post,* Feb. 19, 2001.
9. Adam R. Holz, "Sympathy for the Devil," Plugged in Online, Dec. 16, 2007.

ironically, Mrs. Coulter. In real life, the Magisterium is the name for the teaching authority of the Roman Catholic Church, but Pullman says he is actually referencing Milton's *Paradise Lost*. Nevertheless, the story is unambiguous in its disdain for God, which the book calls "The Authority," and the Church, which is an oppressive and totalitarian enterprise.

The *New York Times* gave *The Golden Compass* an unabashedly positive review, and even implored its director to jump on the sequels! Manohla Dargis writes, "The sequels are a welcome idea," and that " 'The Golden Compass' is an honorable work and especially impressive, given the far smaller, more intimate scale of his last film as a director, 'About a Boy.'"

But, for toning down the anti-Church subtext of the book, Dargis also acknowledged that "agnostics and atheists may, for starters, regret the explicit absence of the Church (others may see lingering traces)."[10] Sorry, moviegoing atheists—this movie isn't quite the unrelenting attack on God you were probably hoping for.

Newsweek was also predictably heavy on praise. In its fall movie preview, it gave *The Golden Compass* a strongly worded endorsement. "If you're not familiar with author Philip Pullman's mesmerizing young-adult trilogy 'His Dark Materials,' this adaptation of the first book might seem like a bid to recapture some 'Lord of the Rings' box-office magic. But this isn't some two-bit knockoff. Literary critics around the world consider Pullman to be a modern-day Tolkien, and 'His Dark Materials,' the tale of an irascible girl named Lyra who investigates why children are disappearing all over England, is Pullman's masterpiece."[11]

So, where *Narnia* was a mere *Lord of the Rings* wannabe, and

---

10.   Manohla Dargis, "Bless the Beasts and Children," *New York Times*, Dec. 7, 2007.

11.   "Fall Preview. First to Worst," *Newsweek*, Sep. 3, 2007.

C. S. Lewis's acclaim did nothing for his modern-day critics, *Newsweek* predicted—a full three months before it came out—that *The Golden Compass* would give Tolkien a run for his money.

In another *Newsweek* promo piece, Devin Gordon discussed the criticism of *The Golden Compass*'s attack on Christianity, which he decided should be taken no more seriously than those doing the critiquing. "The film stands accused of being both anti-Catholic and not anti-Catholic enough—though no one making either claim has actually seen it. The loud, bristling organization known as the Catholic League is urging families to boycott a film in which the word 'Catholic' is never uttered."

Well, the phrase "Death to Christ" is never uttered either, but when Pullman himself admits, "My books are about killing God," [12] is it really all that ambiguous?

And just as the liberal media unleashed its attack dogs on C. S. Lewis, Pullman, everybody's favorite atheist, would be vaulted to, well, sainthood by the *New York Times, Newsweek,* and the *New Yorker.*

Newsweek featured a counterintuitive "explanation" of Pullman by Donna Freitas, who is coauthor of the book *Killing the Imposter God: Philip Pullman's Spiritual Imagination in* His Dark Materials.

Freitas asks, "Is Philip Pullman merely the author of an atheist manifesto for kids? He most certainly is, if you believe the conservative Christian groups, such as the Catholic League, that are sponsoring boycotts of 'The Golden Compass.' I see him in an altogether different light. Although Pullman identifies himself as an atheist, I prefer to think of him as a sort of 'reluctant theologian.' 'His Dark Materials' is a resounding call to open ourselves up to the under-

---

12. Steve Meacham, "The Shed Where God Died," Sydney Morning Herald Online, Dec. 13, 2003.

dogs of Christian theology—the feminists, the liberation theologians, the eco-minded, and the young lay theologians immersed in the messy work of what Christianity has to say to the poor, the disenfranchised, the women, the children, the earth—to all those groups without a voice, without a language or even images that speak to their circumstances."

Um, okay. All that is fine and good, and not an entirely uninteresting perspective. Freitas can "prefer to think of him" however she wants. But to purposefully distance Pullman from what he has himself described as an attack on faith and Christianity is to ignore his own stated objectives in favor of putting them in the context of some kind of esoteric soul-searching project that might mildly criticize an unnamed, nondenominational theology. That is to say, it's absurd. Furthermore, the insinuation that only conservative Catholic groups would consider his work anti-God skirts the inconvenient fact that Pullman has admitted as much, and like-minded atheists celebrate that very aspect of his work.

And for the *New York Times,* he is "the man who dared make religion the villain," "thrillingly ambitious," and an ideal tutor for young readers' exploration of faith. Quoting a London critic, Sarah Lyall writes, "Erica Wagner said she hoped that younger readers would understand the philosophy underpinning the story, whose text is peppered with allusions to Milton, Blake, Coleridge, Ruskin and the Bible, among others. 'One can only hope that where Pullman leads they will follow, and discover the dissenting tradition from which these books spring. This is remarkable writing: courageous and dangerous, as the best art should be.'"[13]

Michael Dirda wrote of *The Golden Compass* in the *Wash-*

---

13. Sarah Lyall, "The Man Who Dared Make Religion the Villain," *New York Times,* Nov. 7, 2000.

ington Post, "We are talking about a novel that can be mentioned in the same breath as such classics as Madeleine L'Engle's *A Wrinkle in Time,* Philippa Pearce's *Tom's Midnight Garden,* and Alan Garner's *The Owl Service.* Actually, Pullman's book is more sheerly, breathtakingly, all-stops-out thrilling than any of them." [14]

And the *New Yorker* followed with a celebratory feature story on Pullman and his "secular fantasy for children." [15]

And what did all this unbridled puffery do for the movie version of Pullman's *The Golden Compass?*

It had the second-highest monetary budget net loss of all domestic box-office bombs in the United States, having cost $180 million to make and losing nearly $110 million, coming in just behind Oliver Stone's *Alexander.* [16] *Variety* called its U.S. opening numbers "not so golden." [17] And it was panned by the few movie critics who weren't trying to preemptively foist its genius on the moviegoing public, one of whom—Kyle Smith of the *New York Post*—said, "The film is not as silly as it sounds; it's much sillier. The best you can say about 'The Golden Compass' is that it's merely the second-dullest Nicole Kidman/Daniel Craig film this year." [18]

As badly as the liberal media may have wanted *Narnia* to fail and *Compass* to succeed, it seems as though the moviegoing public would have its own say in the matter.

The dueling films of Lewis and Pullman, and the liberal press's reaction to them, provide a perfect lens through which to view the

---

14. Michael Dirda, "The Edge of the World," *Washington Post,* Aug. 3, 1997.

15. Laura Miller, "Far From Narnia," *New Yorker,* Dec. 26, 2005.

16. BoxOfficeMojo.com.

17. Pamela McClintock, " 'Compass' Charts Not-So-Golden Bow," *Variety,* Dec. 9, 2007.

18. Kyle Smith, "Broken Compass," *New York Post,* Dec. 6, 2007.

so-called mainstream media's aversion to faith, in pop culture or anywhere else. Lewis was a heathen, and his books were religious propaganda, while Pullman was a genius, and his books are "magical realism."

Popular culture is a messy amalgam of mainstream American values that gets repackaged and regurgitated through countless filters, one of which is politics and another of which is the media. Because of that, it's often hard to tell the difference between what average Americans believe, like, and dislike and what the folks doing the filtering believe, like, and dislike. Movies like *Narnia* and *The Golden Compass* prove that theorem inarguably true. Movies that fare well at the box office don't always do well with critics. And movies that the liberal media likes to promote might fail to get moviegoers in the seats. Complicating all this is the liberal, secular agenda pushed by the reporters, critics, and pundits who discuss all these cultural products under the auspices of either fair and accurate journalism or interesting critical commentary. So often these taste arbiters fail on both counts.

But the weekend movie review has dangerously become yet another place to visit criticism on Christians. *The Passion of the Christ* was deemed too religious (and boring) by critics, even though Christian America flocked to see it. Christian criticism of *The DaVinci Code,* much of which was inarguably valid unless you *don't* consider it blasphemous to suggest Christ was merely some dude, was brushed off by the press, who routinely characterized the opposition as radical fundamentalists. The treatment of *Narnia* and *The Golden Compass* by the media just proves how brazen reviewers have become—they are crafting their write-ups before the movie even comes out, promoting one, blasting another—and not because of their cinematic integrity, but because of how they deal with God. The film that rejects God gets the good press, while the film that defends him is dismissed.

Movie reviewers, like music and art reviewers, can hide behind sub-jectivity, which makes proving their bias a little more difficult. But at the very least we know that they're hopelessly out of touch with mainstream America. Just one more reason they should be stripped of their "mainstream" title.

VI

THOU SHALT FORNICATE

To hear the liberal media tell it, there's no real debate on the abortion issue anymore. It's been all but solved—after all, a pro-choice Democrat is in the White House! Indeed, no one *really* believes abortion is wrong anymore. And the few who do are fanatical Christians like Sarah Palin, whose backwoods religion actually convinced her that she should carry a Down syndrome baby to term, instead of aborting it. Those Christians sure are kooky.

But are they the minority?

On May 15, 2009, Gallup released the results of a new poll, which found that more Americans considered themselves "pro-life" than "pro-choice" for the first time since Gallup began asking the question in 1995. Further, fewer said abortion should be legal "under any circumstance."

According to the poll, 51 percent of Americans call themselves pro-life, while only 42 percent called themselves pro-choice. "The new results, obtained from Gallup's annual Values and Beliefs survey, represent a significant shift from a year ago, when 50 percent were pro-choice and 44 percent pro-life. Prior to now, the highest percentage identifying as pro-life was 46 percent, in both August 2001 and May 2002."[1]

The poll was released in advance of President Obama's speech at the University of Notre Dame, a Catholic school that had recently become ground zero for a debate on abortion. While many of the students and faculty there supported his visit, some Catholic bishops and cardinals, as well as many Catholic worshipers around the country, were angry that the school had invited Obama, an ardently pro-choice president, to speak at its commencement ceremony.

Francis Cardinal George, archbishop of Chicago, called the invitation an "extreme embarrassment" to Catholicism, for which right-to-life issues are the most fundamental. Archbishops in Milwaukee and Newark made similar statements. And pro-life students at Notre Dame formed an opposition group called ND Response to protest the invitation.

Their collective outrage was understandable. Obama is one of the most liberal pro-choice Democrats on record, and someone whose abortion position is, even by some liberal accounts, extreme. He supports partial-birth abortion. He voted no on an Illinois measure that would make it illegal to kill a baby that survived an abortion. And he has suggested that doctors could be forced to perform abortions even if it was against their religious convictions. To call Obama "pro-choice" is to call Paris Hilton "a little overexposed." Needless to say,

---

1. Lydia Saad, "More Americans 'Pro-Life' Than 'Pro-Choice' for First Time," Gallup.com, May 15, 2009.

the president's views have left many—even non-Catholics—worried that he will actively attack the pro-life cause.

POLLS, SCHMOLLS

Despite how well the Notre Dame invitation illustrated the fact that the abortion issue has *not* been solved, the liberal media wasn't buying it. When the Gallup poll stating that the country is, in fact, predominantly pro-life came out, what was the *New York Times'* response?

Well, it didn't actually report on the poll. Instead, it printed an opinion piece a week later by Dalia Sussman, called "Tracking Public Opinion on Abortion: It's Tricky." In it she writes, "Every now and then a single polling result on a particular issue is broadly seized upon by the media and pundits, as well as by proponents and opponents alike on the issue—either to advance an agenda or to reveal flaws in the poll. Sometimes both motives operate in tandem. Last week's Gallup result on abortion was just such a case. The poll does not necessarily indicate a marked shift in Americans' views on this highly complicated issue."[2]

Well, yes, it did. Unless she's calling Gallup's pollsters liars, that's exactly what it indicated. In fact, Gallup's wording was "significant shift." Tracking public opinion on abortion is "tricky" only if you don't like the opinion. The move by the *New York Times* to discount the findings as a bunch of bunk was repeated throughout the mainstream press.

The *Chicago Tribune's* Eric Zorn wrote that abortion polls are generally unreliable and constantly shifting. The new abortion

2. Dalia Sussman, "Tracking Public Opinion on Abortion: It's Tricky," *New York Times,* May 21, 2009.

numbers showing a pro-life majority weren't convincing to him. What was? Another poll, of course. "If you're looking for a more telling number to unpack, try 68: That's the percentage of respondents who told pollsters from CNN/Opinion Research over the weekend that they do not want the Supreme Court to overturn Roe vs. Wade." So, he said, "The pendulum swings slightly around the midpoint but doesn't gather much momentum either way."[3]

Zorn's logic is the kind of astounding feat of acrobatics we usually see only under a tent: Abortion polls are inaccurate, unless they indicate a pro-choice majority, in which case they're not only reliable, but "more telling."

But instead of quibbling over the inaccuracies of polling, CNN dealt with the Gallup poll in a far more direct way—it conducted its own poll to show that even if Gallup's was right, it wasn't hurting Obama's numbers.

Three days after the Gallup poll, CNN found "six in ten Americans continue to approve of how Barack Obama is handling his job as president—and despite the controversy over Obama's appearance at Notre Dame on Sunday, Catholics have a high opinion of him. Obama's position on abortion has no effect on how most Americans—and how most Catholics—view Obama."

And even though the poll showed Obama's overall approval ratings to be down, CNN was still able to put a positive spin on it. " 'Overall, the poll indicates that Obama's rating may be down a bit since early April,' says CNN Polling Director Keating Holland. 'But 62 percent is still a vote of confidence from most Americans.'"[4] The message CNN wanted to deliver was clear: Voters have anointed Barack Obama America's new savior. So abortion foes who defi-

---

3. Eric Zorn, "Abortion Polls Back and Forth," *Chicago Tribune*, May 19, 2009.

4. "CNN Poll: Abortion Not Hurting Obama," CNN, May 18, 2009.

antly choose to worship another Messiah are on the wrong side of history.

The abortion issue perfectly illustrates the liberal media's bias. It no longer reports. It persuades. It will go to great lengths to convince America that its opinions—in this case, on abortion—are right, more intelligent, the most popular, widely accepted, the mark of progress, better for the country, and numerous other qualifiers used to shame and humiliate the opposition into consent and submission.

IS IT US V. THEM? OR US V. US?

Insisting that the abortion debate is over and that the country is pro-choice is just one tactic the liberal media uses. But it also uses another—insisting all pro-lifers (the nominally few that there are) are radical, right-wing Christians.

But two pesky phenomenological varmints—history and reality— paint a different picture. In fact, the pro-life position used to be a Democratic one, mostly because the pro-life position was shared by most Americans, even the first-wave feminists of the nineteenth century. Pro-life Democrats made up a considerable portion of the Democratic Party's membership in the U.S. Congress and Senate in the sixties and seventies. Democrats including Hubert Humphrey and Sargent Shriver even ran on pro-life platforms. John F. Kennedy was believed to be pro-life, and he nominated a pro-life judge, Byron White, for the Supreme Court. Jimmy Carter is staunchly pro-life, as was Pennsylvania governor Bob Casey. And Democrats like Ted Kennedy, Bill Clinton, and Al Gore used to be pro-life—before they ran for office. Now even Harry Reid, the Democratic Senate majority leader, is a vocal proponent of the pro-life cause.

Groups like Democrats for Life of America—yes, that's a real organization—look to restore the party to one that protects life, including that of unborn children. There are also myriad groups that combine otherwise liberal interests with the pro-life cause, like the Pro-Life Alliance of Gays and Lesbians or the Pro-Life Union for Secularity.

In June 2009, nineteen pro-life Democrats in the U.S. House of Representatives sent a letter to House Speaker Nancy Pelosi, who once argued that contraception should be part of an economic stimulus plan, urging Democrats not to include abortion in the federal health-care plan proposed by President Obama. "As the debate on health care reform continues and legislation is produced, it is imperative that the issue of abortion not be overlooked," wrote the lawmakers. "Plans to mandate coverage for abortions, either directly or indirectly is [sic] unacceptable."

Citing a study proving that limits on abortion funding have reduced abortions by one-third, the letter continued, "Funding restrictions save lives by reducing the number of abortions. The Guttmacher Policy Review, a leading pro-choice research organization noted 'that about one third of women who would have had an abortion if support were available carried their pregnancies to term when the abortion fund was unavailable.'"

The letter was signed by Reps. Dan Boren (D-OK); Bart Stupak (D-MI); Colin Peterson (D-MN); Tim Holden (D-PA); Travis Childers (D-MS); Lincoln Davis (D-TN); Heath Shuler (D-NC); Solomon Ortiz (D-TX); Mike McIntyre (D-NC); Jerry Costello (D-IL); Gene Taylor (D-MS); James Oberstar (D-MN); Bobby Bright (D-AL); Steve Driehaus (D-OH); Marcy Kaptur (D-OH); Charlie Melancon (D-LA); John Murtha (D-PA); Paul Kanjorski (D-PA); and Kathleen Dahlkemper (D-PA).

For the liberal media, that there are actually nineteen pro-life Democrats is newsworthy enough, you'd think, to get a mention in a major newspaper or on a major news network. But that they sent a letter to the Speaker of the House urging her to change a controversial part of the health-care legislation is definitely worth a couple of column inches or seconds of air time. The result? Crickets. Nothing—not one mention by the liberal media, for whom it was inconvenient to acknowledge that the pro-life cause is not just one that is taken up by crazy, right-wing Christians. In fact, a 2009 Gallup poll reported that 33 percent of Democrats say they are pro-life. That's compared to 26 percent of Republicans who say they are pro-choice. That's right, there are more pro-life Democrats than pro-choice Republicans. "Life" might be a more conservative position than "choice" is, but it's certainly not *just* for Republicans.

And how Christian is it really? Well, every major religion condemns abortion but for the most extreme cases—Hinduism, Buddhism, Islam, Orthodox Judaism, *and* Christianity. But in America, where Christianity is the dominant religion, one might assume the pro-life position is entirely an evangelical one. Not true—those who said they were pro-life in the 2009 Gallup poll were also asked if they were Christian or Other/None. Thirty-one percent said "other/none." A third of those who identified themselves as pro-life aren't even Christian. So while many Christians are pro-life, it's clear not all pro-lifers are necessarily Christian.

Secular support for the pro-life position is neither hard to find nor outlandish. The Pro-Life Union for Secularity lists a number of reasons on their website for why someone who doesn't necessarily believe in God might still err on the side of life: Abortion violates the constitutional right to life; science has made a compelling argument for life beginning at conception; abortion is psychologically, emotionally, and physically damaging to women; many women come to regret their decision to have an abortion; there are thousands of parents who want to adopt, but have to spend years on a waiting list; legal abortion has, in some cases, led to the rise in multiple abortions; and so forth.

But these facts—that there are pro-life Democrats, that there are pro-life non-Christians, that there are secular applications of the pro-life argument—don't stop the liberal media from excoriating pro-life proponents as crazy, right-wing Christians.

MSNBC's Keith Olbermann bestowed upon WorldNetDaily blogger Jill Stanek his "Worst Person in the World" title in June 2009, accusing her of posting the addresses of two late-term abortion doctors online. She did not, in fact, post their addresses, but she did post photographs of one of their centers, which both the *Los Angeles Times* and the Associated Press had also done.

Regardless, Olbermann said that for her indiscretions, she should be arrested and jailed: "Miss Stanek has now posted pictures and addresses of the only two remaining physicians who will provide late-term abortions when the woman's life is in danger. So here's a little switch, Miss Stanek. You'll never understand that in a just world, to tell a bunch of crazy people, like your readers, where they can find somebody and abuse, threaten, or kill them, that that should be enough of a crime to put you in jail for the rest of your life."[5]

In addition to insulting Stanek, and all the readers of conservative WorldNetDaily, earlier that same week he accused the pro-life movement of waging "a religious jihad by fundamentalist crusaders who believe that murder is justified, their acts of violence having the intended effect of changing behavior."[6]

Olbermann's leg-thrilling partner in crime, Chris Matthews, a Catholic himself, also jumped into the fray with both feet. Worried that President Obama's pro-choice nominee for health secretary, Kathleen Sebelius, would become the unfair target of pro-life activists, he asked, "Is she gonna get through the, the terrorism of the,

---

5.   Keith Olbermann, MSNBC, *Countdown with Keith Olbermann*, June 4, 2009.
6.   Keith Olbermann, MSNBC, *Countdown with Keith Olbermann*, June 1, 2009.

of the antiabortion people?" And then, having realized the possible ramifications of calling pro-life America—nearly half the country—"terrorists," he said, "I mean verbal terrorism."[7]

Is there such a thing as "verbal terrorism"? Apparently, there is for Matthews. For everyone else, it's simply called "free speech."

But Rachel Maddow continued the terrorism trope after Dr. George Tiller, who performed thousands of late-term abortions, was murdered by an antiabortion extremist, an act that countless pro-life proponents immediately condemned. Making no distinctions between Scott Roeder, Tiller's assassin, and anyone else on the pro-life side of the debate, and linking Roeder to the larger political Right, she said: "There's an anti-abortion terrorist movement in the United States that operates relatively openly. They advocate and their members commit acts of violence, including murder, against Americans who are not breaking the law, who are engaged in protected legal activity on American soil. These acts of violence are politically motivated. They are designed to change American policies and to terrorize Americans."[8]

And in 2008, the pro-choice group National Organization for Women honored none other than CBS News anchor Katie Couric, who was famously outed once by Whoopi Goldberg as having marched with her in a pro-choice rally. Couric also came under fire in 2006 for responding to a statement by a Columbine shooting victim's father—he said that abortion has minimized the country's view of life—by editorializing that some viewers may find that opinion "repugnant."[9]

---

7. Chris Matthews, MSNBC, *Hardball with Chris Matthews*, March 2, 2009.
8. Rachel Maddow, MSNBC, *The Rachel Maddow Show*, June 8, 2009.
9. Steven Ertelt, "CBS News' Katie Couric Labels Pro-Life View on Abortion 'Repugnant,'" LifeNews.com, Oct. 5, 2006.

ABSTINENCE? WHAT'S THAT?

It's not just the abortion issue around which the liberal media rallies against Christian conservatives. Any discussion of reproductive rights gives ample opportunity to characterize Christians as out-of-touch simpletons living in the dark ages, or worse, as God-fearing puritans who put the lives of our youth in immediate danger. Sex education and arguments over what we teach our kids in public school about sex have, like abortion, become a reliable fulcrum for the liberal media's assault on Christian values.

In 2008, Nicholas Kristof mocked abstinence—the only form of birth control that works every time—in a column titled "Can This Be Pro-Life?" "There is something about reproductive health— maybe the sex part—that makes some Americans froth and go crazy. We see it in the opposition to condoms to curb AIDS in Africa and in the insistence on abstinence-only sex education in American classrooms."[10] For Kristof, apparently, teaching children that perhaps they should wait until they're older to have sex is frothing and going crazy—the kind of thing that should land you in a psych ward.

But the idea that proponents of abstinence education are crazy (literally and figuratively) is hardly uncommon in the liberal media, which decided long ago that abstinence is silly and doesn't work, that everyone who matters agrees on that, and that those who don't are crazy Christians ignoring the enthusiastic stampede of progress— which includes, apparently, an upswing in teenage sex.

This isn't because they really care all that much if you're morally opposed to abortion or premarital sex, or whether you're encouraging

---

10.   Nicholas Kristof, "Can This Be Pro-Life?" *New York Times*, Oct. 8, 2008.

your kids to make responsible decisions about sex. They paint pro-life and pro-abstinence Christians as crazy because they don't want to have to live up to those standards. And they don't want Christians making them feel guilty about it. To put it even more bluntly, it's not that they don't think abortion and premarital sex are sins—it's that they don't want to be called sinners. It's an unconvincing argument. Imagine if hardened criminals held a press conference from their prison cells and announced that the laws of the American justice system shouldn't apply to them—because they really want to break them. The liberal media is behaving like a bunch of bank robbers, and they want you to say robbing banks is okay. And they'll dig up statistics to prove that criminalizing bank robbers makes them want to rob banks even more.

When a *Mathematica* report in 2005, which looked at data in the federally funded National Longitudinal Study of Adolescent Health, suggested that teenagers who had taken a pledge of abstinence were almost or just as likely to acquire a sexually transmitted disease as those who hadn't pledged, the liberal media jumped on it.

The *Pittsburgh Post-Gazette* declared excitedly, "Abstinence-only programs fail and deceive our kids."[11]

The *Washington Post* cried that the report "sparked an immediate, bitter debate over the wisdom of teaching premarital abstinence."

No one seemed to care that the report was talking about abstinence pledges, not abstinence programs.

But what about the *other* report? The one issued around the same time by the *Journal of Adolescent and Family Health*? The one that studied an actual program designed to restore dignity to teenagers by promoting abstinence from sex, drugs, and alcohol?

This report, aside from Mona Charen's lonely coverage of it in

---

11. Mona Charen, "Abstaining on Abstinence Data," *Washington Times*, May 1, 2005.

the right-leaning *Washington Times,* never saw the light of day in the mainstream media. And why? Because it showed that abstinence programs worked.

Through one-on-one mentoring and group lessons, girls in the Best Friends program in Washington, D.C., were eight times less likely to use drugs and six times less likely to engage in premarital sex when compared to other D.C. girls comparable in age, income level, race, and family structure.

As Charen reported, "As the girls reach high school, they meet leading women like Colin Powell's wife Alma, anchorwoman Lark McCarthy and restaurateur Margaret Auger. The most promising win college scholarships financed by Best Friends donors. At the annual 'Recognition Ceremony,' usually at D.C.'s Kennedy Center, older girls get their first opportunity to dress in evening gowns and be received as dignified young ladies."

But, she wrote, "Dignity is not what the condom crowd wants. Therefore, this is probably the first you've heard of the impressive study."

No matter. When another study on the flimsy success rate of abstinence pledges came out, the liberal media once again used it as proof that abstinence writ large doesn't work.

Ellen Goodman in the *New York Times* cited a study by Janet Rosenbaum of Johns Hopkins, who found no difference in sexual behavior between teens who took an abstinence pledge and those who didn't. She didn't study abstinence programs—just pledges. But Goodman treated them as one and the same—as if studying the success rate of New Year's resolutions to lose a few pounds is the same as studying the success rate of a medical weight-loss program.

"The only difference was that the group that promised to remain abstinent was significantly less likely to use birth control, especially condoms, when they did have sex. The lesson many students seemed to retain from their abstinence-only program was a negative and inaccurate view of contraception."[12] She then goes on to excoriate the whole of abstinence education as ineffective, and backed by Republicans with a Christian agenda.

"All in all, abstinence-only education has become emblematic of the rule of ideology over science." Indeed, for Goodman, the debate wasn't one between science and science—or the scientific studies proving whether abstinence programs actually worked. It was between "ideology," a cute proxy for "right-wing religion," and that unimpeachable and decidedly left-wing body that is Science with a capital "S."

Another *New York Times* column—this one by Olivia Judson, author of the officious-sounding *Dr. Tatiana's Sex Advice to All Creation: The Definitive Guide to the Evolutionary Biology of Sex*—echoed Goodman's theme, alleging that George W. Bush "intimidated" scientists into promoting his right-wing Christian agenda by pressuring them to endorse conservative legislation. That's right—the man who did more to fight AIDS in Africa than any other human in recent memory, whose wife promoted the use of condoms to women in South Africa, the man who rapidly increased funding for the National Science Foundation and National Institutes of Health in his first years of office, and created myriad education programs to better high school math and science, is antiscience.

Judson writes, "The most notable characteristic of the Bush administration's science policy has been the repeated distortion and suppression of scientific evidence in order to fit ideological preferences about how the world should be, rather than how it is. The distortion and suppression of science is dangerous, and not just because it means that public money gets wasted on programs, like abstinence-only sex 'education' schemes, that do not work. It is dangerous because it is an assault on science itself, a method of thought and inquiry on which

12. Ellen Goodman, "American Teens and Sex," *New York Times,* Jan. 7, 2009.

our modern civilization is based and which has been hugely successful as a way of acquiring knowledge that lets us transform our lives
and the world around us." [13]

There are plenty of reports that say abstinence education—not
merely pledges—does work. But the liberal media doesn't want you
to know about them. In Georgia, for example, teen pregnancy rates
have been cut in half, dropping for eleven straight years since the state
mandated abstinence education.

An Institute for Research and Evaluation report in 2007 also
refuted the findings of the 2005 *Mathematica* report, pointing out
damning flaws in its research and claiming that "several major errors
. . . made the study non-representative of American sex education." [14]

This report found that "within the United States, sexual activity
rates have been going down among teenagers for about the last 12
or 13 years, and that coincides with when the abstinence education
started. Abortion, pregnancies and out of wedlock birth rates have
also been going down among teens during that same time period.
However, pregnancy, abortion and out of wedlock births have been
rising for the older age group, between 19–25, a group that has not
been targeted by abstinence programs."

But where did these reports show up? Not in the mainstream
media.

The *Washington Post* did jump on a twenty-page letter written by
a pediatrician named John Santelli, who believed the statistics cited
in abstinence-only education were inaccurate. Santelli's letter claimed
that the assertions in the report—that condoms fail to prevent HIV
infection 31 percent of the time during heterosexual sex; that the
chances of getting pregnant while using a condom are one in six; and

13.   Olivia Judson, "Back to Reality," *New York Times,* Dec. 2, 2008.
14.   Elizabeth O'Brien, " 'Comprehensive' Sex Education Is Ineffective: Abstinence Works, Major
National Study Shows," LifeSiteNews.com, June 13, 2007.

that condoms break or slip off nearly 15 percent of the time—were wrong.

For the *Washington Post*, the abstinence programs weren't trying to lower teen pregnancy, reduce instances of sexually transmitted disease, or make our children healthier people. They were the result of the Bush administration's push to promote a "conservative ideology." [15]

But there are problems with "comprehensive" sex education—in which the option to abstain from sex accounts for only 5 percent of the curriculum—that the liberal media simply can't reconcile. Like, for instance, the fact that while *it* might support "comprehensive" sex ed, parents don't. Then again, what's the fun in letting parents choose what kind of education their kids receive when the liberal media can choose for them?

When they were actually asked, research showed that when parents were told what "comprehensive" sex education is, they overwhelmingly disapproved of it. Maybe that's because it uses graphically explicit lesson plans to advocate safe sex, it teaches children how to engage in sexual acts without actually having sex, and it promotes an acceptance of graphically sexual homosexual acts. To children.

For these reasons it's not surprising a Zogby poll in 2003 found that 75 percent of parents objected to the Centers for Disease Control's "comprehensive" program, and 60 percent of parents objected to the Sexuality Information and Education Council of the United States' (SIECUS) "comprehensive" program. Seventy-five percent of parents disapprove of condom-based sex education in general, and 73 percent of parents said they actually preferred an abstinence-based curriculum. [16]

In this instance, the *New York Times* was quick to publish the

---

15. Christopher Lee, "Inaccurate Statistics Cited in Abstinence-Only Education," *Washington Post*, April 29, 2007.

16. Mary Beth Bonacci, "Comprehensive Is Not Always Good," *Arlington Catholic Herald*, April 16, 2003.

findings—so it could excoriate them as the work of Christian special-interest groups out to scare parents into abstinence approval. Diana Jean Schemo's story featured mostly critics of the Zogby findings, including Tamara Kreinen, president of SIECUS, whose sex education curriculum parents said they didn't like. "Obviously, they polled for what they thought was most shocking."[17]

Not only that, the *New York Times* desperately tried to link the study to the religious Right. For the liberal media, the Zogby poll on abstinence education simply *had* to be rigged. And it knew just who was pulling the strings. In three different instances, Schemo said the Zogby poll was "sponsored" or "released" by "a coalition of conservative groups," "Christian" organizations, and "a consortium of conservative Christian groups."

Except that it wasn't. In fact, the *New York Times* later had to issue a correction: "An article on Thursday about parental attitudes toward sex education referred incorrectly to one sponsor of the survey, the National Abstinence Clearinghouse. It is a secular organization, not a Christian one."

Far-left publications like *The Nation* have been overt promoters of a radical sex agenda, featuring stories like Jessica Valenti's in 2009 that lambasted so-called virginity movements as "comical," "ridiculous," "sexist," "antifeminist," "regressive," and "ripe-for-mockery," and its proponents as "religious leaders and legislators" who are "a bit unhinged."[18] For Valenti, who is author of *The Purity Myth: How America's Obsession with Virginity Is Hurting Young Women* and editor of Feministing.com, teaching abstinence as an option *at all* is tantamount to waging war on our children. And even the new hip, young, modern, liberal president isn't spared her wrath.

---

17.   Diana Jean Schemo, "Explicit Sex Education Is Opposed by Most Parents in Survey," *New York Times*, Feb. 18, 2003.

18.   Jessica Valenti, "The Virginity Movement, Rebranded," *The Nation*, July 6, 2009.

"The good news in all of this is President Obama's budget cutting most abstinence-only education funding and seeking to redirect the funds to 'teen pregnancy prevention programs.' The bad news is that 25 percent of the $164 million marked for teen pregnancy prevention would be open to abstinence-only programs, and the language in the budget doesn't make room for initiatives to curb sexually transmitted infections." It isn't enough to simply cut most abstinence-only funding—Valenti wants abstinence killed off.

For Valenti, teaching children how to have sex is a moral imperative. "It's about stopping a movement committed to the regression of women's rights, enforcing gender norms and teaching America's youth—especially young women—that sexuality is wrong, dirty and dangerous." Well, isn't it dangerous at fourteen?

But at least *The Nation* is fairly open about its political leanings. In the magazine's classified section in the back, it features ads for "Liberal Liaisons," in which "Green Singles" can have their "fetishes and fantasies fulfilled." It also features ads selling anti-Bush and anti-war merchandise, and books like *Scamming God* and *Jews, Mormons, Muslims, Murder, Mayhem and Money: And Where God Came From.* This, even though the magazine's founding prospectus of 1865 declares, "*The Nation* will not be the organ of any party, sect, or body. It will, on the contrary, make an earnest effort to bring to the discussion of political and social questions a really critical spirit, and to wage war upon the vices of violence, exaggeration and misrepresentation by which so much of the political writing of the day is marred."

BRISTOL PALIN—AND NOT A MINUTE TOO LATE

The debate over abstinence in sex education grew to a frenzied pitch when it was announced that Sarah Palin's teenage daughter Bristol was pregnant at seventeen. And because her mother was a Christian Republican who supported abstinence education, it was the perfect chance to deflate the momentum of the McCain/Palin ticket that was steamrolling over the Democrats after the Republican National Convention. For the liberal press, Bristol was proof positive not only that Sarah Palin was unfit to lead the country, but that teaching abstinence was a total waste of time.

The *New York Times* printed no less than three page-one stories on her pregnancy. The Huffington Post, CNN, MSNBC, the *Los Angeles Times*, and countless others reported her statement that "abstinence is not realistic" as their lead story. But when she clarified her statement a few days later, saying that the goal of abstinence, while not always attainable, was "the only effective, 100% foolproof way you can prevent pregnancy," and that she planned to "promote abstinence and say, this is the safest choice. This is the choice that's going to prevent teen pregnancy and prevent a lot of heartache,"[19] much of the mainstream media chose not to report her new message.

But *New York Times* columnist Gail Collins did take the opportunity to lambaste Sarah Palin for her daughter's indiscretions: "Surely, when it comes to combating teen pregnancy, the Palin family has done enough damage already. What worse message could you send to teenage girls than the one they delivered at the Republican convention: If your handsome but somewhat thuglike boyfriend gets you with child, he will clean up nicely, propose marriage and show up at an important family event wearing a suit and holding your hand. At which point you will get a standing ovation."[20]

Apparently, the message that Sarah Palin did send to many teenage girls—that abortion shouldn't be used as birth control, that the

19.   Bristol Palin, *Good Morning America*, ABC, May 6, 2009.

20.   Gail Collins, "Bristol's Abstinence Campaign is a Bad Idea," *Dallas Morning News*, May 8, 2009.

support of one's family can make a tough situation bearable, and that abstinence would have saved her daughter from such a dilemma— was not the kind of message Collins appreciated.

In the *San Francisco Gate,* a writer and sometime fetish model named Violet Blue wrote that Bristol's decision to promote abstinence in the wake of her own pregnancy proved the religious Right's voice on the issue should no longer count. "The eight years America suffered from the strong-arm tactics of the Bush administration to enforce so-called abstinence education as a form of sex ed in public schools [proves] that we still have a long, long way to go to undo the harm abstinence programs have done." [21]

For those who still hoped to keep abstinence as part of the sex education message, Violet Blue had this advice: "The so-called family groups and righty Republicans are up in arms and proposing amendments (that so far have been struck down) to save abstinence funding for the 2010 budget. They're not dissuaded, and are still trying. I mean, practicing. To which I'll be giving our best advice—that they better pull it out, and pray."

For dozens of mainstream news publications and major news outlets, Bristol represented the folly of abstinence education because her mother was a Christian Republican governor. It would have been a convincing argument—except that Bristol didn't get an abstinence-only education. At Wasilla High School, she was taught about safe sex practices, such as condoms and birth control, as well as about abstinence. Her boyfriend, Levi Johnston, admitted on the *Tyra Banks Show* that they did not use a condom as they had been taught. If Alaska were to get the kind of abstinence programs Sarah Palin had pushed for as governor, maybe that state's teen pregnancy rate would be in decline, too.

So what is the liberal answer to lowering teen pregnancy?

---

21.   Violet Blue, "Pull Out and Pray," *San Francisco Gate,* April 9, 2009.

Not abstinence, of course. The push by people like *The Nation*'s Jessica Valenti to teach our kids not only about sex, but about how to have it, is positioned by the liberal media as the mark of cool—and responsible—modern parenting. It's the anti-Palin, whose backward ideas about waiting until marriage (or carrying a disabled child to term) make her a convenient counterweight to the liberal media's "cool mom" idolatry.

Liberal author Ayelet Waldman wrote on NPR.com in 2009 about her views on sex education: "Conservatives lay the blame on our permissive culture, where teenage sex permeates the airwaves and even young children get the message that sexy is the new cute. . . . But study after study has shown that teaching abstinence just doesn't keep kids from having sex."

Her solution? She gave her fourteen-year-old daughter a box of condoms.

"A while ago I ordered some birth control for myself and my husband. When the box arrived, it included a freebie: a pack of 50 candy-colored condoms. I was about to throw them away, but after an internal debate that seemed at once to encompass every attitude, preconception, goal and belief I have about parenting, I took the bag and put it on the very top shelf of the cupboard in the kids' bathroom."[22]

There you have it. Times, they are a changin'. Abstinence is out, and safe sex is in. Then again, so is abortion. Popular culture sits firmly in opposition to traditional values, like waiting until marriage for sex and protecting life. And the teenage celebrities who do espouse those views, like Miley Cyrus, are practically dared by the liberal media to make the kind of mistakes for which it will then ridicule them relentlessly (witness the evolution of the once-virginal Britney Spears). When traditional viewpoints, like supporting life or advocating absti-

22.   Ayelet Waldman, "Sexy Witch or Cereal Box? Which Is Your Teen Girl?" NPR.com, March 20, 2009.

nence, are made synonymous with a Christian, right-wing, or fringe worldview (even though statistics prove otherwise), the liberal media reveals its deep-seated abhorrence for religious America. Indeed, our cheerleading activists in the liberal media hope we will throw out our traditional values as sentimentally as we'd throw out a used condom, so that they don't have to be judged for their values. Immorality is much easier to live up to than morality, and the liberal press resents Christians for taking a moral stand against anything. The mainstream media has turned its back on Judeo-Christian values, and hopes you will, too.

VII

THOU SHALT FALL SPECTACULARLY
FROM GRACE

Hypocrisy, over the past few years, has become the favorite rallying cry of the liberal press, and no group is more often accused of it than Christian America.

When conservative Christians—in particular public figures—fall from grace due to some transgression in their personal lives, their morality is called into question, as is their right to have morals in the first place. "Hypocrisy!" the outraged blowhards cry, as they self-righteously point and then secretly laugh. David Shuster's short-lived MSNBC program, *1600 Pennsylvania Avenue*, featured a regular segment ominously, and kind of comically, called "Hypocrisy Watch," and it would do just this—point and laugh at the country's new creepy, crawly societal ill, the "hypocrites." And not surprisingly, over less than four months of 2009, thirty-four of the new Hypocrisy Arbiter-in-Chief's forty-eight offenders were Republicans or conservatives. Only four were Democrats or liberals. Because liberals are just way more sincere.[1]

The allure of the conservative Christian hypocrite for the urban liberal media elite is fairly predictable: It's another opportunity to shame Christians to the far fringes of American civilization—where oddities like tractor pulls, agriculture, and Sunday Mass are still inexplicably clinging to relevance—and simultaneously out them as liars, frauds, and holier-than-thou zealots. After all, Christians, to the secular Left, are far more dangerous when they actually practice what they preach—so taking them down a peg when they don't reassures the Bill Mahers and Keith Olbermanns of the world that their secular bully pulpits maintain a protected status. "Phew," they say. "We will live to laugh and point another day."

So when a Republican politician, who has the audacity (some might call it courage) to say that he believes some actions are moral, while others aren't, and then that politician himself acts immorally, he is immediately called a hypocrite by the liberal press, and the whole of the Republican Party is thrown to the lions along with him. "So much for family values," the left-wing pundits shrug and shake their heads, and then excitedly snicker during the commercial break and high-five under the news desk.

Their collective glee isn't diminished any when Democratic politicians are caught in flagrante delicto, because these aren't the guys who ever "said" they had morals to begin with, nor did they ever suggest you should. So their transgressions are okay—politically ruinous, maybe, but hardly out of line with the rest of the country, which the liberal media points out is a collection of adulterers and philanderers

---

1. "Ignoring Democratic Hypocrisy, Zinging GOP," Media Research Center, www.mrc.org, April 6, 2009.

anyway. For having values Republicans are hypocrites, and for having none Democrats are merely "representative."

But it seems that, thanks to the continuous circulation of political scandals and controversies in the press, and the affinity for sensationalist hype the media depends on, many in the mainstream press have forgotten what hypocrisy actually means. Or maybe the better explanation is that they never knew what it meant to begin with. ("Tonight on 'Hypocrisy Watch': Liberal hypocrites in the press learn that 'hypocrisy' doesn't mean what they think it means, and that calling people 'hypocrites' is actually 'hypocritical' and inaccurate. Oh, the hypocrisy.")

Hypocrisy means professing beliefs, feelings, or virtues that one does not actually hold or possess. The key is in the second part of the sentence—"does not actually hold or possess." That means, for example, that a politician who cheats on his wife is a hypocrite only if he preached incessantly that cheating on one's wife was wrong, but didn't actually believe that it was. Douchebag? Yes. Hypocrite? Not necessarily.

To contrast, a man who says cheating is wrong, and then cheats on his wife, but still genuinely believes that act of infidelity to be wrong, is not a hypocrite. He's merely a sinner, or a wrongdoer, or someone who fell short of his ideals. He is essentially the majority of people on this planet.

There's a difference—but it's one that's apparently too nuanced for the liberal press to contend with on a regular basis. So instead, conservative Christian wrongdoers are condemned as hypocrites for having values that they do not always live up to. It's an especially easy argument to make when the rules of liberalism don't require its followers to have any ideals, and instead rely on an ever-shifting system of moral relativism that never really implicates anyone personally.

Democratic politicians who find themselves in the midst of an adulterous affair, or in the company of prostitutes, or canoodling with underage girls, or getting divorced, can be cads and dirtbags for sure—but to the liberal media they're never hypocrites, because they never actually "said" they believed any of that stuff was wrong. The liberal solution is to avoid making statements that can later be called hypocritical.

I talked to Dinesh D'Souza, best-selling author, scholar, and conservative commentator, about this, and he put it this way: "Did anyone accuse Bill Clinton of being a hypocrite when he got into trouble with Monica? No, because his actions were probably right in line with his ideals." Because he didn't campaign on a platform of "family values," and, like most liberals, probably thinks, "Hey, infidelity happens," cheating on his wife wasn't falling short of his values—it was right in step with them. So all he had to do was apologize—no one said, "Well, so much for liberal family values."

So when the liberal media declares, after every unfortunate transgression by a conservative Christian politician, that Republicans are no longer the party of family values, they are wrong. Republicans still stand for family values, and Democrats still do not. Wayward Republican Christians do not make the whole of the party debauched hypocrites, they simply show that some of them are sinners. But you'll never hear a liberal pundit like Olbermann say as much, because he has no concept of or use for "sin." There are only "mistakes," the stuff liberals do, and "hypocrisy," the stuff conservatives do.

THE ARGENTINIAN TRYST THAT WILL
KILL CONSERVATISM (HOPEFULLY)

When South Carolina governor Mark Sanford ran off to Argentina for an exotic tryst with his lover—who was not, in a shocking turn of events, his wife—the liberal media had a hypocrisy field day. It was true that Sanford was a conservative Christian who had railed against Bill Clinton for his affair with Monica Lewinsky, and it was true that his behavior was wrong and very disappointing. In a column I wrote for Politico, I called for his resignation—not so much because of the affair, but because of his bizarre behavior after it, which actually made me question both his sanity and his ability to effectively run his state.

But he was not a hypocrite. He believed the affair to be wrong, which was in keeping with his Christian beliefs, and he failed at upholding his values. He'd have been a hypocrite if he'd said, after having wagged a judgmental finger at the country in criticism of infidelity, "I'm not ashamed of what I did. For you, it's wrong. For me, it's okay." But he was ashamed—he was so ashamed that he treated us all to a very informative and truly uncomfortable press conference in which we all cathartically laughed and cried along with the unraveling governor. No matter for the liberal media—he, and others like him, had shown once again that the religious Right was one big hypocritical mess.

Salon.com wrote not one, but four (!) stories declaring as much, which begs two questions: Was anything else happening that week, and how many versions of the same exact column does a magazine really need to publish to make a point?

Joan Walsh wrote, "It's hard not to notice how the worst family-values hypocrites tend to be Republicans, from Newt Gingrich and Bob Livingston, to Mark Foley and Larry Craig, to David Vitter, John Ensign and now Sanford. If they can't practice what they preach, maybe these Republican hypocrites should at least stop preaching."[2]

That's "hypocrites" twice in as many sentences! But what Walsh misses is that "the worst family-values hypocrites" don't just "tend to be Republicans," they're *only* Republicans, because Democrats don't campaign on family values. Except, I guess, for John Edwards. And that went really, really well.

---

2. Joan Walsh, "Mark Sanford's Slow-Motion Crack-Up," Salon.com, July 1, 2009.

Gene Lyons echoed Walsh's sentiments, saying, "It's Republicans who are prone to preaching about other people's intimate lives. ... Like most Southern Republicans, Sanford talked like a biblical fundamentalist: piously condemning others' sexual sins and boasting about his own righteousness."[3]

In yet another Salon story, Gary Kamiya wrote about "the strange nakedness of Mark Sanford." "From Bob Livingston to Newt Gingrich, the hypocrisy of sanctimonious, Bible-thumping, family-values-espousing GOP politicians who get caught with their pants down has become a national joke. Until Republicans abandon their judgmental moralism about all things sexual, their marital peccadilloes will inspire schadenfreude, not sympathy."[4]

For Kamiya, the solution was simple: The GOP should "abandon their judgmental moralism." Conservatives and Christians, on the other hand, might suggest that Republican politicians—and everyone else in the world—do a better job of practicing their morals, but for the Left, better just to throw them out altogether.

Charles Blow made a similar statement in the *New York Times* railing against Republicans for their conservative stances on various social issues, and for being fallible human beings at the same time, how dare they.

"While conservatives fight to 'defend' marriage from gays, they can't keep theirs together. ... Conservatives touted abstinence-only education, which was a flop, when real sex education was needed, most desperately in red states. ... They could avoid this hypocrisy by focusing more on what happens in their own bedrooms and avoiding the trap of judging what goes on in everyone else's."[5]

Again, what Blow is talking about isn't hypocrisy. But nonethe-

---

3. Gene Lyons, "Sex Scandals Are Bipartisan," Salon.com, July 2, 2009.

4. Gary Kamiya, "The Strange Nakedness of Mark Sanford," Salon.com, June 25, 2009.

5. Charles M. Blow, "The Prurient Trap," *New York Times*, June 26, 2009.

less, in essence, like Mr. Kamiya, Mr. Blow believes the easy answer is for conservative Christians to abandon their values, stop trying to make America a more decent place, and just work on "what happens in their own bedrooms." The liberal media's insistence that Christians avoid "the trap of judging" other people is both presumptuous and a gross misunderstanding of Christian morality. Christians aren't just required to live their values, they're required to promote their values above others. And this makes perfect sense—if the Ten Commandments are good for Christians, why wouldn't they think they'd be good for everyone else? The beauty of American democracy for non-believers is that they have to adhere only to the laws (even if many of them also just happen to be Commandments). So it's preposterous to think that Christian America is going to say "Adultery is bad for me, but fine for you." But the secular Left doesn't just want Christian America to keep its beliefs to themselves—they want Christian America to applaud when they trample on them.

But the best Salon story of the bunch came from Joe Conason, a favorite voice of the liberal elite, and author of *The Hunting of the President: The 10 Year Campaign to Destroy Bill and Hillary Clinton*. His take on the Sanford scandal, thinly veiled by the column's headline, "Remind Me: Which Party is 'Decadent' and 'Sick'?" was that the religious Right should just come out already and call themselves what they really are: liberals!

Whenever the latest Republican politician is caught with his zipper undone, a predictable moment of introspection on the right inevitably ensues. Pundits, bloggers and perplexed citizens ruminate over the lessons they have learned, again and again, about human frailty, false piety and the temptations of flesh and power. They express concern for the damaged family and lament the fall of yet another promising young hypocrite. They resolve to restore the purity of their movement and always remember to remind us that

*this is all Bill Clinton's fault. What they never do is face up to an
increasingly embarrassing fact about themselves and their leaders.
They're really just liberals in right-wing drag.*[6]

The idea that conservatives behaving badly might as well be liberals is bizarre, not for the fact that it's liberals who usually admit to
this, but for the discomfiting pride with which they seem to do so. Jon
Stewart mimicked that sentiment on *The Daily Show*, saying, "Oh,
marital infidelity. [Sanford is] just another politician with a conservative mind and a liberal penis." Ha ha ha, liberals are immoral.

Later, Conason bitterly bemoans the fact that conservative politicians like Sanford somehow get to stick around in public office
after admitting to their affairs—as if Bill Clinton had to get a job
grilling up Moons Over My Hammy orders at Denny's. (Seriously,
where's that guy been all these years? Boy, is that name a blast from
the past.)

Conason whines, "Even after confessing to the most flagrant and
colorful fornication, the worst that a conservative must anticipate is a
stern scolding, followed by warm assurances of God's forgiveness and
a swift return to business as usual."

Echoing *Salon's* general tone of disgust for those hypocritical
conservative Christians like Mark Sanford, Maureen Dowd also
jumped on the opportunity to assail the religious Right as a bunch of
phonies and sanctimonious frauds in the *New York Times*. She imagines that Sanford's alter ego, a guy she names "Marco," gets to act out
all of "Mark's" inner fantasies. "Mark was the self-righteous, Bible-
thumping prig who pressed for Bill Clinton's impeachment; Marco
was the un-self-conscious Lothario, canoodling with Maria in Bue-
nos Aires.... Mark is a conservative railing against sinners; Marco
sins liberally. Mark opposes gay marriage as a threat to traditional

---

6. Joe Conason, "Remind Me: Which Party is 'Decadent' and 'Sick'?" Salon.com, June 26, 2009.

marriage. Marco thinks nothing of risking his own traditional marriage, and celebrates transgressive relationships."[7]

Ms. Dowd exaggerates a bit for effect, as she is wont to do. It's not clear that Sanford sinned "liberally," nor is it likely that he thought "nothing" of what the consequences might be, or that he "celebrates transgressive relationships," whatever that means. But you get her point—he's a hypocrite.

On CBSNews.com, Marc Ambinder went so far as to suggest Sanford might just be the straw that breaks the hypocritical conservative Christian camel's back. With similar transgressions that same year by Nevada senator John Ensign and Louisiana senator David Vitter, Sanford risked ruining the party's good name for good: "This may be a tipping point: a few examples of conservative moralists who cheat on their wives (Vitter, Ensign) can be, perhaps, accepted as evidence that human beings are normal. But at some point, the liberal talking point about GOP hypocrisy starts to have the ring of truth. . . . The usual 'blame the culture of New York and Washington' line, which was used to explain the indiscretions of the two most recent New York Democratic governors and of Senators Ensign and Vitter, don't apply to Sanford. He was as South Carolinian as all get out."[8]

And *Newsweek*'s blogger Holly Bailey sounded a similar call: "What's happened with Sanford and Ensign is no doubt a blow to the party, but Republicans were already struggling with question of identity: What kind of GOP does it want to be? The answer is still unclear. The GOP's claim to be the party of 'family values' has taken a hit—though it was already in a tenuous position. (Do the names Mark Foley, Larry Craig and David Vitter ring a bell?)"[9]

And indeed Ensign, who also admitted he had an extramarital

---

7. Maureen Dowd, "Genius in the Bottle," *New York Times,* June 27, 2009.

8. Marc Ambinder, "Political Fallout from Sanford's Affair," CBSNews.com, June 24, 2009.

9. Holly Bailey, "After Sanford, What Do Republicans Do Now?" Newsweek.com, June 24, 2009.

affair, met a similar fate in the liberal press, of course. Much was made of the fact that Ensign had lived at the "C Street House," a Christian living facility owned by Youth With a Mission D.C., which was hypocrisy on top of hypocrisy on top of hypocrisy.

The *New York Times'* Gail Collins may have put it more delicately, but the theme was the same: "We hardly need to point out that Ensign was one of the people who demanded that President Bill Clinton resign over the Lewinsky affair, that he votes against financing for education and contraception services to combat teenage pregnancy and that he supports a constitutional amendment banning same-sex marriage. In the world of politics, hypocrisy is a hard market to corner, but lately the Republicans have been making a Microsoft-like effort to do it." [10]

Religion and political scholar Dinesh D'Souza said that the chasm between mainstream Christian America and the liberal secular press also stems from the view in the liberal media that Christianity is merely a malleable political tool that's problematic only when it's actually someone's worldview.

"People generally hold the belief that liberal Christianity is insincere—but for them, that's a compliment. The media likes it that these guys don't really believe all the stuff they say, and so do their constituents. On the right, though, moral character trumps your political value—if you're a believer, and you mess up, it doesn't matter how good a politician you were, how many bills you passed, or how much spending you cut. All that matters is the moral fall. On the left you can be a believer if it never informs actual morality. So liberals can say, 'My faith compels me to combat global warming,' and that's okay. But if they said, 'My faith compels me to oppose abortion,' that isn't. Liberals have to reassure other liberals—in the media especially—that

---

10.   Gail Collins, "What Happened in Vegas," *New York Times,* July 10, 2009.

they're insincere about their religious convictions, and that they're only opportunistically using religion for political purposes."

Again, it isn't enough for the liberal press that Christians shut up about their views. They want Christians to approve of theirs. The liberal media wasn't offended by Bill Clinton's infidelity. They were offended when we didn't applaud him for it. Christians, regardless of the constant charges of hypocrisy that will be levied against them, need to stick to their guns. Don't be fooled—they want you to totally abandon your beliefs.

THE DEMOCRATS: GO FORTH IN SIN (WE WON'T TELL ANYBODY)

Of course, it's not as though the last couple of years have been stellar for Democrats either. New York governor Eliot Spitzer resigned in 2008 after being implicated as a customer of a prostitution ring in Washington, and former Democratic presidential candidate John Edwards finally admitted to having fathered a child with another woman, after spending months denying he'd even had an affair and allowing his campaign staff to continue working on his presidential bid. But there were others—less colorful perhaps, but others nonetheless. You may or may not have heard much about them. Here's a brief rundown:

In 2008, Florida congressman Tim Mahoney admitted to having "numerous" affairs, "certainly more than two," after reports alleged that he offered to pay $121,000 in hush money to a mistress.

Former Kansas attorney general Paul Morrison admitted to having an affair with an administrative staffer, who claimed he pressured her into revealing sensitive information about the district attorney.

Marc Dann, the attorney general of Ohio, also had an affair with a staffer, but refused to resign, despite persistent calls to do so by

Democratic governor Ted Strickland. The Ohio Democratic Party also called for his resignation, voted to remove their endorsement of him, and stripped him of his membership in the Ohio Democratic Party Executive Committee. Only after articles of impeachment were filed did Dann agree to resign.

New York governor David Paterson, who took over after Spitzer was identified as "Client No. 9," admitted one day after his inauguration that both he and his wife had had extramarital affairs.

Detroit mayor Kwame Kilpatrick was charged with eight felony counts, including perjury, misconduct in office, and obstruction of justice in connection with, in part, an extramarital affair he had with his chief of staff. Later, two additional felony counts would be filed for assaulting and interfering with a law officer.

And Sam Adams, the Portland, Oregon, mayor, admitted to having lied about an affair he had with an eighteen-year-old male legislative intern.

But the scandals weren't just sexual. There was Illinois governor Rod Blagojevich's spectacular meltdown, of course, and the bizarre Roland Burris takeover that followed. Democratic congressmen Charles Rangel, John Murtha, Pete Visclosky, James Moran, and William Jefferson were all investigated in 2009 for corruption and campaign donations controversies. Edwards, Mahoney, Morrison, Paterson, Kilpatrick, Rangel, Murtha, Visclosky, Moran, Jefferson, Blagojevich, and Burris.

Indeed, 2008 was a busy year for Democrats, just as busy as it was for Republicans. But because Republicans campaign on family values, their transgressions were far worse—and got far more press. According to the Media Research Center, the coverage of these scandal-plagued Democrats on ABC, CBS, and NBC's morning and evening shows from January 1 to July 1 of 2009 paled in comparison to that given to Mark Sanford. Murtha had three mentions, William Jefferson, two, and Rangel, Visclosky, and Moran got no coverage at all. Meanwhile, Mark Sanford's affair got forty-nine hits on network news.[11]

Another noticeable incongruity was the media's coverage of Edwards's affair in comparison to the coverage of rumors—which proved to be totally unsubstantiated—that John McCain had been unfaithful.

Even though reports of Edwards's relationship with Rielle Hunter first broke in 2007 (thanks not to the *New York Times* but to the *National Enquirer*), the mainstream press largely ignored them until Edwards had to admit in late 2008 that they were true. (Paternity tests on Hunter's baby would later reveal just how true.)

But the *New York Times* reported on February 21, 2008, that there *might* have been adultery between McCain and a lobbyist, citing innuendo from unnamed former McCain aides who were "convinced the relationship had become romantic." And, despite McCain's denials, all three networks were quick to jump on the unsourced, breathlessly speculative story.

According to the Media Research Center: "CBS Early Show host Harry Smith touted a 'bombshell report that Republican front-runner John McCain may have had a romantic relationship with a lobbyist who was a visitor to his office and traveled with him on a client's corporate jet.' ABC's George Stephanopoulos said it could be deadly. On a scale of one to ten, with ten being fatal, he warned it was a 'six or a seven . . . a damaging story, there's no doubt about that.' NBC's Tim Russert said the story would 'play out today in a very big way.' NBC's Brian Williams began with insinuation: 'Good evening. When it hit the Internet last night and the front page of the New York Times this morning, it was the shot heard 'round the political world. It's a story

---

11. Rich Noyes and Tim Graham, "Networks Mostly Mute on Democratic Scandals," Media Research Center, www.mrc.org, July 2, 2009.

about a female lobbyist in Washington and her relationship, business and perhaps otherwise, with Senator John McCain.'"[12]

For Edwards, rumor wasn't enough for the press to go on—even when there was video and photographic proof. But for McCain, all the liberal media needed was the speculative insinuation of the *New York Times*. It's a sad day when we can tout the good journalism of the *National Enquirer* over that of the Gray Lady.

DIVORCE IN HOLLYWOOD: A MAN-BITES-DOG STORY

It's not just conservative Christian politicians, though, that the liberal media loves to target as hypocrites. It's citizens, too. When Mel Gibson, who is admittedly problematic for a number of often-hilarious and sometimes scary reasons, announced he was getting divorced in 2009, the liberal media ate it up. Never mind that Hollywood celebrities get divorced with the regularity of a sunrise, this one was special—because Gibson is a devout Catholic.

Abortion activist Frances Kissling wrote in Salon.com, "Why is it that these right-wing family-values guys are always the worst sinners? Newt Gingrich, Ted Haggard, Larry Craig and now Mel Gibson."[13]

Gibson is one of "the worst sinners"? Really? Putting him up against murderers, rapists, child molesters, terrorists, and evil dictators, is Mel Gibson really the worst? Moreover, are Gingrich, Haggard, and Craig?

MSNBC contributor Tony Sclafani also seemed a little *too* bent out of shape.

12. "TV Waited on Edwards' Adultery But Leaped on McCain Rumors," Media Research Center, www.mrc.org, Aug. 12, 2008.

13. Frances Kissling, "Mel Gibson's Family Values," Salon.com, April 26, 2009.

I've never been the type to throw things at the television screen out of anger. But I'll admit I did shout something nasty at my TV when I caught Mel Gibson yukking it up with Jay Leno and calling himself "Octo-Mel" since his pregnant girlfriend is carrying his eighth child. My anger, of course, was directed at Gibson's hypocrisy. Not so long ago, Gibson was the world's best-known Traditionalist Catholic, talking about his preference for the old-style teachings of Vatican I (no divorce, no Russian girlfriends while still married). These days, he's not yet divorced and living the kind of life he preached against. What's worse is that Gibson seems unrepentant, to use church lingo.[14]

Is Gibson's marital trouble and infidelity really cause to throw objects at one's television? Does so-called Christian hypocrisy really get these liberal media types *that* worked up? Or is it possible there's a little disingenuous pretending for the readers and for the cameras, that's as if to say, "I am outraged! And you should be, too! Won't you join me in collectively loathing the religious right?"

What's bizarre, and disappointing, is that it's not the divorce or the infidelity the liberal media finds problematic. That, they're perfectly fine with. It's that Christian conservatives have the temerity to stand for something at all. And when they fail to live up to their own standards, as most of us do, the liberal media just loves to watch them fall, proof yet again that they were right all along: Having standards is a silly waste of time.

Forget about the Hollywood celebutards—they're a lost cause. But shouldn't we, as Americans, want our political leaders to, at the very least, *say* they have values? Don't we want them to stand for something instead of nothing? Isn't Mark Sanford's public struggle with his conscience for cheating on his wife more admirable than

---

14. Tony Sclafani, "Hypocrisy, Thy Name is Mel Gibson," MSNBC.com, June 1, 2009.

Bill Clinton's seeming indifference to it? Both made mistakes, but only Sanford called his a sin. Clinton's was merely a "lapse in judgment." When the mainstream media mocks and scolds the "sinners" but ignores or even celebrates the "judgment-impaired," it signals to the rest of America that it's having morals in the first place that gets you in trouble. So why bother?

It's not the job of the media to tell us that our values as a Judeo-Christian nation are out of fashion, irrelevant, or hypocritical. Insisting at every turn that Christian America defend its beliefs is abusive—Christian America should be demanding that the secular Left defend *its* beliefs, not the other way around. If conservative values like fidelity are so outdated to the liberal press, and if Christian values are so fundamentally backward, why doesn't anyone ask Keith Olbermann or Chris Matthews to defend their values? What are they, anyway? Besides being pro-Clinton and anti-Sanford, what do they really believe in? The answer *should* be, Who cares? But if the liberal media's going to scrutinize the values of a huge swath of Americans, then shouldn't they lay theirs out on the table, too?

VIII

THOU SHALT BURN FOX NEWS IN EFFIGY

In fall 2009, President Obama and his team of angry pit bulls—David Axelrod, Anita Dunn, Rahm Emanuel, and Robert Gibbs—waged a war on Fox News. The administration decided—in what would become, even according to most liberals, a silly and highly unpresidential moment—that it would orchestrate a synchronized and organized attack on the news juggernaut, which has long led in prime-time ratings. All at once, they descended on the *other* networks to tell the country that Fox News is just a vehicle for the GOP and should not be trusted or taken seriously. Even the liberal press had to tell the president he couldn't, much as he wanted to, kick the Fox team out of the White House press pool. Fox, of course, had a field day with it. And most agreed eventually that it had been a colossal waste of time and energy on the part of the president. Even Joy Behar, on her CNN *Headline News* show, said to me, "Well, that was a mistake."

But the White House war on Fox is nothing new. The liberal press has been doing it for years. Consider, for example, the liberal media monitoring website News Hounds: "We Watch Fox So You Don't Have To." It's not very sophisticated. Nor is it very serious. Honest and responsible media critics know that to be trusted for fair analysis you can't just target one news organization over and over again. There's a word for that in the news business: bias. Yet News Hounds, once attached to MoveOn.org and now maintained by regular citizen-activists Ellen, Priscilla, Julie, Alex, Dan, and Brian, want you to know they don't think Fox News is fair or balanced.

The gang over at News Hounds is objectionable, and not because I've had the honor of being a personal, frequent target of their rigorous analysis, which makes use of thoughtful terms like "dick," "political prostitute," and "crybaby." Nor is the problem that the spelling and grammar are atrocious, and the discourse reminiscent of a pimply-faced high schooler's MySpace page. The problem with News Hounds is the sheer hypocrisy of the site and sites like it for waging a vitriolic war on Fox and then bashing the whole of the American Right along with them. As part of their campaign to bring Fox News down (though I don't think anyone at Fox News is too worried), News Hounds just loves to slam their reporters, pundits, and viewers as crazy Christians, and in the ugliest language possible.

They've called former presidential candidate, Arkansas governor, and pastor Mike Huckabee a "christofascist," a "hypochristian," and "Jesus' Huckster." They've called *Fox & Friends*, the network's morning program, "that old-time religion show" that "sure does love those victimized Christians. (Somebody call me a whambulance!)" They routinely slam Fox's "neocon and rapture-ready fundamentalist Christians," claim Fox "whines" about "persecuted Christians," and calls the Christian Fox News personalities like Sean Hannity, Gretchen Carlson, and Bill O'Reilly "wingnuts" and "Nazis."

While News Hounds is decidedly fringe, it is a microcosmic representation of the sentiment often expressed by the larger liberal media, which at least has the good taste to couch its anti-Christian vitriol in gentler language. Usually. The mainstream liberal media has decided that the rest of the media is full of kooky, fanatical Christians who won't shut up about Jesus, and that any reported attacks against American Christians are entirely fabricated, ginned up by the conservative media itself to carry out their own sociopolitical agenda of martyrdom and woe-is-me victimhood. The same group that regularly allows its own secularism and antireligious ideology to color its news coverage is angry and indignant that its nonliberal counterparts mention God once in a while. Ted Turner reportedly called his CNN employees who wore ashes on their foreheads on Ash Wednesday "Jesus freaks," prompting the resignation of some prominent reporters. What's good for the goose apparently isn't so good for the gander.

This systematic campaign by the liberal media has been surgical in its precision—if by "surgical," you mean broad, sweeping, and relatively careless, the kind of surgery you'd do with a machete, not a scalpel. The first tactic is to redefine Fox News. Because Fox News in particular is a reaction against the slavish bias of the liberal media and aims to more widely represent American viewpoints (and effectively, judging by its ratings), the network is routinely and inaccurately skewered by the liberal press as an overactive, bionic arm of the GOP. And because of that, it is also, de facto, an arm of the Christian Right.

So the nonliberal media is stacked with fanatical Christians advancing illegitimate story lines about the supposed anti-Christian bias of the American Left. In part, the liberal media's allegations are true— there are openly Christian reporters, pundits, editors, and producers at Fox News, the *Weekly Standard,* the *New York Post,* the *Washington Times,* and elsewhere in the nonliberal landscape of American media. But the part that the Left won't acknowledge is that Christians are, in fact, *everywhere.* In a nation of 173,402,000 of them, you're bound to run into a few. Yes, even—gasp!—in a newsroom.

But here's, in part, why this doesn't add up: Some of the country's—and Fox's—leading conservative commentators aren't Christian. Mark Levin, Dennis Miller, Jonah Goldberg, Ben Stein, Bernard Goldberg, Bill Kristol, Michael Medved, Dennis Prager, Charles Krauthammer—all wildly popular, none Christian.

But of course the deeper allegation here isn't really that Christians have infiltrated the nonliberal press. It's that they dare to talk about it. The fact that some of these journalists and pundits, as well as non-Christian reporters, find stories once in a while that deal with Christianity might just be good reporting, right?

Openly Christian pundits like Bill O'Reilly, Sean Hannity, Laura Ingraham, Glenn Beck, Ann Coulter, Dr. Laura Schlessinger, Brit Hume, Mike Huckabee, Joe Scarborough, Rush Limbaugh, and even Michael Savage, who is Jewish but defends Christian America, aren't supposed to reference their faith when talking politics and culture, even when the liberal media devotes ample time to denouncing it. The double standard is impressive, if totally disingenuous. But why isn't anyone at MSNBC, CNN, the *New York Times,* or *Newsweek* regularly defending Christian America? Why don't these media outlets feature pundits and columnists like Sean Hannity and Ann Coulter, who aren't ashamed of their Christian faith and talk to Christian Americans as if they matter? In fact, it feels like they go out of their way *not* to feature these very voices.

The dirty secret is that the liberal media simply loves it when Sean Hannity talks about Catholicism, or Glenn Beck talks about Mormonism, or Mike Huckabee talks about Southern Baptists, or any of them talk about God at all—because the conservative pundits have just opened the door for the Huffington Post and MSNBC to classify them all not just as conservative crazies, but as conservative Christian crazies, a bonus-points twofer that enthusiastically forgoes nuance or honesty in favor of the nasty shock-value sensationalism the liberal media relishes. That it thinks it's winning favor with audiences by slamming Christians as crazy just highlights the myopia that has driven much of the liberal media into financial ruin and ratings obscurity.

FAIR, CIVIL, AND ACCURATE?

The liberal media likes to attack its more popular, profitable cousins in the right-wing press whenever it gets the opportunity, and it isn't very nice about it. The typical campaign goes something like this:

Sanctimoniously declare the right-wing media is unfair, uncivil, and inaccurate.

Give examples of purported right-wing bias.

Call right-wing media nasty names.

Watch ratings soar!

The plan is flawed for a number of reasons, not the least of which is that ratings are not soaring. What the liberal press has called "right-wing bias" isn't actually—it's just *not* the usual left-wing bias that we've all grown so accustomed to from the mainstream media. For the Left, right-wing bias, supposedly, means covering hardworking Middle America (how dare it?!) and religious America—which is the overwhelming majority of people in this country. It's not so much a right-wing conspiracy as it is a brilliant marketing strategy to deliver news and commentary that actually matter to the bulk of the country, and not just the so-called sophisticates in New York and Los Angeles.

And second, calling the right-wing media "uncivil" would elicit sympathy only if the left-wing media weren't so nasty itself. In the *Washington Post*, Tom Shales, reviewing Alexandra Pelosi's documentary *Friends of God*, about religious America, calls Bill O'Reilly "Fox's nut-in-residence." Reverend Jerry Falwell, according to Shales, "looks like a parody of a mean, blubbery Southern politico." And religious America is "sometimes scary as hell." Of course, as he says this, he also writes that the so-called attack on Christianity is literally crazy, "a seemingly paranoid hostility that maintains Christians are the most persecuted group in America."[1]

So when the liberal media talks about the nonliberal media, mounting that flawed campaign, it's not all that credible.

David Brock, author of *The Republican Noise Machine: Right-Wing Media and How It Corrupts Democracy*, wrote about his book in Salon.com, which has a particular affinity for criticizing conservative Christians, in 2004.

He claimed that the media is dominated by right-wing religious fanatics, so much so that the folks who eschew those media outlets don't even realize exactly what they're missing. "When I say this, in a more respectful way, to folks outside the right wing, I usually get either of two responses. Those who receive their news from the *New York Times* and National Public Radio give me blank stares. They are living in a rarefied media culture—one that prizes accuracy, fairness, and civility—that is no longer representative of the media as a whole. Those who have heard snippets of Rush Limbaugh's radio show, have caught a glimpse of Bill O'Reilly's temper tantrums on the Fox News Channel, or occasionally peruse the editorials in the *Wall Street Journal* think I'm a Cassandra. They view this media as self-discrediting and therefore irrelevant. They are living in a vacuum of denial."[2]

To review, he's saying the *New York Times*, in which Paul Krugman

1. Tom Shales, "Soldiers of the Cross," *Washington Post*, Jan. 25, 2007.
2. David Brock, "The Mighty Windbags," Salon.com, May 11, 2004.

wrote that Republicans are "embarrassing to watch," "crazy," "clue-less," "bad for the country," and the "subject of considerable mockery, and rightly so," is accurate, fair, and civil. Accuracy means, appar-ently, issuing correction after correction for wrongly criticizing some conservative special-interest groups as Christian, when they weren't. Fairness means, apparently, totally ignoring conservative protests but splashing liberal ones all over the front, middle, and back pages. And civility means, apparently, snobbishly treating the religious Right as if they were the backwoods rednecks from *Deliverance.*

Brock goes on to further describe his new project, one that prizes the accuracy, fairness, and civility of the left-wing press: "It is also about the beliefs of those who populate right-wing media and the beliefs that people derive from it. My conclusion is that right-wing media is a massive fraud, victimizing its own audience and corrupting the broader political dialogue with the tacit permission of established media authorities who should, and probably do, know better."

In 2004 and 2005 Christian America was particularly bothered by the growing secular assault on Christmas, which the liberal media routinely assailed as either entirely in their heads, or the work of an-gry anti-Semitic right-wing talking heads.

In the *New York Times,* and on Christmas day, Frank Rich called Christian outrage "manufactured" and "irrational hysteria" propagated by news outlets that were tired of defending President Bush's foreign policy. "If you worked at Fox News," he wrote, "wouldn't you want to change the subject from the war in Iraq to a war in which victory is a slam-dunk?"[3]

Covering the issues important to Christian America isn't, for Frank Rich and the *New York Times,* about speaking directly to a vast majority. It's about pandering to them in the wake of a 2004 election that reinstated "a born-again president whose base is typified by these

---

3.   Frank Rich, "I Saw Jackie Mason Kissing Santa Claus," *New York Times,* Dec. 25, 2005.

holy rollers and the Christmas demagogues of Fox News." "Ever since, politicians of both parties, Fox News anchors and any other huckster eager to sell goods, an agenda or an image have increased the decibel level of their pandering to 'people of faith.'"

The war on Christmas gave the liberal media a golden opportunity to target not just Christian America, but the right-wing press. And boy did they take it.

Time magazine's Joel Stein wrote about John Gibson's book, *The War on Christmas: How the Liberal Plot to Ban the Sacred Christian Holiday Is Worse Than You Thought,* and Fox's coverage of the war on Christmas in the *Los Angeles Times,* slamming Gibson's title— "Seriously, the guy couldn't even afford an editor for the title?"[4]—and accusing Gibson and Bill O'Reilly of organizing a boycott of stores that used the phrase "Happy Holidays" instead of "Merry Christmas." In his column, called "Oy to the World," Stein reveled in the opportunity to lambaste American Christians as stupid and childish rubes.

"I think it's adorable that you ring giant, white pipe cleaners around streetlights and make everything taste like peppermint and thought the world was going to end when the calendar went to three zeros in a row. It's like living with children. . . . We Jews find it a little embarrassing that adults can still make such a big fuss over Christmas. To us, Jesus was just a cool guy everyone liked because he died young. And even 16-year-old girls eventually take down their James Dean posters."

So, not exactly civil—but was it at least accurate and fair?

The *Los Angeles Times* later issued a correction, acknowledging that neither Gibson nor O'Reilly ever organized such boycotts. Accurate, fair, and civil—not exactly.

Look at it this way: O'Reilly, a conservative Christian who is paid to have opinions, isn't allowed to defend Christian America without

---

4.   Joel Stein, "Oy to the World," *Los Angeles Times,* Dec. 6, 2005.

being called a liar, anti-Semitic, or a "nut." If President Bush couldn't defend Christian America without being ridiculed by the liberal press, and Bill O'Reilly, who has the most-watched cable news show on television, can't defend Christian America without being ridiculed by the liberal press, how can Christian America defend itself without being ridiculed by the liberal press?

The short answer is, it can't. Christian America can either get used to being unceremoniously mocked at every turn, which seems to be the strategy thus far, or it can do something about it. Over the last few years, simple declarations of faith have tellingly become more like acts of revolution. Saying "Merry Christmas" to someone who has said "Happy Holidays" is now part of a rebellion, not just a polite greeting. "God Bless America" isn't just a motto, it's an aggressive declaration. Wearing a cross around your neck isn't just a fashion choice, it's a bold act of tyranny. And this has happened because the liberal media has shamed Christians back into their churches and homes, railing against a religious president or a religious television pundit, telling average Americans that if presidents can be targeted, so can you. Now acknowledging faith isn't just an act of piety, it's an act of war. When the faithful represent the vast majority, the war should be easily won, but not if the majority stays home. So what's the battle plan? Become the "crazy Christian" the liberal media insists you are. Don't get quieter, get louder. Just like the tea partiers took to the streets against government waste, so should Christians against media bias. Christian America should make the media realize how mainstream Christians actually are, when they're left alone.

THOSE CRAZY CHRISTIAN NUTBALLS

Certainly Christmas isn't the only time when the nonliberal media is assailed for its insistence on covering Christian America or defending Christianity against rank secularism. When President Obama repealed President Bush's stem cell restrictions in 2009, the moment was one of particular relevance to Christians, who consider the use of embryonic stem cells a devaluation of the sanctity of life. For Salon, that stalwart defender of the anti-Christian Left, Fox's decision to acknowledge that aspect of Obama's decision was somehow inappropriate.

"At this point, it seems like Fox News has just gone ahead and dropped that whole pretense of being 'fair and balanced.' Of all the people Fox could have had on to talk about the president's move to overturn his predecessor's ban on federal funding for stem cell research, they turned to former Christian Coalition Executive Director Ralph Reed."[5]

Apparently Salon would have preferred Fox to interview the head of the American atheists? Because the liberal media totally ignored the religious implications of Obama's stell cell decision, despite the country's overwhelming Christian majority, Fox News was excoriated as unfair and imbalanced for daring to address it.

And when Proposition 8 passed in California, banning same-sex marriage in that state, the liberal media once again took to blaming the nonliberal media for somehow prodding Christian America into homophobic hysteria. It wasn't that the state of California didn't favor gay marriage, it was that Fox News didn't.

Mark Morford wrote a scathing critique of Christian America and Fox in the online outlet of the *San Francisco Chronicle:* "The most amusing, laughable example of panicked wailing of all [is] the fiery gyrations and frustrations of the right-wing extremists, the shrillest of the shrill, the hysterics of Fox News' fringe nutball militia. Much to the humiliation of moderate Republicans, the spotlight has now shifted to the most nauseating, preposterous voices the right-wing

5. Alex Koppelman, "Fox News' Stem Cell Expert: Ralph Reed," Salon.com, March 9, 2009.

punditry has to offer: from the Brothers Limbaugh to O'Reilly, and now on to freakshow Glenn Beck and even Michael Savage, and all hitched to a ragtag squad of fanatic bloggers and conspiracy theorists like Alex Jones, and all currently fanning the flames of violent extremism and paranoia like never before."[6]

And his examples? Well, he had none. Not a single quotation from any of his aforementioned "nutballs." But there you have it—that's the way the liberal media does fairness, accuracy, and civility. We're all very impressed.

It's not just Fox that's regularly in the crosshairs of the liberal press for purportedly propping up Christian America. AM radio, dominated by wildly popular conservative talk show hosts, is also a frequent target.

In 2008, Marc Fisher wrote about the funny little quirks and oddities of AM radio in the *Washington Post*, suggesting that the kind of rhetoric these shows deliver is behind the times and counterproductive. "To spend a week listening only to AM radio, as I recently did, is to explore a world not unlike that of the Internet, where what's dominant is not reasoned and careful conversation, but the wild and woolly, voices crying out to be heard in a soundscape of plenty."[7]

What was he talking about? Christian radio, which—inexplicably —dares to espouse Christian views and ask questions of import to Christian America.

He writes, " 'Is masturbation okay?' talk host Marsha Sumner asks her panel on Heaven 1580 (WPGC), a gospel and Christian station."

For posing a question asked at church meetings, Bible study

---

6. Mark Morford, "Fear the Rainbow!" *San Francisco Gate,* April 10, 2009.

7. Marc Fisher, "In the Internet Age, AM Radio Needs Fine-Tuning," *Washington Post,* May 4, 2008.

groups, and Catholic schools around the country, Marsha Sumner is suddenly a "wild and woolly" voice of irrationality.

But there was more shock and horror in store for Fisher during his quick tour around the AM dial.

"Another Christian station, WFAX (1220) in Falls Church, features a preacher breathlessly explaining why he's reluctant to pay his taxes. 'We Christians are taught to pay our government for good leadership, but the Bible nowhere tells us we should pay our taxes for evil,' he says."

When Air America Radio, that failed after-school project of the liberal Left, was railing against President Bush and the Iraq War, mounting conspiracy campaign after conspiracy campaign against the government, including that the United States was behind the attacks on September 11th, this, to the sanctimonious arbiters of the media, was legitimate subject matter for talk radio conversation. But when a preacher discussed political policies in a biblical context—on a Christian radio station—this is of far lesser value to listeners?

And in a story about the waning relevance of AM radio, Fisher also casually references a conversation between talk show host Laura Ingraham and Ben Stein about creationism, as if to say, look how bizarre, parochial, and outdated these rubes are. He fails to mention that the *Laura Ingraham Show* is ranked eighth among most-listened-to radio programs, with an average of 5.5 million weekly listeners.[8]

But Fisher doesn't explain himself or elaborate on the content he finds questionable or silly or problematic on those Christian stations. He just drops those sound bites into his story because he thinks you will find them amusing and even a little scary. What he and countless others like him don't understand is that average Americans find the shrill and paranoid invective spat out by Janeane Garofalo, Al Franken, Joy Behar, Rachel Maddow, and Rosie O'Donnell far scarier

8. "The Top Talk Radio Audiences," *Talkers* magazine, Nov. 2008.

than anything Laura Ingraham, Sean Hannity, or Ben Stein ever have to say.

IF A BOOK LANDS ON THE BEST-SELLER LIST, DOES ANYONE REVIEW IT?

The bias against Christian right-wing media personalities is also evidenced by the way their inarguable successes are covered in the liberal media. Glenn Beck, Bill O'Reilly, Ann Coulter, Laura Ingraham, Sean Hannity, and Rush Limbaugh are called nuts and "fringe," despite the fact that their television and radio shows, their business ventures, and their books have been proven huge successes with the American public.

The venerable *New York Times Book Review* is particularly revealing. The liberal bias against these stars is on full view as reviewers revile the content of their books as extreme and unrepresentative, or wholly ignore them, even while those same books sit atop the *New York Times* best-seller list.

The *New York Times* did not review Ann Coulter's *Guilty* or *Treason* or *High Crimes and Misdemeanors*. It did not review Glenn Beck's *An Inconvenient Book, Common Sense,* or *Real America*. It did not review Dr. Laura Schlessinger's *The Proper Care and Feeding of Marriage, In Praise of Stay at Home Moms,* or any of her other books. It did not review Sean Hannity's *Let Freedom Ring* or *Deliver Us From Evil*. It did not review Mark Levin's *Liberty and Tyranny,* or Dick Morris's *Catastrophe,* or Michelle Malkin's *Culture of Corruption* or *Unhinged*. And it did not review Laura Ingraham's *Shut Up and Sing* or *Power to the People*.

The *Times* did review a series of Coulter counterbooks, writing, "The latest testament to Coulter's notoriety is the appearance of no less than three books devoted to bashing her. In 'Soulless,' 'Brainless' and 'I Hate Ann Coulter!,' Susan Estrich, Joe Maguire and 'Unanimous' seek to outdo one another in exposing what they see as her uniquely malign influence on American politics and culture."[9]

And on the rare occasion that the *Times* does review a conservative author, the seething vitriol is hardly disguised. Liesl Schillinger reviewed Coulter's *How to Talk to a Liberal (If You Must)*, under the headline "All Their Fault," writing dismissively, "Coulter is the only opponent she's prepared to hear out; indeed, she writes early in the book that she doesn't really want to talk to liberals since 'in most cases I don't even like them.' Well, in the words of mean girls everywhere: the feeling is mutual."[10]

Janet Maslin was similarly condescending when she reviewed Coulter's book *Slander*. "Reading her strictly for opinion on issues is thus akin to appreciating Playboy strictly for its articles. Much of this book's entertainment value exists on a lower plane."[11]

But Maslin also reviewed Al Franken's book *Lies (And the Lying Liars Who Tell Them)*. To end the suspense, she pretty much loved it. "In the kicking, spitting spirit of current all-star political discourse, Al Franken gives as good as he gets. His quintessential ad hominem attack title, 'Rush Limbaugh Is a Big, Fat Idiot,' has already established his flair for the requisite games."[12]

Book reviewers, and any other kind of critics, are of course allowed to like what they like and dislike what they don't. But the *New York Times Book Review* should exist to review books that people are reading—Michelle Malkin, Sean Hannity, Laura Ingraham, Mark Levin, and Glenn Beck are best-selling authors. And when a conservative Christian's book is reviewed, it should be assessed by virtue of

---

9. Jacob Heilbrunn, "Start Me Up," *New York Times*, Nov. 26, 2006.

10. Liesl Schillinger, "All Their Fault," *New York Times*, Oct. 31, 2004.

11. Janet Maslin, "Lining Up Right and Left As a Political Ball Game," *New York Times*, July 18, 2002.

12. Janet Maslin, "Franken Retorts, You Decide," *New York Times*, Sep. 1, 2003.

its writing, not its politics. Coulter is a hack, but Franken is a witty social commentator. Alas, to pretend there's any accuracy, fairness, or civility in what the *New York Times Book Review* publishes is to totally ignore the facts.

There are differences between Fox News and, say, MSNBC, that should be addressed here. Both cable news networks have their stable of outspoken talking heads who rail against the Left and the Right for a living—and do a great job at it. But Fox News also has serious news programs, like the *Fox Report with Shepard Smith,* and *Special Report,* once with host Brit Hume and now with Bret Baier, that balance out the prime-time slots and deliver hard, unbiased news. The regular panelists on *Special Report* are also serious journalists, and include Mort Kondracke, Charles Krauthammer, Bill Kristol, Fred Barnes, Mara Liasson, Nina Easton, and Juan Williams, some of whom are more liberal than conservative. MSNBC doesn't have this. Their prime-time schedule has liberal talking heads Ed Schultz, Chris Matthews, Keith Olbermann, and Rachel Maddow. Worst of all was when MSNBC tried to pretend some of these pundits were serious newsmen, staffing Matthews and Olbermann on the 2008 presidential election, until, thanks to some memorable leg-thrilling, that backfired. Big-time. So when the liberal media throws the right-wing-bias label up on Fox News, and then conflates that as it so often does with a Christian bias, the allegations are all the more ludicrous.

Conservative pundits on Fox News and elsewhere, like Sean Hannity, Bill O'Reilly, and Ann Coulter, don't need defending—not by viewers and readers, not by the liberal media, and certainly not by me. They are enterprises unto themselves who have somehow found a way to make a living speaking directly to Christian America un-apologetically and passionately, and for that they've been handsomely rewarded.

But if the liberal media wants a share of the kind of success that Fox News, conservative talk radio, and conservative print media have had, it might want to avoid attacking their rivals as crazy Christians who are shoving their religious views down the country's throat. Americans already know that Laura Ingraham is a Christian. And they love it. Furthermore, America's news consumers should understand that an attack on Fox News and other nonliberal outlets like talk radio is actually an attack on American values. Fox, the *Wall Street Journal*, the *Washington Times*, Rush Limbaugh, and others who haven't pledged allegiance to mainstream media liberalism are standing up for the majority—they are unafraid to acknowledge that the country is religious, that it is predominantly Christian, and that there's nothing embarrassing or dangerous about that. And they aren't engaging in the kind of soft bigotry of the leftist media outlets that attack the faithful for their beliefs. Needless to say, the liberal media should be very careful not to encourage the White House to take up its war on Fox News again—lest they be next.

IX

THOU SHALT HAVE STANDARDS—
DOUBLE STANDARDS

When history remembers the presidential election of 2008, it will undoubtedly recall as its main story line the election of a black man to the highest office in the country, and deservedly so. It will remember Oprah Winfrey and Jesse Jackson weeping at Barack Obama's Hyde Park acceptance speech. It will remember Obama's speech on race. It will remember the words of a ninety-year-old black woman who said she never thought she'd see the day when a black man lived in the White House.

But it wasn't actually race that dominated the media headlines during the 2008 election and the months that preceded it. It was religion. One could argue we spent more time talking about God during the campaign than we did about anything else—not because it's polarizing, or makes for particularly good TV, but because it matters a great deal to a great many Americans.

And that year, more than ever before, the secular liberal media used religion to get its candidate elected, exposing its own ugly biases and prejudices in ways most of us couldn't have imagined in the twenty-first century. And as badly as the media covered race (and boy, did it), the way it treated religion was worse, and may have lasting and far-reaching implications that could affect many political elections to come.

When Obama told a liberal San Francisco crowd that rural folks in Pennsylvania cling to "guns and religion" during tough times, it almost ended his run for the White House. Christian America was outraged, and even the liberal press was forced to cover his galling misstep.

Obama's own religious views would become a topic of much conversation over the course of that year, but for the liberal media his religion, his church, and his values were entirely acceptable, while another candidate's were dangerous and fanatical.

The 2008 presidential campaign offered American voters a textbook example of the way the liberal media cheaply politicizes faith to its advantage: the dueling accounts of Obama's Christianity and Sarah Palin's. To put it bluntly, Palin was eviscerated by the liberal press during the 2008 presidential campaign. The mainstream media will contend that it was so hard on her because she was an unknown when announced as John McCain's vice presidential running mate, but that assertion just doesn't pass muster. The media is still hard on her, even after dispatching hordes of investigators to Alaska to uncover every minor and insignificant detail of her life. When her book, *Going Rogue,* came out in November 2009 (it was a bestseller before it hit the shelves), they slammed her again. But Barack Obama, despite his critically acclaimed debut on the national stage at the 2004

Democratic National Convention, was also an unknown, with even less experience in public office and no executive experience at all.

Furthermore, polling shows that Obama's positions on both domestic and foreign policy issues were far outside the mainstream, more extreme than those of most Americans and most of his colleagues in the Senate, while in contrast Sarah Palin's were far more representative. An evenhanded media should also have held Obama to account for some disconcerting relationships with nefarious and radical extremists, such as the domestic terrorist William Ayers, the corrupt Tony Rezko, and a socialist network of Chicago intellectuals that would later come to reveal some of his sweeping ideological worldview. The media should have vetted Obama much more rigorously, asking the nation if his views, rather than his cult of personality, were really what they supported.

But it didn't, of course. The media was so enamored of this charismatic, young, pontificating Democrat that it decided very early on that Obama was its guy. And because so few questions were asked, the media declared full-throatedly that his brand of Christianity made him relatable, contemplative, introspective, and morally accountable, while Palin's made her categorically controversial, extreme, radical, and dangerous.

Women in the liberal media made Obama out to be a handsome—sexy, even!—progressive family man, while men in the liberal media made Palin out to be a cheap and often pornographic sex object. Men in the liberal media insisted Obama was a wordly genius and master orator, while women in the liberal media called Palin a stupid, unsophisticated, rifle-wielding hick. Supposedly objective journalists like Chris Matthews were openly and unabashedly impressed by Obama, while others, like Charlie Gibson and Katie Couric, were openly and unabashedly disapproving of Palin.

And to help sell these messages they all united around one

common theme: the unimpeachable superiority of his values and the so-called extremism of hers.

The hyperventilating over Sarah Palin began almost immediately. Her church is strange, she speaks in tongues, she believes in witchcraft, she talks to God, she refused an abortion, she believes in creationism, she bans books, she cures homosexuals, she hunts God's creatures from helicopters. It's hard to say whether the attacks on Palin by the left-wing media were a sincere reflection of secular paranoia or just smear tactics—the answer's probably a little of both. But one thing's certain—the belief of the mainstream media that her Christianity would scare people reflected the kind of out-of-touch myopia and hatred for actual morality that effectively sealed the media's fate for good. It no longer represents you, and it can no longer be trusted. In the course of one admittedly long election cycle, the mainstream media destroyed any credibility it once had.

PENTECOSTALISM TRUMPS BLACK LIBERATION THEOLOGY IN ROCK, PAPER, SCISSORS

The constant and hysterical meme from the liberal media was that Sarah Palin's religion was "extreme." In reality, her faith is noteworthy only for its ordinariness. She was born and raised Roman Catholic until her family converted to Pentecostalism when she was a teenager. She belonged to a Pentecostal church in Alaska, the Wasilla Assembly of God, and in 2002 left to join the Wasilla Bible Church and the Juneau Christian Center.

Pentecostalism is an umbrella movement within Christianity that places special emphasis on a direct personal experience of God, but with no central church or unifying theology many Pentecostals consider themselves to be Christian, or part of a broader Christian denomination.

When asked, Palin describes herself not as Pentecostal, but as a "Bible-believing Christian." She takes her Christian faith very seriously, which is to say, she believes in God, prays fervently, regularly seeks his guidance and the spiritual guidance of her ministers, and shares her experiences with her constituents, not unlike millions of other American Christians, countless American elected officials, and even the majority of our past presidents.

To call Palin's religion "extreme" is to call the broad Christianity of the majority of Americans extreme. "Extreme" is Jonestown. "Extreme" is suicide bombers. "Extreme" is child brides. "Extreme" is Hitler's atheist eugenics. "Extreme" is, in fact, Obama's black liberation theology.

Barack Obama was raised secularly, his mother and stepfather nonpracticing Methodists and Baptists whom he describes as atheists. Obama says he discovered through his community organizing efforts with black churches that he identified with the black liberation theology of the Trinity United Church of Christ in Chicago, where he was baptized in 1988 at age twenty-seven and was an active member for twenty years.

Dr. Robert A. Morley, a theology scholar, wrote of black liberation theology ten years before Barack Obama came onto the national stage, "The goals . . . are to turn religion into sociology, Christianity into a political agenda, Jesus into a black Marxist rebel, and the gospel into violent revolution."[1]

He also writes that it "cries out for political liberation instead of spiritual salvation," "thinks more of Marx than it does of Jesus," "is more interested in black culture than in Jesus Christ," and "defines 'blackness' and 'whiteness' in the Marxist sense of class struggle."

"Black Theology believes that history is as relative as morals. Thus

---

1.   Robert A. Morley, "The Truth About Black Liberal Theology," Research and Education Foundation, 1994.

BT rewrites history to foster its own socio-political goals. This is why BT does not hesitate to teach lies and to practice academic chicanery. The 'truth' is not their concern. To manipulate young blacks into racist rage is always their real goal."

To listen to Obama's former spiritual adviser and Trinity Church pastor Reverend Jeremiah Wright—who married Barack and Michelle and baptized their two daughters—is to fortify those very claims.

In the days following the terrorist attacks on September 11, 2001, Wright told his congregation that Malcolm X was right—America's chickens were coming home to roost.

"We bombed Hiroshima, we bombed Nagasaki, and we nuked far more than the thousands in New York and the Pentagon, and we never batted an eye. And now we are indignant, because the stuff we have done overseas is now brought back into our own front yards. America's chickens are coming home to roost."[2]

In another sermon, he said: "The government still thinks a woman has no rights over her own body, and between Uncle Clarence who sexually harassed Anita Hill, and a closeted Klan court that is a throwback to the 19th century, handpicked by Daddy Bush, Ronald Reagan, Gerald Ford, between Clarence and that stacked court, they are about to undo Roe vs. Wade, just like they are about to undo affirmative action. The government lied in its founding documents and the government is still lying today. Governments lie."

In the course of that sermon, he also said that the United States government purposely infected African-Americans with syphilis and invented AIDS to kill off the black population. And in one of the most chilling and memorable excerpts from that sermon, Reverend Wright tells his congregation: "The government gives them the drugs,

---

2.   Roland Martin, "The Full Story Behind Rev. Jeremiah Wright's 9/11 Sermon," *Anderson Cooper 360*, CNN, March 21, 2008.

builds bigger prisons, passes a three-strike law and then wants us to sing 'God Bless America.' No, no, no, not God Bless America. God damn America—that's in the Bible—for killing innocent people. God damn America, for treating our citizens as less than human. God damn America, as long as she tries to act like she is God, and she is supreme. The United States government has failed the vast majority of her citizens of African descent."

In comparing Palin's broad Christianity with Obama's black liberation theology, the differences are self-evident and inarguable: Palin's faith and practices are far more representative of the country's than Barack Obama's, insofar as he told us what they were. It wasn't until the Wright sermons hit the digital airwaves that he really had to address religion in any meaningful way. And even then, he first defended the pastor, and broke ties with Wright and his church only once polling showed the country disapproved of Wright's radical views. The reality is, Barack Obama doesn't seem to hew to any particular faith exclusively. He left Trinity Church, has since flirted with its polar opposite in Rick Warren and Carey Cash's Christian evangelism, and has even embraced the teachings of Judaism when it was politically expedient. He has yet to pick a D.C. church for his family, and has said he doesn't plan to. Barack Obama's theological worldview is a confusing, muddled amalgam of pseudointellectual social movements, and it's mostly political posturing. The truth is, we have no idea what Barack Obama actually believes because it's quite likely he doesn't, either.

But to hear the liberal media tell it, Palin's faith was crazy, and Obama's was either totally incidental to his politics or helped positively shape him into a responsible, sensitive, and cultured world leader.

SPEAKING IN TONGUES, AND OTHER
THINGS PALIN NEVER DID

Much of the liberal media targeted Pentecostalism, which, according to Palin, is not her religious identification, when discussing her faith.

The *Chicago Tribune*'s Manya A. Brachear wrote, even as she admitted that "many of Palin's beliefs mirror those of evangelical Christians," that "Pentecostals occupy a distinct subset of evangelical Christianity. They believe they can be 'baptized in the Holy Spirit' just as Jesus Christ's apostles were in the New Testament's Book of Acts. Gifts of the spirit include speaking in tongues, prophecy and faith healing."[3]

The speaking-in-tongues bit was particularly intriguing to the liberal media, even though Palin never practiced that particular rite herself. Max Blumenthal wrote in the Daily Beast that Palin's one-time Assembly of God church in Wasilla emphasized "practices such as holy laughter (hysterical giggling that supposedly represents the spirit of God flowing through the bodies of believers) and drunkenness in the spirit, where worshippers emulate the experience of intoxication so melodramatically that Charles Bukowski would reel in embarrassment."[4]

Blumenthal also discussed a sermon given by a Pentecostal pastor who, he said, spoke in tongues, and Palin's "apparent belief in witchcraft."

Salon.com's Sarah Posner echoed this theme in her scathing account of "Palin's Pentecostal roots" in a piece called "Where She Was Saved." (The word "saved," used by millions of evangelical Christians to describe their acceptance of Jesus Christ as their savior, is common

---

3. Manya A. Brachear, "How Religion Guides Palin," *Chicago Tribune,* Sep. 6, 2008.
4. Max Blumenthal, "Inside Sarah's Church," Daily Beast, Sep. 5, 2008.

code by the liberal media to telegraph "crazy." Barack Obama also found Christ, but no one in the liberal press refers to his spiritual awakening as being "saved.")

Posner, like others in the media, had to admit that Palin was more evangelical than Pentecostal, but no matter—Pentecostalism was still the problem for Salon, which declared, "The church where Sarah Palin grew up and was baptized preaches some of the most extreme religious views in the nation.

"Although they share religious doctrine with other evangelicals, Pentecostals' religious experiences include such 'spirit-filled' expressions as speaking in tongues, receiving divine prophecy and revelation, casting out demons and witnessing miracles."[5]

Time magazine also ran a piece asking, rhetorically of course, "Does Sarah Palin Have a Pentecostal Problem?"[6]

And Salon's Juan Cole commented on Palin's Christian faith by setting up a joke: "What's the difference between Palin and Muslim fundamentalists? Lipstick. A theocrat is a theocrat, whether Muslim or Christian."[7]

In *Newsweek*, under the headline "An Apostle of Alaska," a consortium of nearly a dozen "reporters" seemed alarmed by the fact that Palin was religious from a young age, and even used scripture in her high school yearbook quotation (gasp!). Her faith, they claimed, also gave her the egomaniacal gumption to think she, of all people, should run for political office: "Her sense of personal mission may be rooted in her religious upbringing. She was raised in a tradition that tended to emphasize an intimate connection with God, through the Holy Spirit—a tradition that puts the believer at the center of the spiritual drama, in direct communion with the Lord. Formed

5. Sarah Posner, "Where She Was Saved," Salon.com, Sep. 11, 2008.

6. Amy Sullivan, "Does Sarah Palin Have a Pentecostal Problem?" *Time,* Oct. 9, 2008.

7. Juan Cole, "What's the Difference Between Palin and Muslim Fundamentalists?" Salon.com, Sep. 9, 2008.

in such a milieu, it is not surprising that someone like Palin would have a heightened sense of self, and of the possibilities of self, for she was taught from her earliest days that she could be directly moved by God."[8]

The *New York Times* was particularly ruthless in its portrayal of Palin as a fanatical Pentecostal. In one story, which the paper inexplicably published twice, on two different days under two different headlines, because it really, really wanted you to read it, reporters Kirk Johnson and Kim Severson worked hard to convey that she is an ultraconservative biblical literalist who—and here's the kicker—relies on the holy text to make many of life's decisions.[9] (Just to be clear, you're meant to find this scary.)

And Maureen Dowd, truly the paper's Middle American "voice of the people," wrote, respectfully: "I wandered through the Wal-Mart, which seemed almost as large as Wasilla, a town that is a soulless strip mall without sidewalks set beside a soulful mountain and lake. I stopped by Sarah's old Pentecostal church, the Wasilla Assembly of God, and perused some books: 'The Bait of Satan,' 'Deliverance from PMS,' and 'Kissed the Girls and Made them Cry: Why Women Lose When They Give In.' (Author Lisa Bevere advises: 'Run to the arms of your prince and enter your dream.')"[10]

US News & World Report also, of course, found Palin's beliefs, "which stray a bit from the mainstream," problematic.

ABC News ran an alarmist piece called "Did Sarah Palin Try to Ban Library Books?" which probed a rumor that she wanted a book on gay tolerance censored.

MSNBC picked up an AP piece expressing outrage that Palin's

8.   Multiple reporters, "Sarah Palin: An Apostle of Alaska," *Newsweek*, Sep. 6, 2008.
9.   Kirk Johnson and Kim Severson, "In Palin's Life and Politics, Goal to Follow God's Will," *New York Times*, Sep. 5, 2008, and Sep. 7, 2008.
10.   Maureen Dowd, "Barbies for War!" *New York Times*, Sep. 16, 2008.

church, unbelievably, preached against homosexuality, not unlike millions of other Christian churches across the country, even while admitting that "gay activists in Alaska said Palin has not worked actively against their interests." Nonetheless, "Sarah Palin's church is promoting a conference that promises to convert gays to heterosexuals through the power of prayer," read the lead. And here's the vast wealth of dirt MSNBC and the AP were able to scrounge up on this one: "Palin, campaigning with McCain in the Midwest on Friday, has not publicly expressed a view on the so-called 'pray away the gay' movement. Larry Kroon, senior pastor at Palin's church, was not available to discuss the matter Friday, said a church worker who declined to give her name."[11]

Now, that is some good reporting. Nevertheless, Katie Couric also felt compelled to ask Palin about it. This was the exchange:

Couric: Your church sponsored a conference that claimed to be able to convert gays into heterosexuals through prayer. Do you think that gays can be converted, Governor?

Palin: Well, you're absolutely wrong, again, on the facts. My church, I don't have a church, I'm not a member of any church. I get to visit a couple of churches in Alaska when I'm home, including one, Wasilla Bible Church, and that's the one that you're talking about.

Couric: Right. I think James Dobson's group . . . had a convention or a meeting there. And your church . . .

Palin: No, I think they . . .

Couric: . . . supported it.

Palin: The Wasilla Bible Church had a flyer that was part of a bulletin or something. . . .

---

11. Associated Press, "Palin Church Promotes Conversion of Gays," MSNBC, Sep. 5, 2008.

Couric: But you know what? That doesn't even matter. Let me just ask you the question.

Palin: Well, it matters, though, because, Katie, when the media gets it wrong, it frustrates Americans who are just trying to get the facts and be able to make up their mind on, about a person's values. So it does matter. . . .

Couric: . . . you're correcting us.

Palin: But you are talking about, I think, a value here, what my position is on homosexuality and can you pray it away 'cause I think that was the title that was listed in that bulletin. And, you know, I don't know what prayers are worthy of being prayed. And I don't know what prayers are gonna be answered or not answered. But as for homosexuality, I am not going to judge Americans and the decisions that they make in their adult personal relationships.

I have, one of my absolute best friends for the last thirty years who happens to be gay. And I love her dearly. And she is not my "gay friend." She is one of my best friends who happens to have made a choice that isn't a choice that I have made. But I am not gonna judge people. And I love America where we are more tolerant than other countries are. And are more accepting of some of these choices that sometimes people want to believe reflects solely on an individual's values or not. Homosexuality, I am not gonna judge people.[12]

Despite Couric's continued pressing of Palin on the issue, and despite Palin's repeated insistence that she doesn't know if homosexuality can be "prayed away," and doesn't judge homosexuals, Palin's churchy homophobia was a persistent story in the liberal media.

---

12.   Katie Couric interview with Sarah Palin and John McCain, CBS, Sep. 30, 2008.

SHE SAID WHAT? THE PRAYER
HEARD ROUND THE WORLD

Nothing was more troubling to the liberal media than an address Palin gave to a graduating class of students at her former church, in which she asked them to pray for the military. The "breaking" story and so-called smoking gun was literally everywhere.

This was the damning quote: "Pray for our military men and women who are striving to do what is right. Also, for this country, that our leaders, our national leaders, are sending them out on a task that is from God. That's what we have to make sure that we're praying for, that there is a plan and that that plan is God's plan."

The Huffington Post's Sam Stein and Nico Pitney led with the headline "Palin's Church May Have Shaped Controversial World-view," and wrote, "Her speech in June provides as much insight into her policy leanings as anything uncovered since she was asked to be John McCain's running mate. Speaking before the Pentecostal church, Palin painted the current war in Iraq as a messianic affair in which the United States could act out the will of the Lord." [13]

The Huffington Post went on to call her faith "politically explosive," "eyebrow-raising," and "provocative."

Palin's convocation to the graduating class was hardly controversial, of course. She was asking her congregation to pray for our soldiers overseas. Her belief that God has a "plan" for this war or anything else is in keeping with nearly every monotheistic religious worldview. Anyone who legitimately believes that God does *not* have a divine plan, and thus, that the world is a chaotic and spontaneous unraveling of events, is, frankly, either an atheist or an anarchist.

---

13. Nico Pitney and Sam Stein, "Palin's Church May Have Shaped Controversial Worldview," Huffington Post, Sep. 2, 2008.

Nor was her speech without precedent. President Franklin Roosevelt publicly invoked God on D-Day, praying that "by Thy grace, and by the righteousness of our cause, our sons will triumph."

President Lincoln also reportedly said, "Let us not pray that God is on our side in a war or any other time, but let us pray that we are on God's side."

And President Kennedy made a similar statement against the threat of communism in his inaugural address in 1961, saying to the nation, "With a good conscience our only sure reward, with history the final judge of our deeds, let us go forth to lead the land we love, asking His blessing and His help, but knowing that here on earth God's work must truly be our own."

As Glenn Beck put it on CNN, "Palin is clearly praying that we're doing the right thing in Iraq, something sensible for an introspective woman of faith concerned about the lives of our troops to do. She's not saying that she just received a text message from heaven's Black-Berry ordering her to launch missiles. Sorry to disappoint you."[14]

Nonetheless, the liberal media was outraged. NBC's Michael Levine wrote about it in an online piece that made the speech out to be some kind of major campaign flub, melodramatically writing twice in his report that the McCain campaign "had no knowledge of it." Levine interviews an unnamed "political operative," who says authoritatively, "It's pretty uncomfortable stuff. It's bad. It's really bad. It's going to be interesting to see how this plays out."[15] Well put!

Keith Olbermann and Rachel Maddow had a field day with the speech on MSNBC's *Countdown with Keith Olbermann* and *The Rachel Maddow Show* on the same night. On Olbermann's show, he says, "Perhaps the fate of the McCain/Palin campaign lies in the hands of a power much greater than America's constitutionally designated

14.   Glenn Beck, "The Sarah Palin Smear-Fest," CNN.com, Sep. 12, 2008.
15.   Michael Levine, "The Palin Church Video," NBC.com, Sep. 2, 2008.

democracy. In fact, your votes may not matter at all. Your prayers, however, that's a whole different ball of wax. In our number-one story on *Countdown,* Sarah Palin, messenger and messiah."[16]

He then asks Maddow rhetorically, "Should we be terrified?"

To that, Maddow responds in part, "What she needs to be asked about, what we need to figure out whether it's worth worrying about is whether she thinks that God is directing her public policies, whether she believes in the separation of church and state, whether she believes that she has been elected to public office in order to do the will of her religion and if God is speaking through her. Then I think there's cause to worry."

The rest of the exchange was predictably inflammatory:

Olbermann: Well, we just had one of those presidents, and it hasn't worked out so well. But this, listening to her, and this doesn't just apply to the tape we just saw, but throughout the last, the ten days of Sarah Palin, she's Elmer Gantry. She's Amy Semple McHockey Mom. Which group is larger, do you think? Do we have any idea, those who will look at those tapes, whose eyes will then roll back in their heads and in tongues they will say I like this woman or this candidate, or Americans who will then shout a three-word question, beginning with "What the—?"

Maddow: Well, we are one of the most religious countries in the world, in terms of the privately held religious beliefs of our citizens. But we're also not that psyched about extremism. Extremism of any kind, particularly religious extremism, particularly in this world. So I think having faith is seen as a nice thing to know about a person who's running for office.

---

16. Keith Olbermann and Rachel Maddow, *Countdown with Keith Olbermann,* MSNBC, Sep. 8, 2008.

Of course, there's no religious test for office, but Americans think that says something nice about your character and what kind of person you are. But if you believe that God is directing troop movements in Fallujah, I think that Americans, by and large, will react with the "what the" reaction rather than the neat-o reaction to that.

On Maddow's show later that night, the scurrilous pundit who once said conservatives would "celebrate" the anniversary of the 9/11 terrorist attacks with a "teabag party," reduced Palin's prayer to a source of mockery, as per usual: "This past June, Governor Palin, speaking at her longtime church in Wasilla, Alaska, said that the commander-in-chief for our side in the Iraq War is a mighty general whose initials are G-O-D."[17]

After playing the clip of Palin's speech—again—Maddow, intrepid journalist that she is, had simply this to say: "A task that is from God, God's plan for Iraq. Wow."

Wow indeed, Rachel. Thanks for bringing to the world's attention—and so respectfully—a total nonstory about a Christian politician who prays for our men and women in uniform. To quote you, "Wow."

BARACK OBAMA IS LIKE JESUS, BUT BETTER

Now contrast all that with the way Obama's Christianity was portrayed by the mainstream press, and the secular and liberal bias is inescapable. The liberal media—your watchdogs—really wanted Obama to win, and they'd even use God to make sure he did.

A July 2008 cover story in *Newsweek* called "What Obama Be-

---

17.   Rachel Maddow, *The Rachel Maddow Show*, MSNBC.com, Sep. 8, 2008.

lieves" set out to assure all the well-meaning voters out there that his religion was exactly the kind they wanted, wholesome and mainstream, right as rain and pure as pie. The piece reads like something out of a promotional bio for a vaunted spiritual world leader—it is meant to be moving and inspiring, and speak directly to Christian voters. It is, *Newsweek* humbly and objectively promises, "a fascinating look at the spiritual life of a man who was raised secular but chose to become a Christian."[18]

In it, Lisa Miller and Richard Wolffe don't mince words. They just love this guy.

"Obama has spoken often and eloquently about the importance of religion in public life," they decide.

"The story of Obama's religious journey is a uniquely American tale," it goes on, as if right out of a Ken Burns documentary, with an acoustic guitar, violin, and fiddle accompaniment, gently strumming a pastoral tune from the heartland. "It's one of a seeker, an intellectually curious young man trying to cobble together a religious identity out of myriad influences. Always drawn to life's Big Questions, Obama embarked on a spiritual quest in which he tried to reconcile his rational side with his yearning for transcendence. He found Christ—but that hasn't stopped him from asking questions."

This went on for an epic thirty-four hundred words—more than Chekov needed to write "The Lottery Ticket" and "A Slander," combined.

Here are some especially poignant excerpts, and translations for all the Christian voters out there, too dumb to get what *Newsweek*'s scholars are trying to say:

"Obama says his spiritual quest was driven by two main impulses. He was looking for a community that he could call home—a sense of rootedness and belonging he missed from his biracial, peripatetic

---

18.   Lisa Miller and Richard Wolffe, "What Obama Believes," *Newsweek*, July 14, 2008.

childhood. The visits to the black churches uptown helped fulfill that desire."

Translation: Obama is, like, deep and introspective.

"He became obsessed with the civil-rights movement. He'd become convinced, through his reading, of the transforming power of social activism, especially when paired with religion. This is not an uncommon revelation among the spiritually and progressively minded. . . . When Gerald Kellman recruited Obama to go to Chicago as a community organizer, he remembers, the young man was 'very much caught up in the world of ideas.' He was devouring Taylor Branch's 'Parting the Waters,' which is part history of the civil-rights movement, part biography of Martin Luther King Jr."

Translation: Obama is, like, really smart. He even reads and stuff.

"In Chicago, Obama found that organizers and activists there (and elsewhere) were employing a progressive theology to motivate faith groups to action. Using the writings of Paul Tillich and, especially, Reinhold Niebuhr—and also King, African-American and Roman Catholic liberation theologians, and Christian fathers like Saint Augustine—local religious leaders emphasized original sin and human imperfection."

Translation: Black Liberation Theology is really just like Catholicism!

"Was it a conversion in the sense that he heard Jesus speaking to him in a moment after which nothing was the same? No. 'It wasn't an epiphany,' he says. 'A bolt of lightning didn't strike me and suddenly I said, "Aha!" It was a more gradual process that traced back to those times that I had spent in New York wandering the streets or reading books, where I decided that the meaning I found in my life, the values that were most important to me, the sense of wonder that I had, the sense of tragedy that I had—all these things were captured in the Christian story.'"

Translation: Don't worry, Obama's not one of those crazy "saved" evangelicals.

"For one thing, Trinity insisted on social activism as a part of Christian life. It was also a family place. Members refer to the sections in the massive sanctuary as neighborhoods; churchgoers go to the same neighborhood each Sunday and they get to know the people who sit near them. They know when someone's sick or got a promotion at work."

Translation: Whatever you've heard about Trinity Church, it isn't true.

"Should Obama beat John McCain, he has history on his side. Presidents such as Lincoln and Jefferson were unorthodox Christians; and, according to a Pew Forum survey, 70 percent of Americans agree with the statement that 'many religions can lead to eternal life.'"

Translation: If you liked those guys, you'll just adore Barack Obama.

So it is written, so it shall be done. In the same issue, *Newsweek* also featured an interview with the presidential hopeful (*Newsweek* was sure hoping, too) called "What Barack Obama Prays For." Don't worry. Unlike Sarah Palin, he doesn't pray for the troops in Iraq and Afghanistan, so he's in the clear with the liberal media elite.

He did admit he prayed that he is "carrying out God's will, and not in a grandiose way, but simply that there is an alignment between my actions and what he would want." This, somehow, didn't raise the kind of red flags it did for Palin, or for George W. Bush before her. Only Democrats can safely carry out God's will without rebuke, it seems.

As nasty as the *New York Times* was to Sarah Palin for her "bizarre and extreme" religious views, it was just that kind to Obama. After Obama delivered a speech on race and religion, the *Times* delivered a theatrical editorial lavishing praise on the senator for what it called his "Profile in Courage."

"There are moments—increasingly rare in risk-abhorrent modern

campaigns—when politicians are called upon to bare their fundamental beliefs. In the best of these moments, the speaker does not
just salve the current political wound, but also illuminates larger,
troubling issues that the nation is wrestling with. Senator Barack
Obama, who has not faced such tests of character this year, faced
one on Tuesday. It is hard to imagine how he could have handled it
better." [19]

While Sarah Palin's prayer for the military was creepy and fanatical, in his speech, Obama managed to address religion in a way that
"raised the discussion to a higher plane."

In another piece, the *Times* congratulated Obama for his work
as a community organizer with a number of Chicago churches,
years he spent "guiding others and finding himself," according to reporter Serge Kovaleski. "It is clear that the benefit of those years to
Mr. Obama dwarfs what he accomplished." [20]

In another, the *Times* is simply overjoyed to report the super-
terrific good news that an "ex-GOP official" and Catholic you've
never heard of had endorsed him. "It made waves," the *Times* insisted,
"especially among Roman Catholics." [21]

And in yet another, Samuel G. Freedman writes about all the
nasty "untruths" conservatives were spreading about Obama's unimpeachable, wholesome brand of Christianity, which he said were, of
course, racist "echoes of a distant time." [22]

19.   Editorial, "Mr. Obama's Profile in Courage," *New York Times,* March 19, 2008.

20.   Serge Kovaleski, "Obama's Organizing Years, Guiding Others and Finding Himself," *New York Times,* July 7, 2008.

21.   Peter Steinfels, "For Ex-GOP Official, Obama is the Candidate of Catholic Values," *New York Times,* Aug. 29, 2008.

22.   Samuel G. Freedman, "In Untruths About Obama, Echoes of a Distant Time," *New York Times,* Oct. 31, 2008.

PASTOR PROBLEM? WHAT PASTOR PROBLEM?

But when word got out that Obama's longtime pastor, Reverend Wright, was himself a racist, anti-American Black Liberation Theologist, did the liberal sycophants in the mainstream media do an about-face? Hardly. The *Times*, along with the rest of the liberal media, was quick to reassure the country that it wasn't Obama's problem. And why? Because that's exactly what Obama tried to do. After Obama and the liberal media spent months trying to convince us that his unflinching dedication to Trinity Church and his beloved pastor of twenty years meant that he was just like you and me, suddenly Reverend Wright was persona non grata.

"On Tuesday, Mr. Obama drew a bright line between his religious connection with Mr. Wright, which should be none of the voters' business, and having a political connection, which would be very much their business. The distinction seems especially urgent after seven years of a president who has worked to blur the line between church and state."[23]

Sarah Palin's fleeting connection to a Pentecostal church was tantamount to a death sentence. But the church Obama sat in for twenty years, and the pastor whom Obama said he could "no more disown . . . than he could disown his white grandmother," was, for a *Times* editorial, "none of the voters' business."

Obama defended Reverend Wright for weeks. "I don't think my church is actually particularly controversial," he said at a campaign stop. He said Reverend Wright "is like an old uncle who says things I don't always agree with." And old uncles, as everyone knows, may be crazy, but they're also harmless.

NPR, for one, was more than happy to believe him. In a broadcast

---

23. Editorial, "Mr. Obama's Profile in Courage," *New York Times*, March 19, 2008.

of *All Things Considered*, the program decided that concerned voters had the story all wrong when it came to Wright.

It categorized Reverend Wright's brand of Christianity as benign, merely a "loud, passionate, physical affair," and quoted a professor who reassuringly explained that the "whole point of it is to challenge the powerful and raise questions for society to think about."

And of course, anyone who didn't understand that was racist. "If white people are surprised by the rhetoric, it's because most have never visited a black church." And Obama was "uniquely situated to bridge those two cultures because of his biracial heritage."[24]

CNN's Anderson Cooper also didn't think the story was that big a deal. "At issue now, a video of a sermon given by Barack Obama's minister at the Trinity United Church of Christ in Chicago. We're running it because—like it or not, legitimate or not—it has become an issue. All this seems to have nothing to do with actual issues that the country is facing, which these candidates should be talking about and we probably should be talking about."[25]

David Gergen repeated that sentiment, even during live coverage of Wright's speech to the National Press Club: "Every time he appears, he just gives legitimacy and a hunger by those who oppose Barack Obama to re-run those tapes, to keep him at the center of controversy, to let this overhang and define Barack Obama, when it has, you know—it has very, very little to do—it's a very marginal piece of who Barack Obama is and what he stands for. And it takes attention away—we have huge, huge problems facing this country. I think it's time for him to get off the stage and frankly, for the media, I suggest, to move on."[26]

And ABC News wanted to assure you that Trinity Church and

24. Barbara Bradley Hagerty, "Chicagoans: Reports Misrepresent Obama's Church," *All Things Considered,* NPR, March 18, 2008.

25. Anderson Cooper, *Anderson Cooper 360*, CNN, March 13, 2008.

26. David Gergen, CNN, April 28, 2008.

Reverend Wright weren't all that bad. They quoted one unnamed "congregation member" as saying, "I wouldn't call it radical. I call it being black in America." And they quoted yet another unnamed "congregation member," who said of Wright, "He has impacted the life of Barack Obama so much so that he wants to portray that feeling he got from Rev. Wright onto the country because we all need something positive."[27]

Something positive . . . right. Like saying "God damn America." Puts a smile on your face, doesn't it?

When the inevitable finally happened—Obama denounced Reverend Wright to remain a viable political candidate—the *New York Times* and other liberal outlets should have written about it with honest objectivity, explaining what actually happened: The man who was Obama's longtime spiritual confidant has turned out to be crazy, so the politically expedient thing to do was to dump him.

Instead, the *Times* wrote about the stunning move with rhetoric that was downright somber, mourning the moment as if Obama's ultraconservative parents had just forced him to break up with a longtime girlfriend whom they disapproved of but everyone else really, really liked. It reads like an obituary.

"A tightly knit relationship finally came apart—Mr. Wright had married Mr. Obama and his wife, Michelle, and baptized their children. Theirs was a long and painful falling out, marked by a degree of mutual incomprehension, friends and aides say. . . . In recent months, the candidate has tried to distance himself from Mr. Wright and his often radical views, even as he felt compelled to understand and explain his former pastor to a larger, predominantly white political world."[28]

---

27. Brian Ross and Rehab El-Buri, "Obama's Pastor: God Damn America, US to Blame for 9/11," ABC News, March 13, 2008.

28. Michael Powell and Jodi Kantor, "A Strained Wright-Obama Bond Finally Snaps," *New York Times,* May 1, 2008.

If that sounds like something you'd hear in grief therapy, the lunacy of this bizarre postmortem was totally lost on the *Times*. And on ABC's David Wright. In an April 30 broadcast, he said in pained tones: "Imagine having to publicly denounce the minister who married you, who baptized your kids, who prayed with you the day you announced your candidacy for president. . . . For Obama, whose own father abandoned him as a child, this must have been another painful break."[29]

VICTORY IS OURS! SO LET'S KEEP FIGHTING

After the election, the divided rhetoric continued. Even though Palin was back in Alaska, safely confined to the governor's mansion, or so thought the liberal media, Chris Matthews was still picking a fight. Just a week after the election, he played a clip of Palin discussing her ambitions for the next presidential race: "You know, faith is a very big part of my life and putting, putting my life in my creator's hands. This is what I always do in life. Okay, God, if there is an open door for me somewhere—this is what I always pray—I'm like, don't let me miss the open door. And if there is an open door in '12 or four years later and if it's something that's gonna be good for my family, for my state, for my nation, an opportunity for me, then I'll plow through that door."

That Palin admitted that her faith guides her life goals appalled Matthews, and he implied that Palin shouldn't answer questions about her future honestly, but should instead censor all that God-talk when she's in the public sphere.

"Is, is this commentary about theocracy and going to God for approval? We've been through that with President Bush who said he

---

29.   David Wright, ABC News, April 30, 2008.

didn't take advice from his father, he got it from another father. And we've been through this sort of Joan of Arc period. Are we gonna get another piece of this where God's leading candidates to run for president? I mean that sort of keeps us out of the conversation doesn't it? I mean, seriously, I mean God is telling her to run? And she's saying it openly on a secular television show? This isn't the religious hour."

"Talking about God in a political setting is troubling to a lot of people. If you're talking about a big tent, this looks more like the church tent, not the big tent. . . . I'm not talking about faith, I'm talking about using it politically and talking about it this way, as if that's a determinant. You know we've [*sic*], 'God is on our side,' kind of talk is very dangerous in the world because a lot of our enemies talk like that. And I think it's just a dangerous way to talk. Just a thought." [30]

Months later, in March 2009, he was once again hot and bothered by Palin's insistence on mentioning God from time to time. And he had the *Washington Post*'s Lois Romano and *Mother Jones*'s David Corn on board to collectively groan with him.

This time they were talking about another Palin comment, in which she admitted she didn't have anyone she thought she could pray with inside the McCain campaign. [31]

Romano called that "bizarre" and "judgmental," and asked "Why did she need to pray with anyone? I think she was clearly pandering to the only base she has, which is the religious right." Matthews said that because she prayed, Palin wasn't "normal."

In the same segment, the three wise sages also discussed Republican National Committee chair Michael Steele's admission that he will also listen to God's advice when it comes to the next presidential election.

To this, Romano resoundingly declared, "He's gone off the

---

30. Chris Matthews, *Hardball*, MSNBC, Nov. 11, 2008.
31. Chris Matthews, *Hardball*, MSNBC, March 26, 2009.

reservation." And Corn said ominously, "Any time someone says 'I'll do this if God wants me to,' I get suspicious."

Matthews closed the televised Mensa meeting of the minds with this provocative pearl: "Why does everything sound like the '700 Club,' with this party now? I mean, everything seems to be a religious discussion."

Clearly, the mainstream media would have us believe that Palin's minimal connection to Pentecostalism makes her scary, while Obama's significant connection—at least according to him—to the Black Liberation Theology of Jeremiah Wright must be ignored. Meanwhile, Palin's inarguable devotion and her daily commitment to putting faith into action makes her "extreme," while Obama's work as a community organizer, his "uniquely American" spiritual journey, and all the scholarly reading up he's done on religion make him devout and downright saintly. *Newsweek's* Evan Thomas once said on Matthews's program, "I mean in a way, Obama's standing above the country, above—above the world. He's sort of God."[32] The double standard would be shocking if it weren't so predictable.

The larger question, though, is why does the liberal media accept with little or no skepticism the Christianity of liberal Democrats like Barack Obama, Jesse Jackson, Al Sharpton, Hillary Clinton, John Kerry, Bill Clinton, and John Edwards, but categorically reject and dismiss the Christianity of conservative Republicans like Sarah Palin, George Bush, Mike Huckabee, Mitt Romney, Bobby Jindal, and John McCain, as fanatical and extreme? And, worse, why does it think you won't notice?

Former Speaker Newt Gingrich described to me the inconsistency in coverage of Obama and Palin as follows: "The elite media found comfort in someone who went to church for twenty years and could

---

32. Evan Thomas, "Hardball," MSNBC, June 4, 2009.

claim with a straight face that he had not heard the sermons. Senator Obama is an elite figure. His experiences at Columbia and Harvard, his style and elegance, his facile use of language, his authorship of two books, his eloquence on the stump, all marked him as a sophisticated person. Governor Palin was seen as smart but not sophisticated. She was an authentic representative of Wasilla, and Wasilla represents a frontier tradition. Senator Obama, in contrast, had taught at the University of Chicago Law School. He was, by definition, a member of the club and therefore his religious statements could be shrugged off as subsumed inside a larger acceptable ethos. Governor Palin's entire experience was alien and jarring to the elite media."[33]

In other words, the liberal media was more comfortable with Obama's values because they were couched in highbrow, intellectual verbiage, which reassured the media that however serious or unserious he was about his faith, it couldn't be that scary. He was simply too smart. Palin's faith, on the other hand, wasn't really all that extreme. It was just rural. Her Wasilla plain-speak and political outsiderness, so obviously uninformed by the elite universities of the liberal Northeast or the halls of power in Washington, contrastingly telegraphed to the media that however serious or unserious she was about her faith, it was probably scarier than even they could imagine. To them, she was simply too dumb.

But Gingrich also implied that there's something inherent in Christianity that the liberal media recoils from, because it requires an abdication of power and self-importance.

"Christianity is disturbing [to the liberal media]. Christianity is an act of faith in a larger universe and a universal God. Christianity is an act of submission and subordination. Christianity establishes explicit limits to behavior and belief. If you want a self-centered, hedonistic life or you want to change the rules to fit this year's cultural

---

33. Interview with author, Sep. 10, 2009.

whims, Christianity is profoundly challenging because it limits your ability to choose within a framework defined by God rather than defined by your immediate needs."

The great divide we witnessed in the coverage of faith during the presidential election of 2008 was informed by all of this—by an elitism inherent in the media profession, by secular paranoia and anti-Christian bias, by class warfare, by liberal ideological subjectivity within the press. But the implications go far beyond the election. How can voters ever trust the media to accurately and fairly report on politics or faith ever again, when it made it so clear that faith is merely a political weapon?

The fact is, religion is just that for the mainstream media—a weapon. It is trotted out with a straight face when it can make the media's favorite candidate seem more "of the people," and it is maniacally attacked when the media fears that the other candidate actually *is* "of the people." That Barack Obama's faith seems inauthentic isn't a problem for the media, it's a selling point! Because once again it means they are safe from judgment. Sarah Palin has fixed values—she can name them and defend them. Barack Obama has values when they're convenient. The problem for voters is that they can't trust either—the mainstream media or Obama—because both ascribe to value systems that shift whenever the political tides deem it necessary. What are you really watching when you turn on MSNBC? And who are you really voting for when you pull the lever for someone like Obama? You're watching a network that would just as soon mock and attack you if you fell out of line with their ideology of the day. And you're voting for someone who would just as soon abandon you if you became a political liability. It isn't Christians who are judging you—it's liberalism, in the media and in the halls of power.

And the liberalism of the secular press will continue to judge and mock you until your values are totally eradicated. They'll be satisfied when we finally have a presidential candidate who just comes right out and says "I believe in nothing." They'll be satisfied when Christian candidates are so scared of the badgering they will get for their beliefs that they decide not to run. They'll be satisfied when Mormonism and Pentecostalism and Evangelism have been so thoroughly bashed that a Mitt Romney and a Sarah Palin and a George Bush seem as plausible as Jesus himself getting elected president. And they'll be satisfied when you, the Christian voter, feel so alienated from the political landscape that you simply decide to stay home on Election Day. If religion-baiting by the liberal media continues to go unchecked in presidential politics, this is all going to get a whole lot worse.

Christians should take a good, hard look at the way they have been underserved and undermined by the mainstream media, the supposed watchdogs of the state. Can they really be called watchdogs when they so obviously have a dog in the race?

X

THOU SHALT NOT SPEAK HIS NAME, UNLESS TO BASH IT

The religion beat, once a staple of every major newspaper and the pride of countless local papers across the country, has been in its death throes for a few years. In 2009, the *Dallas Morning News* reassigned its religion beat writers to cover suburban schools after closing down its critically acclaimed religion section. And the year before, religion reporters at the *New York Daily News, San Diego Union-Tribune, Milwaukee Journal Sentinel, Orlando Sentinel,* and elsewhere were laid off. William Lobdell, former religion writer at the *Los Angeles Times*—yes, they had one—recalled, "When I first was put on the religion beat for the Los Angeles Times, I was the fourth full-time reporter covering faith for the newspaper. Today, there is one reporter, who in months past has often been pulled to cover other types of stories."[1]

In 2008, Michael Paulson of the *Boston Globe* took top honors in the Religion Newswriters Association's awards for religion reporting and writing. But he was the only first-place award winner from a major mainstream news publication. Other first-place prizes went to Canada's *Ottawa Citizen*, Kennewick, Washington's *Tri-City Herald*, and the *Salt Lake Tribune*.

Even the television landscape, which was never very friendly to religion reporting, has taken a hit. Back in the late 1990s Peggy Wehmeyer was hired by ABC as the first-ever network religion correspondent, and, as a woman of strong Christian faith herself, became a favorite among politicians and religious leaders. During the Clinton administration, when the president turned to two evangelical pastors for guidance during the Lewinsky scandal, only Wehmeyer was granted interviews with the two men.

When asked about the loneliness of her field, and the scrutiny that comes with it, Wehmeyer said, "It's infuriating. There are journalists who wonder if I have some secret agenda because I happen to be a person of faith. And I say, 'Do you think political reporters can't be objective covering politics because they vote?' Of course not. If anything, my faith, which demands that I be fair and honest, makes me a better reporter. What's the alternative—to have religion covered by an atheist who has no interest in God?"[2] Unfortunately, she was let go in 2001 when ABC News partnered with BeliefNet to conduct cowritten and coproduced reports on religion.

But the slow abandonment of regular religion reporting in the mainstream press hasn't happened because no one cares about religion

---

1. William Lobdell, "The Death of the Religion Beat," Williamlobdell.com, Aug. 29, 2008.
2. Skip Hollandsworth, "My Faith Makes Me a Better Reporter," *USA Today*, Dec. 4–6, 1998.

anymore, or because secularism has rendered religion un-newsworthy. The religion beat is yet another casualty of the dying print industry that has yet to come up with lasting ways to compete in the internet age, and it's a sad loss to print journalism, to the religious community, and to the country at large.

The loss of the religion beat around the country also risks sending a dangerous message to news consumers—that faith has disappeared and religious issues aren't worth covering. Of course, the zeitgeist tells just the opposite story. In a country still so polarized over domestic policies with explicit religious implications—gay marriage, abortion, abstinence education, prayer in school, stem cell research, and even the environment—religious ideology is often the stage on which those arguments are hashed out, not only by philosophers and scholars, but by political candidates, religious leaders, and their congregations.

And there are local stories that can have a huge impact on small communities around the country—the changing over of pastors, a church's help after a natural disaster, church-funded youth outreach programs, a visit by an important spiritual leader. These are stories about the heart of a community, and if no one's there to cover them, it's like a piece of the community is missing.

But it's not just that the local church bake sale will be ignored. It's also that religious arguments—within the church and mosque and synagogue and outside them—aren't being covered. Ninety-eight percent of the world believes in God, but America's newsrooms are slowly phasing him out, and American consumers will be worse off and less informed because of it. For all the insistence by the liberal press that Americans need to know more about the world beyond San Francisco and Manhattan, how much can they really know when religion—a sociological phenomenon that binds almost all cultures from every civilization together—is conspicuously absent from their morning paper? And how will American communities connect with

each other if we start pretending that none of us have a value system anymore? After all, if the media isn't covering it, it must not
be important. Community-building doesn't happen over an *American
Idol* episode or Jon Stewart's "Moment of Zen." It happens around
establishing and sharing values—deciding what's really important to
us. The religion beat covered those discussions, and in their absence,
what's left? Movie reviews, technology trends, and the police blotter.
Saving the religion beat will be an uphill battle in the high-tech information age, but it's one worth fighting.

Religion beat reporters—genuinely objective writers covering the
subject—are being replaced, at least at major publications, by opinion
writers. So covering religion (like covering politics) is becoming less
and less a fact-based endeavor, and more and more a partisan one.
This trend should prompt an honest look at the way religion is being
covered, not just in print, but online and over the airwaves. In a country full of Christians, it's possible that the death of the religion beat is
about more than just the bottom line, but party lines as well.

The religion beat was (and is, where it still exists) a surprising bastion of objectivity. Reporters like Eric Gorski of the Associated Press,
Cathy Grossman of *USA Today,* and Michael Paulson of the *Boston
Globe* write about all sorts of issues—the Catholic priest sex scandal,
women in the clergy, Catholic school enrollment rates, local church
charities, and marriage trends. They tell of news out of the Vatican,
religious controversies, interfaith squabbles, and trends in religious
practice, and they interview religious leaders from T. D. Jakes to Rick
Warren, Desmond Tutu to Ralph Reed. They don't exist explicitly for
the faithful, just as crime reporters don't exist explicitly for criminals.
They are there to cover stories, stories about religious America and
the intersection of God and country. And their presence in the paper
is a signal to readers that religion in this country matters, regardless of
on what side of the aisle—the religious aisle—you may fall.

Thanks to these shoe-leather reporters, the religion beat goes on in some places. But elsewhere, religion writers in many liberal news magazines, in left-wing newspapers, and on liberal cable news outlets are now religion columnists. There's less news, more opinion. They aren't really there to cover the religion beat—they're there to stomp all over it. For the most part, it seems as though these writers and commentators have been asked by their editors to take a side, which admittedly isn't a new or surprising phenomenon in the liberal media, but something that has turned religion columns and religion news into secular and explicitly anti-Christian propaganda, a tool to reinforce the liberal left's insistence that God is dead and Christianity is over with, and no longer relevant in the twenty-first century.

So religion stories read more like indictments of religion, as commentators hurl invective against the religious Right, conservative religious political candidates, Christian Middle America, and religious leaders with whom they disagree.

Make no mistake, these are partisan political pieces wrapped up in a religion beat bow, and it's not accidental. It's yet another way editors and producers can attack Christian America under the guise of "news," and by staffing someone on a religion column, they can maintain the cunning appearance of tolerance and fairness. It's only when you start to read and watch these columns and commentators regularly that you see just how intolerant and unfair they really are. They are there for the sole purpose of marginalizing Christianity to an underground subculture.

Readers and viewers don't need a story about religion to be covered by someone religious, or for that reporter or columnist to share their religious views. They just want their faith acknowledged with honesty and objectivity. So why are writers who so clearly loathe Christianity the ones so often chosen to cover it?

NEWSWEEK AND THE BEAT-UP-ON-RELIGION BEAT

Newsweek's Lisa Miller has a regular column called *Belief Watch* in the magazine and online, and in it she discusses myriad religious issues. In 2009 she wrote about new technological developments in phone applications for the faithful. She also wrote about two pastors and their reflections on the Columbine High School massacre. She's written about the controversy over the Mayan calendar, faith-based initiatives, and Tony Blair's religious awakening.

But far more often than not, her stories reveal an antipathy for Christianity and Christian America that is hard to reconcile with her presumed duties—to cover belief in this country and elsewhere in an honest and objective way.

Miller generally uses her column as a way to paint Christians as either fringe and bizarre or downright dangerous. And she doesn't even try to hide it. When Senator Ted Kennedy died in summer 2009, for example, she practically admitted as much: "Amid all the eulogizing, the death of Edward Moore Kennedy presents an opportunity to reflect on the peculiar nature of American Roman Catholicism and the epochal changes—in piety, in practice, in politics—that have shaken those Catholics through three generations."[3]

In her own words, the death of a prominent Catholic was a chance for a religion writer to write about the "peculiar" nature of a Christian belief system. Why wasn't it an opportunity to reflect on the ways in which Senator Kennedy implemented his faith in everyday life or in his politics, or to reflect on the way Catholic politicians have become more mainstreamed since the era when his brother had to promise the nation that, if elected president, he wouldn't be beholden to the pope?

---

3.   Lisa Miller, "The Believer: Kennedy's Faith," *Newsweek*, Aug. 27, 2009.

Interestingly, forty years after John F. Kennedy gave that famous speech in Texas, John Kerry had to prove just the opposite in 2004—that he was Catholic enough—when running for president. Wouldn't that have been an interesting "opportunity"?

Catholicism and its "peculiarities" are a favorite target of Miller's. In another piece, she talks about the pope's "PR problem," alleging that "Benedict has done little to appeal to an American flock that is in need of a serious spiritual catharsis." And why has he had a hard time "connecting," in Miller's opinion? To put it bluntly, he's ugly, he dresses badly, and he's stupid. No joke.

"It's not just his unfortunate visage that puts people off, or his predilection for the more outré aspects of papal fashion (antique chapeaux and ermine-trimmed capes). . . . It's that Benedict is a Christian believer first and an intellectual second, a man who shows little comfort on the global stage with the messiness of human life and politics."[4]

This one paragraph from this one story begs a very important question: Who is this written for? Not for Catholics, clearly, who are probably unconcerned with the pope's "unfortunate visage" or "outré" fashion. And it's not for the general Christian public either, who realize that intellectual prowess isn't the most important quality a spiritual leader should possess. So clearly, then, it's written for everyone else—non-Christians who might be more titillated by a conversation about papal fashion and the pope's ugly mug than actual faith.

Nonetheless, for these sins, these crimes against fashion, Miller decides, "Benedict is not the man for this job." But most of the nation's Catholics would beg to differ. A 2009 Marist College poll found that 76 percent of Catholics have either a favorable or very favorable impression of Pope Benedict, while 60 percent of Americans in general

---

4. Lisa Miller, "Why This Pope Doesn't Connect," *Newsweek*, April 21, 2008.

reported the same.[5] In 2008, a Georgetown poll put the number even higher, at an 80 percent approval rating among American Catholics.[6] When he visited the United States in April 2008, 60,000 people flooded into Yankee Stadium to hear him speak. Despite these facts, Miller wrote, "the truth is that among American Roman Catholics, excitement about this pope and his trip is remarkably low." Thou shalt not lie, Ms. Miller, and at the very least, Thou shalt not speculate.

Miller also comes up with a list of "Hottest Rabbis" every year ("Is Your Rabbi Hot or Not?"). Not exactly the stuff of searing intellectual scholarship. Hot Rabbis and papal fashion—maybe Miller should write for *Cosmo* instead of *Newsweek*. (The better question—is *Newsweek* just *Cosmo* without the sex tips?)

Miller may not impress religious scholars or the faithful with her hard-hitting Hot Rabbi lists, but that doesn't mean she doesn't try. In another piece, Miller writes rather indelicately about Patrick Henry College, a small Christian school of five hundred in Virginia, where many of the students are hoping to find jobs in politics when they graduate. The school's stated mission is to "prepare Christian men and women who will lead our nation and shape our culture." This is the mission of thousands of parochial schools and small Christian colleges across the nation.

But Miller is wary of writing about such a place, she says, and sanctimoniously lays out her particular dilemma in covering the "complicated" college in the first few sentences of her column: "The challenge for any responsible journalist approaching this subject, then, is twofold. She must approach with compassion, avoiding the stereotyping that so often characterizes books and articles about religious groups. This tendency among reporters to see people of strong faith

---

5. Marist College–Knights of Columbus Poll, June 2009, www.kofc.org/un/cmf/resources/Communications/documents/poll_pope_20090517.pdf.

6. Georgetown University Center for Applied Research in the Apostolate, "Sacraments Today: Belief and Practice Among US Catholics," Feb. 2008.

as freaks or oddities . . . only exacerbates misunderstandings between Red and Blue Staters and fans the flames of the culture war."[7]

She's absolutely right, of course, that journalists often do just that. And it's a real abuse of power. So to that end, she very responsibly writes, "Patrick Henry College is the kind of place that would make most coastal liberals run screaming."

Her second challenge, after trying to show compassion for these odd little Christian students, of course, is to "retain her skepticism, wrestling with the fact that what liberal intellectuals fear most about evangelical Christians is in this case partially true: The students at Patrick Henry College do want to take over the world and they do think that anyone without a personal relationship with Jesus Christ is going to hell."

Never mind that the students of Patrick Henry College do not, likely, "want to take over the world" simply because they are politically minded, any more than political science majors at Princeton or UMass want to take over the world. (And frankly, the unstated missions of some Ivy League programs are far more frightening.) The real problem here is that she essentially declares that the strong Christian beliefs of Patrick Henry College students make them scary. But for this, we are supposed to commend Miller for embarking on the thoughtful journey of a compassionate and responsible journalist?

Finally, she leaves us with a serious question. "Does Patrick Henry College actually pose a threat to American values of pluralism, equality and democracy? Certainly, its students are culture warriors in the extreme—committed to breaking down church-state separation and debunking evolution, as well as to overturning Roe and banning gay marriage."

When a religion writer characterizes Christian college students as "culture warriors" looking to destroy the constitutional boundary

7.   Lisa Miller, "Campus Crusaders," *Newsweek,* Sep. 3, 2007.

between church and state, and whose views on social issues are "extreme" when they actually represent the majority opinion, where's the intellectual honesty? Where's the objectivity? Where's the journalistic integrity? This isn't a column *about* belief, it's a column *against* belief, and *Newsweek* and Ms. Miller should say that at the outset.

But Miller's religion columns aren't just anti-Christian in the way they crassly address Christian America. They're anti-Christian in their subtle attempt to minimize their beliefs and push a secular political agenda. Whether she's covering the so-called death of Christian publishing, or excitedly commending a small strain of progressive Western Islam that allows for interfaith marriage, or declaring evangelicals are desperate, or offering a full-throated "defense of secularism," the choices she makes in what she covers and how reveal an inarguable animus for most of the country's belief system.

With few exceptions, *Newsweek*'s *Belief Watch* column and Lisa Miller exist only to serve the explicit purpose of marginalizing and mocking Christian America into irrelevance. As she wrote in paragraph one, sentence one of a 2009 column suggesting America's religious philosophy is actually more Hindu than Judeo-Christian (yes, seriously), she believes that "America is not a Christian nation."[8] We know at least one person who agrees with her. And we just happened to have elected him president.

CHRISTIANITY: THE FAITH SAN FRANCISCO AND NEW YORK FORGOT

The *San Francisco Chronicle*, which ranks twelfth in the country in circulation, has an online arm called the SFGate, where they run the

---

8.   Lisa Miller, "We Are All Hindus Now," *Newsweek*, Aug. 15, 2009.

kinds of wacky stuff that even a San Francisco newspaper can't get away with.

Among that wacky stuff is David Ian Miller's monthly *Finding My Religion* column, which, because the *Chronicle* gets most of its religion news from the wires now, serves as the publication's only regular original religion feature. And that's a shame. Though David Ian Miller is an able enough writer, the column seems to go out of its way to celebrate every belief system but Christianity, which it dares discuss only with the frequency of a lunar eclipse.

A run-through of headlines from just the past two years reads like an around-the-mystical-world travel itinerary, but a stop in Judeo-Christianville is conspicuously absent:

"Pagan teacher and author of 'Slow Time,' Waverly Fitzgerald talks about rethinking her relationship to time" (Jan. 28, 2008).

"Buddhist scholar Robert Thurman on 'Why the Dalai Lama Matters'" (June 16, 2008).

"A Bay Area woman is drawn to Sufism and whirling like a dervish" (April 21, 2008).

"LSD helped forge Alex Grey's [Tibetan Buddhist] Spiritual, Artistic and Love Loves" (March 24, 2008).

"Mac Geek Mike Lee is a committed atheist living a deeply spiritual life" (Dec. 15, 2008).

"Dattatreya Siva Baba, the YouTube Guru, predicts a new age of enlightenment starting on this month's full moon" (July 14, 2008).

"Reconciling faith, feminism, and Islam—One woman's push for change at her hometown mosque" (June 15, 2009).

"Zen Boyfriend? A new play shows how that creature can be less than heavenly" (March 9, 2009).

"Astrologer Rob Brezsny on what's in our stars—and Obama's"
   (Dec. 30, 2008).
"Coleman Barks, foremost Rumi translator, talks about the Per-
   sian mystic's timeless appeal and his own spiritual life" (Oct.
   1, 2007).
"Yoga Saved Jim Whiting's life" (July 2, 2007).

All these stories might be very interesting reads, and valuable
commentaries on a number of uncommon and minority belief systems. But when this column serves as the only regular original feature
on faith and belief for the publication, shouldn't it address the majority faith of the country more than once or twice a year?

Salon.com is another San Francisco–based liberal outlet that has
chosen to devote an inordinate number of column inches (or online
space, as it were) to bashing Christianity and God as often as it can.

Michelle Goldberg, the onetime senior writer for Salon, wrote
dozens of religion stories that offered her singular views that Christianity is destroying the country. She is the author of *Kingdom Coming:
The Rise of Christian Nationalism*, which she excerpted for Salon in
2006. The headline read like this: "Across the United States, religious
activists are organizing to establish an American theocracy. A frightening look inside the growing right-wing movement."[9] Goldberg is
also author of a book called *The Means of Reproduction: Sex, Power and
the Future of the World*. *Bitch* magazine called it "a stunning book, an
absolute must-read."[10]

Her Salon stories were predictably unkind to the country's Christians. They included a celebration of abortion and "the unlikely forces

---

9.   Michelle Goldberg, "Kingdom Coming: The Rise of Christian Nationalism," Salon.com, May
12, 2006.
10.   Anna Clark, "Michelle Goldberg on Sex, Power & The Future of the World," *Bitch*, March
25, 2009.

that helped spread global family planning,"[11] as well as one on "abortion under siege in Mississippi."

In another, called "The Holy Blitz Rolls On," she interviewed author Chris Hedges, whose book *American Fascists* argues that the Christian right is a " 'deeply anti-democratic movement' that gains force by exploiting Americans' fears."[12]

In that story Goldberg starts off with a dramatic quotation from another of Hedges's books, *War Is a Force That Gives Us Meaning:* "I have been in ambushes on desolate stretches of Central American roads, shot at in the marshes of Southern Iraq, imprisoned in the Sudan, beaten by Saudi military police, deported from Libya and Iran, captured and held for a week by Iraqi Republican Guard during the Shiite rebellion following the Gulf War, strafed by Russian Mig-21s in Bosnia, fired upon by Serb snipers, and shelled for days in Sarajevo with deafening rounds of heavy artillery that threw out thousands of deadly bits of iron fragments."

And what's the connection between Hedges's experience as a war reporter and Christianity? For Goldberg it's obvious: "Given such intimacy with horror, one might expect him to be aloof from the seemingly less urgent cultural disputes that dominate domestic American politics. Yet in the rise of America's religious Right, Hedges senses something akin to the brutal movements he's spent his life chronicling." That's right—for Hedges, and Goldberg certainly, the work of Christian conservatives is akin to that of brutal, genocidal dictatorships.

In the *New York Times,* that august bastion of highbrow reportage, former religion writer Peter Steinfels acts more like a resident taste arbiter and ivory tower intellectual than like a thoughtful analyst.

---

11. Michelle Goldberg, "How Abortion Changed the World," Salon.com, April 10, 2009.
12. Michelle Goldberg, "The Holy Blitz Rolls On," Salon.com, Jan. 8, 2007.

Indeed, he is an academic himself, a professor at Fordham University. And like some art critics I've known, who like to suggest that art is too complicated and arcane to be discussed among the dumbed-down, uneducated masses, he, too, makes sure you know he has the final say on what counts as serious debate.

When *Marie Claire* magazine published a surprising piece on faith that featured five essays by young career women struggling to carve out a space for belief, the *Beliefs* columnist, a Roman Catholic himself, decided it was his role to lecture and ridicule. That the fashion magazine dared an attempt at examining religion—something only the intellectually superior scholars of the *New York Times* and esteemed liberal think tanks are supposed to do—baffled and bemused Steinfels, who did not mince words about *Marie Claire's* audacious move.

"O.K., no one expects Marie Claire to publish Augustine," he writes, sarcastically thanking the magazine's publicist "Jillian" for sending him the story, foolishly assuming that a religion writer for the *New York Times* might be interested to see an article addressing issues of import to him and his readers. "Fashion writing has not loomed large in this column," he condescends. And for suggesting that, in tough economic times, faith might be more important and therapeutic than ever, he scolds the magazine for promoting in other pages "the $4,100 skirt or the $4,995 dress or the $1,250 clutch or the $315 diamond-dust-based body treatment at one spa or the $250 head-to-toe feng shui scrub-down and massage at another."

The *Marie Claire* piece was not rigorous scholarship—but shouldn't religion writers applaud the popular culture for leaving its retail meccas once in a while to discuss the value of faith? For the *New York Times*, religion is not, apparently, the property of the masses, but something totally removed from and high above them, something that only academics should discuss, and not actual American believers. And for Steinfels, it was apparently a turf war he wouldn't even deign to fight.[13]

In other pieces, Steinfels also takes up the role of the officious intellectual scold. He chastises the Bush administration for the president's faith-based initiatives, which only "opened a new front in the culture wars, reignited longstanding constitutional disputes about church and state, and stirred controversies about whether religion was being bent to political purposes."[14] He commends a handful of authors for promoting a "new atheism," and for arguing that "Americans are far more secular—or at least less religious—than is often recognized."[15]

And in another article, he reviews a book about Christian democracy, writing, "If you wanted a book title to speed the pulse of liberal academics, journalists and politicians, you couldn't do much better than 'The Democratic Virtues of the Christian Right.' For many people that's a title akin to 'The Winning Ways of Serial Killers.'"

Newsweek, the *San Francisco Chronicle,* the *New York Times,* and Salon.com are but a few examples of the kinds of anti-Christian venom that is spewed in the liberal media. In the case of the *Chronicle,* the attack is indirect—an attack of omission. In the case of *Newsweek,* it's fairly direct, but sneaky. The mere presence of a "belief" column seems to signal an acknowledgment of the importance of faith in America, but Miller's choices in covering Christianity make her own opinion of it less than ambiguous. Same goes for the *New York Times,* which has positioned Steinfels as some kind of religion arbiter who

13. Peter Steinfels, "For 'Modern Gals,' Religion as Off-The-Rack Therapy," *New York Times,* June 19, 2009.

14. Peter Steinfels, "Despite a Decade of Controversy, the 'Faith-Based Initiative' Endures," *New York Times,* July 31, 2009.

15. Peter Steinfels, "The New Atheism," *New York Times,* Feb. 13, 2009.

can decide what's worthy of his judicious eye and what isn't. And in the case of Salon, the attack is undeniable and overt. Salon covers Christianity, whether through anti-Christians like Michelle Goldberg or a number of other writers on their staff, only in order to denounce it.

Ignoring Christian culture altogether, or covering it only to ridicule and marginalize it, is a terrible abuse of power. The press exists to report on your life and the things that matter most to you—and instead it is announcing that you don't matter, and that your values are illegitimate. There's a difference between respectfully acknowledging the importance of Christian America and Christian issues, and promoting them, and skilled journalists would be aware of that difference. The media is not the arbiter of morality, nor should it stomp on the values that formed this nation. If that has become its new mission, it should say as much, and reclassify itself not as mainstream but as a fringe press.

SOME GOOD ADVICE TO GET BACK IN GOOD STEAD

But the real problem is that there are so few publications and television news networks that feature regular religious commentary that it's hard to prove this sort of rhetoric is more than just sporadic—because the coverage of Christianity *is* often just sporadic. It's the absence of regular religion writing that makes the Lisa Millers, David Ian Millers, Peter Steinfelses, and Michelle Goldbergs more problematic. If they were just four voices in a million, their biases would be less disturbing, because at least there would be some parity.

But there are some publications and programs that do a good job with religion reporting, and those should be acknowledged and praised, for fear that they, too, will go the way of the larger religion beat, and then we'd all be in trouble.

USA Today has the highest circulation of any newspaper in the country, reaching more than two million readers every day. Cathy Lynn Grossman covers the religion beat for the newspaper in a section called Faith and Reason, and she does a great job, delivering honest, thoughtful, and generally objective analyses of the religious issues confronting the country, from the serious (the pope's views on an ethical economy) to the lighthearted (Is Michael Jackson a celebrity "god"?). She offers up, daily, the kinds of stories that matter— both to religious America and to secular America—in a respectful voice.

And the newspaper's weekly *On Religion* column, a place where *USA Today* columnists and guest contributors can weigh in on religious issues, is also an admirable attempt to present a rigorous debate on spirituality and belief. It features controversial writers saying controversial things about God and faith, not always kind to Christianity, but does so in a balanced way, allowing contributors equal time to defend Christianity and to question it. The success of Cathy Lynn Grossman in this milieu helps to explain *USA Today*'s mass appeal, and its circulation success.

As far as television goes, the networks largely avoid stories on Christianity. They may pick up a news item here or there, and Anderson Cooper or Christiane Amanpour may do explosive features now and then on Islam or evangelicals, but there are very few regular religion reports. The one exception is Fox News' Lauren Green, who offers colorful features on religion in America. But the best television coverage of religious issues is *Religion & Ethics Newsweekly*, a PBS show hosted by veteran journalist Bob Abernethy. Week after week it explores complicated and fascinating stories here and abroad and provides a forum for meaningful discussion on a vast array of religious issues, and it has been the recipient of numerous awards for doing so.

The Media Research Center, which monitors bias in the press, suggested four ways in which the liberal media could improve its coverage of religion. They are, at the very least, a good start:

1. Hire a religion reporter.
2. Hire reporters who are religious. As national journalism organizations publicly declare diversity in the newsroom as a requirement for a balanced reflection of the communities they serve, why is that any less compelling for people of faith than other constituencies in the viewing audience?
3. When covering religion stories, use religious questions and approaches, not just secular or political ones. The media elite have taken the separation of church and state into another dimension: the separation of church and culture, or ultimately the separation of church and news.
4. If TV news wants to dabble in theology, the sample of experts interviewed ought to reflect the actual playing field in seminaries and universities, balancing conservative and progressive experts and scholars instead of relying on a preponderance of progressives.[16]

If struggling news outlets like the *New York Times, Newsweek,* MSNBC and countless other operations want to ramp up their circulations and ratings, maybe they should reconsider their decision to marginalize religion and Christianity, or in the worst cases, attack them outright. It's not pandering to regularly acknowledge and discuss Christianity and belief when doing so would service the interests of the majority of the country. No one's suggesting the media should

---

16. Tim Graham, "Religion On TV News," Media Research Center, www.mrc.org, April 6, 2004.

become publicists for Christianity, but its aversion to it isn't just hurting its bottom line—it's hurting its reputation.

That might sound good to those of us who would like to see the liberal media fail, but in the end we should all want a strong free press, and we should encourage and demand that the mainstream media get better at doing their jobs, not worse.

Conclusion

All a revolution requires is faith and a plan of action.

The mainstream media is winning. Over time it has gained your trust, and outlets like MSNBC and the *New York Times* have convinced you that they are your diligent watchdogs, your guardians of truth. And when you walk into work quoting something you heard from Chris Matthews or Katie Couric or read from Paul Krugman, you're participating in the charade.

We can learn some lessons from the not-so-distant past. Targeting conservative America stopped working for the mainstream media eventually, because conservatives—after years of ignoring it—finally got wise and decided to act. The success of Fox News, Matt Drudge, Rush Limbaugh, and other conservative voices are proof of that. So is the steady decline in viewership and readership at the far-left outlets.

But targeting Christian America *is* working. The liberal press does it both subtly and overtly, in the news and in editorials. It is a quiet murmur during an evening news broadcast and it is a loud cackle from Keith Olbermann. It's the absence of an important story, and the bold headline of another. It is smug condescension, and it is pointed hostility. And what are we doing about it? How have we allowed it to get this far?

How is it that we now live in a country where someone like Chris

Matthews feels comfortable condemning a United States governor for saying she prays for advice—something millions of Americans do every day? Or where someone like Katie Couric can imply during an interview that valuing life may be "repugnant"? Or where a beauty pageant contestant is called the c-word for defending traditional values? Or where our president thinks it's okay to cover up the Christian insignia at a Catholic university? America hasn't created this safe environment for the media. Instead, the media, so enamored of itself, has created this environment without your permission.

That's the problem with majorities. They get complacent. They feel invincible. You may see what's going on, but you think, "Our numbers are too great for anything to really hurt us." That's where you're wrong. The media may not be able to shrink your numbers, or keep you from going to church on Sunday or putting up a Christmas tree in your house. But it wants to. By attacking your values, your character, your intelligence, your motives, your class, your sophistication, and your very relevance, the media is telegraphing to the rest of the country and the rest of the world that you no longer matter. And when that happens, democracy is nothing but an afterthought. The twin tenets of democracy are freedom and equality, and the media's marginalization of the Christian majority is an effort to destroy both. Rachel Maddow doesn't want you to have the freedom to worship publicly. The *New York Times* doesn't want your voice to count equally in the battle over abortion or gay marriage, and proved it when it told only one side of those stories. The goal is suppression and submission. And it's only a matter of time before they achieve it.

So what's the plan? You may expect me to suggest that you boycott CNN or cancel your subscription to the *New York Times* or block the Huffington Post on your computer. But ignoring the problem, pretending it doesn't exist if you can't see or hear it, will only make it worse.

When I speak to conservative college students, one piece of

advice I always give them, much to their chagrin at first, is: Watch MSNBC. Read the *New York Times*. Visit Salon.com. You don't know what you're up against if you surround yourself only with opinions that reaffirm your own. And that's what we all have to do—we have to plug in to these so-called mainstream media outlets occasionally to arm ourselves, to see just how dangerous they've become. And then we need to go into our classrooms and talk to our students and teachers about the things we hear and read in the press. We need to tell our friends and our parents and our children and our pastors. We need to write pithy notes about them on Facebook and Twitter. We need to post creative, irreverent videos about them on YouTube. We need to write our elected officials and we need to write letters to the editor. We need to write books and papers and essays and theses and articles and columns. We need to make movies and music and documentaries and television shows about it.

We need to congratulate the media outlets that do a good job and promote them where we can. We need to acknowledge good reporting, and convince our neighbors that journalism isn't sound bites or colorful graphics or an easy shot at stardom. We need to remind our neighbors that journalists are supposed to be informative, not speculative. And we need to insist that our opinion journalists live up to the standards of integrity and decency that should make them role models for our children. And if the mainstream media is going to continue to characterize Christian America as fringe, then we need to characterize the mainstream media as fringe. They can have their opinions—but let's not pretend they're representative anymore. The silence surrounding the mainstream media's attack on Christianity has become deafening. And soon, it will mean the demise of Christian values altogether.

The media is very effectively using the strategy that Hollywood has used to muzzle conservatives for so long—it is making them the butt of every joke, it is painting them as hopelessly out of touch and uncool, and it is using every chance it gets to insist that they are dangerous and fanatical. Conservatives in Hollywood—and I know a bunch—have to speak in hushed tones, meet in private, hide their beliefs, and watch their backs. It won't be long before that's the norm for Christians in America, too.

Someone once said to me that there are two groups that you're allowed to make fun of now without getting in trouble: Christians and Southerners. It's true—but it doesn't have to be.

So what does this mean for non-Christians and nonbelievers like me? Plenty. If you think it doesn't matter that the mainstream media is targeting Christians, because you're not one of them, then you don't care much about American democracy.

A major selling point of American democracy is its free press, a media that is objective, fair-minded, decent, and civil, one that the state will punish, not reward, for its unchecked prejudices. When the president of the United States tries to get Fox News kicked out of the White House press pool, or when it rewards a news outlet for attacking a Christian politician's beliefs, we are no better than Castro's Cuba or Chavez's Venezuela, where the press is just a tool of the administration. And when the press attacks its own citizenry for its values, with the backing of the commander in chief, it's no better than the *Pravda* of the former Soviet Union. The press needs to remember at every step that it works *for* us, and not *against* us. It should, as those five tenets command, respect and not trample on the Judeo-Christian values that formed the basis of American democracy. It should promote the tolerance of all religions, not just minority ones. It should be fair and objective, not hostile and corrupt. It should acknowledge that Christians, by and large, do good works, and that good works should be praised, not mocked. And it should maintain standards of civility and decency, instead of crassly attacking its own readership and viewership. These should be our standards—regardless of to whom you pray or whether you pray at all.

And last, we need to hold our president accountable. He has rewarded corruption, bias, and hostility in the press by praising the work of his loyalists and trying to suppress the work of his opposition. Make no mistake, he is complicit in this war on Christianity, in his effort to water down the fundamental tenets of faith, and to prop up a lack of belief as equivalent to belief itself. They are not equivalent systems. Christianity, like every other organized religion, takes a moral position. It sets standards of moral behavior. It says certain things are right, and certain things are wrong. Christianity holds people accountable for their actions. Atheism does not do this. There's no implied morality in atheism. This doesn't mean atheists are immoral, of course, or that every Christian is a good person. As an atheist I like to think that Judeo-Christian values form the points of my moral compass. I assume for most other atheists it's the same, though they may be loath to admit it. (None of the atheists I know take issue with the Ten Commandments, as long as they're not phrased as such.)

But when the president acknowledges or celebrates American atheism, he is acknowledging and celebrating nobody and nothing. It doesn't *mean* anything to applaud atheism, because atheism isn't a creed or a value system, it's the absence of one. That's okay—but Obama's desire to equate a lack of faith with faith should be very disconcerting. And it's nudging the mainstream media along in its own push for secularism.

So go forth and do good works. But remember that the revolution is all around you—the media has become so ubiquitous and so powerful that it feels it is above reproach. And no one is guarding the guardians.

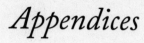
Appendices

Interviews

To better tackle these issues I enlisted the help of a wide variety of thought leaders, including Newt Gingrich, Dinesh D'Souza, Kevin Madden, Martha Zoller, James T. Harris, and Kevin Williamson. Some of their thoughts have been woven into the book. The full texts of their interviews are here.

AN INTERVIEW WITH DINESH D'SOUZA

Dinesh D'Souza is a conservative writer and public speaker who once served as the Robert and Karen Rishwain Fellow at the Hoover Institution at Stanford University. D'Souza is the author of numerous New York Times *best-selling books, including* What's So Great About America? *and* What's So Great About Christianity?

Q. **Does the mainstream media have an antipathy for Christianity? How is American coverage of American religion unique?**

If you look at America and Europe, America is fairly religious by Western standards, among countries in the industrial world. I'd put it on par with maybe Ireland and Poland. But by the standards of the world as a whole, it's actually not that religious. So while America is probably more religious than Europe, the West is far less religious than the rest of the world. And it's true that the elite classes in both Europe and America are thoroughly secular. The difference between American and Europe is, the elite classes in Europe share the views of the ordinary, common man in that sense. Both are secular. That's not the case in America. Here, the elite class and the ordinary, common man do not share those secular views, so there's a split between what the elite believe and what the average person believes.

Now, the media is accountable in an ultimate sense to the capitalist system. But it's not accountable in a direct sense. In that way it's almost like a university. These elite universities, take a Yale, for example, don't really have to prepare their students to get jobs, they're not required to do this, even if that's the unstated intention. If Yale changed its curriculum to totally ignore the need of students to get jobs, it would take a while before people stopped enrolling in Yale. Yale can do a lot of mischief before most Americans would notice. It's the same with the media. Most people don't understand just how interpretive, subjective, and selective the news business is. They don't know just how selective journalists can be. They just hear the news and think, "Well, that's what happened yesterday." There's a lot of room for editors and journalists to interpret. By putting on a straight face, the media can fool a lot of people.

Also, it's a bias that is not overt. It's not a planned bias. It would be much easier to catch if it were. The religion writer, the journalist we're talking about here, is a guy who grew up in, maybe, Austin, Texas. He went to a second-tier college, and he's working at a second-rate newspaper. He's hoping to break into the *New York Times,* and then one day take over Brian Williams's job, right? So he takes his cues from the elite media. He aspires to the kind of urban sophistication he sees among his superiors. So this secularization of the social classes establishes itself in a top-down sort of way. He wants to do things the way the *New York Times* is doing things. If that means turning his nose up at traditional religion, he'll do it.

Q. **The country is nearly 80 percent Christian. These people buy newspapers, watch the news, and listen to talk radio. Yet the mainstream media seems to make conscious choices to speak primarily to the secular few. Why is that?**

There's a major reason: selection bias. Who is the kind of person who goes into a media job? Certain jobs attract certain kinds of people. People who go into finance and business are usually bottom-line kind of people, right? Well, journalism—not a particularly lucrative field—doesn't attract the money guy. It attracts an embittered personality, who feels that the existing social order is out of sync, and he's out to right it. These are generally people who would rather tear something down than build something up. Now, this isn't how it was one hundred years ago. We're just talking about the journalists of our generation.

And second, it's a rootless life. It's not particularly conducive to stable morals and a stable family life, is it? Divorce, while something that's present in American life in general, is omnipresent in the media. This rootlessness turns them against traditional religious values and morals because it's hard to attain them without stability. Do you know any reporters who are happily married, churchgoing, normal guys with a wife and three kids at home? Probably not.

Q. **Was the coverage of Obama's faith next to Palin's faith balanced? It seems like liberal Christianity is okay but conservative Christianity is somehow fringe.**

That's a great comparison. Both Obama and Palin were very green, stepping into a big arena, and in that sense the comparison is very appropriate and accurate. The coverage of Obama was very thin. Palin was scrutinized for very small details—did her husband get a DUI, what about that state trooper, right? And with Obama, who was running for the main job, and therefore should have gotten more coverage, not less, the media ignored much bigger issues, like how did he climb up the greasy pole of Chicago politics, who gave him his start, where is he getting his money, what did he learn in school, all of that. There was a scandalous double standard in just the amount of scrutiny these two people had to endure.

As for liberal Christianity versus conservative Christianity, yes—you're absolutely right. People generally hold the belief that liberal Christianity is insincere—but for them, that's a compliment. The media likes it that these guys don't really believe all the stuff they say, and so do their constituents. On the right, though, moral character trumps your political value—if you're a believer, and you mess up, it doesn't matter how good a politician you were, how many bills you passed, or how much spending you cut. All that matters is the moral fall. On the left you can be a believer if it never informs actual morality. So liberals can say, "My faith compels me to combat global warming," and that's okay. But if they said, "My faith compels me to oppose abortion," that isn't. Liberals have to reassure other liberals—in the media especially—that they're insincere about their religious convictions, and that they're only opportunistically using religion for political purposes.

Q. Is the characterization of Christianity as cultish and fringe by the mainstream media the reflection of deep secular paranoia or is it really just another way the liberal press can paint the right as "extreme"?

Reporters want to separate the Christian Right from, shall we say, mainstream Christian America. This serves a special purpose. The media doesn't want the overwhelming body of Christians to be alert to what the media is doing. They recognize that would be a huge mistake. So they have to pick off the evangelical leaders as extreme and crazy, and hope that that trickles down. Now, the problem for us is, we've had some very problematic national figures that have been particularly vulnerable to this kind of public criticism. And scandals there have really helped the secular Left.

But what we see here is a major redefinition of the meaning of hypocrisy. Hypocrisy in the time of Jesus meant you believed one thing, but behaved contradictorily. And in that case, Jesus wouldn't have said, "Well, might as well forget about your beliefs." He would have said, "Talking about morality and being moral are not the same thing." Hypocrisy today is much different. Take Ted Haggard, the classic example. Is anyone saying Ted Haggard doesn't believe in God? Or that he doesn't believe in a certain set of morals? No, of course not. But his conduct is out of step with his ideals. He believes one thing, very seriously, but may behave differently on a Saturday night. Jesus would have called that a sinner, not a hypocrite. Sinners have moral ideals, and fall short of them. That describes nearly everyone, right? The liberal solution is to say, "Well, let's not have any ideals." Did anyone accuse Bill Clinton of being a hypocrite when he got in trouble? No, because his actions were probably right in line with his ideals. It's a one-sided battering ram that is set up just to hit those on the religious Right. Redefining hypocrisy for political purposes has been very beneficial to the Left, and very detrimental to the Right.

Q. Are Christians ultimately the new persecuted community in America?

Only if they allow it. Christians have been a little namby-pamby, a little weak, in mobilizing as a group. Not mobilizing in a political sense, but in a social and cultural sense, and standing up for

Christianity. And it's not the job of pastors to do it. In fact, it's much better when the laity does it. Christians are an easy target because they don't bite back. A professor of mine in college asked us once, "When you go to the circus, and you see a lion and a lion tamer, which is the one with the real power?" Well, obviously, the lion is dangerous, and could easily kill the lion tamer, this short, balding man in tights, with a little stick. But actually the lion tamer has the power—because the lion doesn't know that he's the more powerful one. Christians have a lot of power, but they don't know it, so instead they allow the short guys in tights to push them around.

And conservatism falls short here. Conservatism constantly services its foreign policy and economic needs, but underservices its constituents' moral needs. Look back over the past few decades, and what can you say conservatism has done for you? Well, on the economic side there's plenty—low taxes, free markets, free trade. And on the foreign policy side, too—end of the cold war, building democracy abroad, missile defense. You can't say anything near the same on the morality side. So for Christians, it's a little bit of unrequited love, a one-way street. They think, We're doing all the work, and the politicians are just taking us for granted. Someone needs to recognize that if conservatism is going to move forward. Conservatives should say, We want to keep the country safe—that's foreign policy. We want to keep the country prosperous—that's economics. And we want to keep the country decent—that's morality.

AN INTERVIEW WITH MARTHA ZOLLER

Martha Zoller is a columnist, author, and radio personality on WDUN AM 550 located in Gainesville, Georgia. Zoller makes regular appearances on CNN, Fox News, and MSNBC, and was named one of Talkers *magazine's Heavy Hundred talk shows in America in 2005, 2006, 2007, and 2009.* The Martha Zoller Show *is syndicated statewide on the Georgia News Network.*

Q. Why does the mainstream media cover Christianity with hostility so often?

It's a combination of things. First, most of the mainstream media are what Bill O'Reilly calls "secular progressives," and they are uncomfortable with faith. Look at the lyrics of mainstream songs on the radio from thirty years ago—there are many references to faith and God; look at the coverage of things like the *Challenger* disaster or earlier and you hear news media make references to the faith or even their own faith in the situation. Listen to the speeches of FDR in wartime and with Barack Obama—they are afraid of offending people because they have become Euro-elitists who look at pretty churches, cover funerals and weddings in churches but it's not a part of their lives. People like Tim Russert and Tony Snow come along and are open about their faith in their reporting and people love it, but the rest of the media doesn't know what to do with it. On the other hand, they, the vultures of the mainstream media, are waiting for a Christian to slip up so they can sneer about the hypocrisy of the faith experience. If you have moral relativism, then you never let anyone down. . . . If you have standards, you always take that chance.

Q. What influences the mainstream media? Does it take its cues from from the American public, from the secular liberal elite, or from Washington?

The halls of media are filled with people who mainly live and work in New York City and D.C., and that's not the real world. In the "flyover" country, churches and synagogues fill the gap in many ways. In "flyover" country we look at it as a plus that someone is a regular attendee of religious services. Just look at how the *New York Times* markets the Sunday edition throughout the country. They run commercials about staying home and reading the newspaper on Sunday. That's not the world I live in.

Q.   **Compare the coverage of Obama's faith during the presidential election to that of Sarah Palin.**

It was absolutely unbalanced in the coverage. The media didn't look at Obama and Jeremiah Wright as being mainstream exactly, but they didn't press him on it, they didn't ask the hard questions—like, if you sat in that church for twenty years, how did you not hear any of this stuff? I talked to a black elected county official and asked him if he'd ever seen a church like Wright's. He said yes, but he resented that it was being marketed as the mainstream in black churches. I asked him what he would do if he heard something like that. He said he would walk out and then meet with his minister the next day and get things changed.

Q.   **What's the point, for the mainstream media, in portraying Christian America as fringe and extreme?**

It's a way to marginalize conservatives. Secular progressives cannot fathom someone believing in God, putting your faith in God and bending with God's will. I wonder if Van Jones will have the kind of scrutiny that Jack Abramoff got. He's just as corrupt. But that's a random thought. . . .

Q.   **Are Christians ultimately the new persecuted community in America?**

As a Christian, I can't be persecuted, because I know where I'm going when I die, and that really bugs them. To stay in power, the liberals have to marginalize Christians, but they don't realize that this is a country built on Christian principles.

AN INTERVIEW WITH JAMES T. HARRIS

James T. Harris is the host of The National Conversation *radio talk show on Wisconsin's number-one-rated talk radio station, 620 AM-WTMJ. He is also a conservative blogger and a regular panelist on* Sunday Insight, *a current-events-driven program that appears on WTMJ's leading Milwaukee television station. He is a frequent guest on* Fox & Friends, The O'Reilly Factor, *and CNN.*

Q. Who's to blame for the way Christianity is covered by the media?

I think it's the fault of Christians. We are in a post-Church era in which what the Church has to say basically falls on deaf ears, even among believers. The Church no longer holds sway concerning the culture's mores. Look at the divorce rate among Christians, the number of Christians living together outside of marriage, and the number of babies born out of wedlock. The numbers are just as high as the rest of the population. It's the culture, stupid! Culture creeps into the Church.

So, it is entirely possible to attribute the antipathy toward Christianity to the effects of a post-Church era, including the antipathy of Christians to their own lives of faith.

Q. Is the mainstream media acting in a calculated way to reach secular America and ignore religious America? Is it responding to something in the zeitgeist?

Did the Scribes, Pharisees, and Sadducees like what Jesus was telling them? Nope. Did they follow the scriptures? Not exactly. Did they understand that the whole law is based upon God's love for us, and loving God above all things and our neighbors as ourselves? In other words, who do you know that wants to be told that they're a sinner? Who do you know that wants someone telling them that God has expectations of behavior that are higher than their own or those of society? The Scribes, Pharisees, and Sadducees were the "elite mainstream media" of their day.

Ultimately, the situation with the mainstream media in regard to Christianity is no different from what the "elite" of the world have always held about Christianity and salvation in Christ alone. They expected that they could earn God's favor and that the Messiah would be a political savior.

It is no accident that those who followed Jesus most readily were not the elite but the downtrodden and poor.

Q. Is the liberal Christianity of someone like Barack Obama acceptable, but the conservative Christianity of someone like Sarah Palin unacceptable?

Liberal "Christianity" has always been considered the "religion of the elite." It is unaccountable to God, it holds the Bible to be a work of fiction, and science is the be-all and end-all of knowledge. So, was the faith coverage provided by the mainstream media fair and balanced? No.

Q. Do you suspect the mainstream media will ever wrap its arms around religious America?

Trust me when I say that the mainstream media wants nothing to do with biblical Christianity, which confesses Christ and holds that humanity is fallen and unable to save itself. What is happening here, it seems to me, is that we "conservatives" who are Christians have allowed the mainstream media to dictate the argument and define the parameters of culture.

Again, it's the culture, stupid! How does 80 percent of the population allow the other 20 percent (and probably only 5 percent) to control the question and the agenda? If anyone can answer that dilemma, they should be able to tell me WWJD!

Q. Are Christians ultimately the new persecuted community in America?

Read the Book of Revelation. Read Matthew chapters 24 and 25. Christians will always, in the end, be persecuted. Nothing new here. Jesus points that out in numerous ways during His ministry, but a review of the Beatitudes in the Sermon on the Mount, Matthew 5:1–12, should make that pretty clear.

Which begs the question, how can 80 percent of the population be persecuted by 20 percent or less of the rest of the population? What is it about biblical Christianity that causes Christians to allow such things to happen? Part of the problem, I think, is that we Christians have allowed our theological, ethnic, and racial separations to get in the way of standing together as witnesses for Jesus Christ. It's supposed to be about Jesus, not liberation theology or social justice. It's supposed to be about . . . Jesus.

AN INTERVIEW WITH NEWT GINGRICH

Newt Gingrich served as the Speaker of the United States House of Representatives from 1995 to 1999. In 1995, Time *magazine selected him as the Person of the Year for his role in leading the Republican Revolution in*

the House, ending forty years of the Democratic Party being in the major-
ity. He is a best-selling author, speaker, and strategist, and founder of the
think tank American Solutions.

Q. Is the antipathy toward American Christianity among
the mainstream media an attempt to push secularism on
Middle America or is it something else?

In both the news media–entertainment world and the academic
world there is a substantial bias against religious belief and faith.
Some of it goes back to the anticlericalism of the French Revolution, which, as Bea Himmelfarb has written, was a fundamentally
more antireligious movement than anything happening in Britain or
America. In Britain and America the Methodist movement and the
Great Awakening made religion more important and more personal.
My book *Rediscovering God in America*, and the two movies Callista
and I have done, *Rediscovering God in America: Parts 1 & 2*, explore
religion from the colonial experience to the Civil War and illustrate
the essentially religious basis of the American experience. The modern secular antireligious movement is a European phenomenon that
has been growing in the United States and is inherently antireligious
and judgmental in a negative way about the experience of faith.

Q. Why do you think there's such a chasm between the main-
stream media's views on Christianity (that it's cultish
and extreme) and mainstream America's, which is nearly
80 percent Christian?

Mainstream media is an extension of the elitist cultural-educational
system and its values are shaped by the hierarchy of beliefs those
systems have. It is alien from and contemptuous of the mainstream
American. Sinclair Lewis's *Babbitt* and *Main Street* capture the con-

tempt of the modern American elite for the people from whom they spring and from whom they earn a living. The cynicism of H. L. Mencken is a good example of the antipopular elitism that has come to characterize both the elite media and the academic world.

Q. **Why did the mainstream media seem to have such a difficult time examining the faiths and values of Barack Obama and Sarah Palin in a balanced, honest, and respectful way? Where was the breakdown?**

The elite media found comfort in someone who went to church for twenty years and could claim with a straight face that he had not heard the sermons. Senator Obama is an elite figure. His experiences at Columbia and Harvard, his style and elegance, his facile use of language, his authorship of two books, his eloquence on the stump, all marked him as a sophisticated person. Governor Palin was seen as smart but not sophisticated. She was an authentic representative of Wasilla and Wasilla represents a frontier tradition.

Senator Obama, in contrast, had taught at the University of Chicago Law School. He was, by definition, a member of the club and therefore his religious statements could be shrugged off as subsumed inside a larger acceptable ethos. Governor Palin's entire experience was alien and jarring to the elite media.

Q. **Is Christianity really all that disturbing to the mainstream media or is it just another way for liberals in the press to marginalize conservatives and make them seem extreme?**

Christianity *is* disturbing. Christianity is an act of faith in a larger universe and a universal God. Christianity is an act of submission and subordination. Christianity establishes explicit limits to behavior and belief. If you want a self-centered, hedonistic life or you want to change the rules to fit this year's cultural whims, Christianity is profoundly challenging because it limits your ability to choose within a framework defined by God rather than defined by your immediate needs.

Q. Are Christians ultimately the new persecuted community in America?

We are now engaged in a great struggle to decide whether America remains a nation endowed by its Creator with certain inalienable rights or becomes a nation repudiating God and repudiating its own history. I am an optimist and believe the secularists will lose.

AN INTERVIEW WITH KEVIN MADDEN

Kevin Madden is senior vice president in the Public Affairs division of the Glover Park Group. Madden most recently served as national press secretary and senior communications strategist for Governor Mitt Romney's 2008 presidential campaign and helped to plan his 2007 "Faith in America" speech. Before that, he served as press secretary to House Majority Leader John Boehner (R-OH) and as communications director to House Majority Leader Tom DeLay (R-TX). He was a national spokesman for the Department of Justice and a former campaign spokesman for George W. Bush.

Q. How much of an influence do you think Washington has on the mainstream media's coverage of religion in America?

Most mainstream news organizations are headquartered in metropolitan areas like New York, Los Angeles, or Washington, D.C. I don't think you can underestimate the social conditioning that occurs in newsrooms on social issues or a topic like religion. Most journalists at these news organizations are conditioned to view issues related to faith through a big-city lens or metropolitan perspective as opposed to how everyday Americans across the country view issues related to faith.

They're also conditioned toward moderation. They expect every issue to have a middle ground, and when it comes to faith they're no different. But people of strong faith hold very calcified views. What makes them passionate about their beliefs and their faith is just how strongly held their beliefs are, whether it's a strong belief in doctrine or a passionate advocacy of the doctrine's practice. Oftentimes, people in journalism or professional politics in New York and Washington are caught up in a "live to work" lifestyle. Our jobs are our lives. But the rest of the country doesn't live like that. In many places where faith is the most important link in the community, people are not defined by their jobs or their title. Their faith is what comes first. That concept is very foreign and even puzzling to many mainstream media organizations. So what develops as a result of these two different worlds is a failure by each party to really understand and relate to the other. The media ends up with a false sense of "extremism" with how it views everyday Americans of strong faith and people of faith communities feel misunderstood and become skeptical of the media's perceived elitism.

Q. How would you characterize the coverage of Romney's faith by the mainstream press? Did he get a fair shake?

I think the coverage was defined by what I would call the "X factor" of the governor's faith, with X signifying the unknown. This was a campaign field that had many potential "firsts." At the outset, there was the potential to see the first African-American president, the first woman president, the oldest president ever elected, and, possibly, the first Mormon president. Well, every reporter knows an African-American, knows a woman, a senior citizen ... but what reporters knew about the Church of Latter Day Saints and Mormons was next to nothing. And so people generally are skeptical or wary of the unknown. They just prefer the comforts and familiarity of what they do know.

So, as a result many reporters tended to frame their introductions of Governor Romney to a wider audience mainly through this lens of his faith. Story after story included lines like "Romney, who is a Mormon, is seeking the Republican nomination," whereas every other candidate escaped similar designations or narrow definitions. Having started the campaign only known by 2 percent of the national electorate, it became challenging to break past this narrow media profile that was so heavily focused on his faith.

The perfect example of this faith-centric reporting bias was an October 8, 2007, *Newsweek* cover story that was titled "A Mormon's Journey. The Making of Mitt Romney."

Would any other candidate have gotten such a headline? A woman's journey? An African-American's journey? A Catholic's journey? Sure, there was some element of each of those traits present in reporting on the other candidates, but they were either championed by the media or just garnered mere mentions as part of a larger bio.

So if we define fairness as equal treatment and emphasis, then coverage of the governor's faith was not proportional to his full biography and the coverage other candidates received on their faith. The difference was that our campaign was not surprised by that. If anything we expected it to be an angle the press would have a certain obsession with. But that just meant we had to be very vigilant when it came to dealing with press inquiries or a hyper-focus on just that part of the governor's background.

Q. **If you're a campaign strategist, how would you advise Christian politicians to go about conveying their faith to the public without coming off, to the media, as extreme? Or can they?**

It's so important to not allow the media or your opponent to define Christian values or beliefs as being against something, as opposed to being for something. You hear it all the time from the media or liberals: antichoice, anti–gay marriage, against the separation of church and state. You literally have to stop reporters and remind them that you are in favor of traditional marriage or that you are a strong advocate for policies that welcome and protect the sanctity of life, as opposed to being "anti" something. We shouldn't allow others to define the genesis of our beliefs. Sometimes we've done it to ourselves by explaining our policy goals as efforts to "stop" liberals or "fight back," which, while surely admirable, too often negatively define our intentions. Christian politicians, or any conservative advocates for that matter, are better off when we recognize the value of persuasion when articulating our beliefs.

AN INTERVIEW WITH KEVIN WILLIAMSON

Kevin Williamson is deputy managing editor of the National Review. *He directed a journalism program at the Institute for Humane Studies at George Mason University, and served for five years as the editor of a Philadelphia newspaper.*

Q. **Is the mainstream media's assertion that secularism is on the rise in America the result of good reporting or wishful thinking?**

I think there is very much an intentional effort from the Left, of which the mainstream media is one faction, to rewrite American history with an eye toward remaking the American present, with Christianity erased from both, or at least much diminished. The media does a relatively poor job of covering faith issues, particularly Christian faith issues, for a lot of reasons, but the fundamental one is that the sort of people who tend to end up working at the *New York Times* or MSNBC are not the sort of people who tend to be much familiar with unsanitized Christianity; they certainly are not the sort of people who practice it.

That is particularly weird in the case of newspapers. Any tiny trend—the couture cupcake boom in New York City, for instance—can count on rapt coverage from the papers. I've been to probably a dozen or so meetings with newspaper executives and editors about declining readership, and they're always going on about the need to cover new trends, usually stale ones: Picture a bunch of graybeards sitting around talking about skateboarding or video games. But four in five of their potential readers profess one sort of Christianity or another—you'd think their instinct of self-preservation would kick in, but it hasn't. And that shows up, I think, in their declining readerships.

Q. Is the media really secular or is it just liberal?

The media princes aren't anti-Christian because they're cynical reporters, they're anti-Christian because they're leftists. The Left's distaste for traditional American institutions is almost lexical. They dislike business, they dislike free enterprise, they dislike our culture, they dislike the real diversity of American life, which is found in its great variety of character from town to town and from place to place. They wish to impose a certain uniformity and conformity on American life, and that means restricting the influence of religion—because religion establishes a sphere of life that is outside the state, independent of the state, and not subject to the state. You cannot impose your own moral code on the nation if there is a bigger, older, more robust competitor on the scene. Religion and tradition are the only real bulwark against the self-appointed improvers and perfecters of our humanity.

And it's not just Big Media. Smaller publications, outside the northeastern corridor, absolutely take their cues, both editorial and stylistic, from the *New York Times*, the *Washington Post*, and the like. If you don't have much experience with them, you would be absolutely shocked at how liberal small-town newspaper reporters are in places like Lubbock, Texas, or York, Pennsylvania. And the religion writers are no exception. If anything, the religion editors often are even further to the left than other journalists, because they often fall into the intellectual orbits of the bureaucrats in the church-management caste, who tend to pick up a lot of liberalism in seminary. (Compare Baylor's faculty to Baylor's students some day, or Notre Dame's, if you want to see a similar dynamic in action.)

Q. Compare the coverage of Obama's faith during the presidential campaign to that of Palin.

I have to imagine that if Sarah Palin had had a white pastor with racial attitudes analogous to the Reverend Wright's, she never would have been governor, much less a name on a presidential ticket. President Obama belonged to a church that embraces a noxious, hateful, explicitly racist theology. It's not quite as kooky as Christian Identity or the Nation of Islam, but it's on the same spectrum. A conservative politician with a white Wright absolutely would be crucified.

Beyond Governor Palin, remember that George W. Bush was characterized as a wacko fundamentalist even though he's a Methodist—the same congregation to which Hillary Rodham Clinton belongs.

Q. How was Romney's faith covered by the mainstream media? Did he get a fair shake?

The media attempted to use Romney's Mormonism against him, of course, and they did so in a sneaky way: by insinuating, without much in the way of evidence, that Republicans were hesitant about him because of the church to which he belongs. I spend a good deal of time around ultramontane Catholics and biblioplangistical Protestants, and I did not once hear a discouraging word about Romney's Mormonism. But the media will use any available cudgel against a Republican threat, even a relatively moderate one like Mitt Romney, prophet of universal health care in Massachusetts. And of course the Mormons were blamed for Proposition 8 in California, so it was especially sweet for the Left to try to use Romney's church as a wedge between him and conservatives. I have my theological beefs with Mormonism, of course, but my experience is that people with some approximation of traditional religious faith have discovered that we have much more in common with one another than we do with the militant secularists, which is why evangelicals, Catholics, religious Jews, and the last of the remaining old-line Protestants have found so many opportunities for cooperation.

Q. Is the mainstream media, in your opinion, capable of covering Christianity with any nuance?

I think conservatism and Christianity are more or less the same thing in the hive-mind of the Left. It doesn't matter what kind of conservative you are—Republican, Jeffersonian, libertarian, neocon—the Left always imagines that there's an Arthur Chillingsworth about to burst out of your Brooks Brothers vest like that creature in *Alien*. So they don't go after Christians because we tend to be conservatives or conservatives because we tend to be Christian—it's all the same to the

Left. But they do have a special hatred, I think, for unsophisticated expressions of Christianity. It gives them the pleasure of condescension and allows them to feel smug. There's not much they love more than feeling smug.

Q. Are Christians ultimately the new persecuted community in America?

Anti-Catholicism, somebody once said, is the anti-Semitism of the urbane sophisticate. With the rise of antineocon hysteria, anti-Semitism itself has made a comeback on the Left, too, but they still have a special hatred of Christians, both as individuals and for what they represent corporately.

A Decade of Lowlights from the Liberal Media: A Worst-of List

It's hard to believe that over the last decade our favorite television news personalities and esteemed print journalists actually got away with these beauties, but they did. If you have any doubt that Christians are in the left-wing media's crosshairs, just peruse this collection of quotations.

You have to teach them both. Darwinism is not some kind of a religious fervor thing. You want your children to go into the world being igno-rant? That's child abuse I think.

—Joy Behar, on *The View*, ABC, May 6, 2009,
likening creationism to child abuse.

The decline and fall of the modern religious right's notion of a Chris-tian America creates a calmer political environment and, for many be-lievers, may help open the way for a more theologically serious religious life.

—Jon Meacham, "The End of Christian America,"
Newsweek, April 4, 2009.

Why does everything sound like the "700 Club," with this party now? I mean everything seems to be a religious discussion.

—Chris Matthews, *Hardball*, MSNBC,
March 26, 2009.

The so-called "family groups" and righty Republicans are up in arms and proposing amendments (that so far have been struck down) to save abstinence funding for the 2010 budget. They're not dissuaded, and are still trying. I mean, practicing. To which I'll be giving our best advice—that they better pull it out, and pray.

—Violet Blue, "Pull Out and Pray,"
San Francisco Gate, April 9, 2009.

In a country founded in part so that religion would be a private matter for every citizen, in a country in which the government is constitutionally prohibited from endorsing any particular religious observation over any other, or even the endorsing the idea of having a religion over not having a religion, having an official, legal National Day of Prayer in America has always been a little awkward. But religious forces have long been powerful here and have long sought to yoke the power of the state to particular forms of religious expression.

—Rachel Maddow, *The Rachel Maddow Show,*
MSNBC, May 7, 2009.

Is she gonna get through the, the terrorism of the, of the anti-abortion people? I mean verbal terrorism.

—Chris Matthews, wondering whether Kathleen Sebelius
would survive confirmation hearings as Obama's
new health secretary, on *Hardball,*
MSNBC, March 2, 2009.

It's been quite a year for women. After all, a Latina has just been nominated to the Supreme Court, only the third woman in history. And I heard she graduated summa cum laude from a little school in New Jersey! Hillary Clinton was the first serious female presidential candidate and made 18 million cracks in the ultimate glass ceiling. And then of course, there's Carrie Prejean, Miss California. No one has done more to motivate gay rights activists since Anita Bryant. (Your parents know who she is.)

> —Katie Couric, commencement address to Princeton University graduates, quoted in Christopher Neefus, "Katie Couric Tells Princeton Grads to Avoid 'Nastiness,'" CNSNews.com, June 8, 2009.

Are we gonna get another piece of this where God's leading candidates to run for president? I mean that sort of keeps us out of the conversation doesn't it? I mean, seriously, I mean God is telling her to run? And she's saying it openly on a secular television show? This isn't the religious hour.

> —Chris Matthews, *Hardball*, MSNBC, Nov. 11, 2008.

She gave the worst answer in pageant history. She got booed. I think that was the first time in Miss USA ever that a contestant has been booed. She lost not because she doesn't believe in gay marriage. Miss California lost because she's a dumb bitch.

> —Perez Hilton, Perezhilton.com, April 20, 2009.

Amid cell phones ringing, video cams rolling and ice cream melting under the Florida sun, a blood-spattered Jesus stumbles through the crowd on his way to Golgotha, where nasty Roman soldiers strip him, nail him to the cross and crucify him—while perspiring tourists look on in Bermuda shorts. After the resurrection sequence, visitors applaud and line up for a photo op, not with Mickey or Minnie, but a disciple or bloody-handed yet friendly centurion. Welcome to Orlando's most unusual theme park, the Holy Land Experience.

> —Joan Branham, "The Crucifixion and Ice Cream," *Newsweek*, May 23, 2008.

The Proposition 8 team is preying on parents' fears that their children can somehow be "turned" gay if they encounter gay people or learn anything about the "homosexual lifestyle" (a phrase used by the religious right that is code for 'burn in hell').

—David Jefferson, "Will My Marriage Last?"
Newsweek, Oct. 30, 2008.

Does it constitute child abuse to lead children in the way of religion?

—Carl Strock, "It's Bibleman! But Is This Child Abuse?"
Schenectady Daily Gazette, April 13, 2008.

To see [Jeremiah Wright's] career completely destroyed by three twenty-second sound bites, all of the work he has done, his entire legacy gone down the drain, has been absolutely devastating to me—to him, sorry. We are still a racist country. I think that so many white people who had never been inside a black church were absolutely shocked by the tone and language that they heard. I think it brought out a lot of latent racism.

—*Washington Post* writer Sally Quinn,
on PBS's *Charlie Rose,* April 30, 2008.

At issue now, a video of a sermon given by Barack Obama's minister at the Trinity United Church of Christ in Chicago. We're running it because—like it or not, legitimate or not—it has become an issue. All this seems to have nothing to do with actual issues that the country is facing, which these candidates should be talking about and we probably should be talking about.

—CNN's Anderson Cooper, on *Anderson Cooper 360,*
CNN, March 13, 2008.

I'd like to tip off law enforcement to an even larger child-abusing religious cult. Its leader also has a compound, and this guy not only operates outside the bounds of the law, but he used to be a Nazi and he wears funny hats. That's right, the pope is coming to America. If you have a few hundred followers, and you let some of them molest children, they call you a cult leader. If you have a billion, they call you "pope." It's like, if you can't pay your mortgage, you're a deadbeat. But if you can't pay a million mortgages, you're Bear Stearns and we bail you out. And that is who the Catholic Church is: the Bear Stearns of organized pedophilia. The Church's attitude: "We're here, we're queer, get used to it," which is fine. Far be it for me to criticize religion.

—Bill Maher, *Real Time with Bill Maher,* HBO, April 11, 2008.

Perhaps the fate of the McCain/Palin campaign lies in the hands of a power much greater than America's constitutionally designated democracy. In fact, your votes may not matter at all. Your prayers, however, that's a whole different ball of wax. In our number-one story on the Countdown, Sarah Palin, messenger and messiah.

—Keith Olbermann and Rachel Maddow, *Countdown with Keith Olbermann,* MSNBC, Sep. 8, 2008.

[Sarah Palin] brings the children up when she needs them to shore up her own image and yet she isn't doing—I mean this is a woman who is a committed Christian, family values is everything. For her faith, often people believe women shouldn't even be working outside of the home. So my feeling is that if she were—put her money where her mouth is, that she would say, "Look, I'm resigning because I want to spend more time with my family."

—*Washington Post On Faith* writer Sally Quinn, on CBS *Early Show,* Sep. 3, 2008.

When doctors pronounced the Rev. Jerry Laymon Falwell Sr. dead at 12:40 P.M. EST Tuesday . . . my first thoughts were not of what to say or write. In fact, my very first thought upon hearing of the Rev. Falwell's passing was: Good. And I didn't mean "good" in a oh-good-

he's-gone-home-to-be-with-the-Lord kind of way. I meant "good" as in
"Ding-dong, the witch is dead."

—Cathleen Falsani, "Sigh of Relief Over Falwell Death,"
Chicago Sun-Times, May 18, 2007.

Well, I thought her answer—not the answer at the pageant, but later,
when she said, "Satan was trying to tempt me with that," I think that
says a lot about our country because, you know, here's a person who be-
lieves in Satan, as does, I would guess, 60, 70, 80 percent of this county.
This dumb, dumb, country believes in demons and some creature with
horns and a tail and a pitchfork who's going to make you burn in a
mythical place if you don't believe in an imaginary friend. That's really
the root problem of it, isn't it?

—Bill Maher on CNN, *Reliable Sources,* May 24, 2009.

The GOP campaigns as the party of family values and Senator Craig's
bathroom bust underscores the hypocrisy. There is former Republican
congressman Mark Foley, who built his social life on male pages; con-
servative pastor Ted Haggard, who had trysts with a male prostitute,
Republican senator David Vitter, who campaigned as a family man but
later acknowledged encounters with a woman who police described as a
prostitute. It all adds moral insult to the injuries being suffered today by
the victims of Hurricane Katrina.

—David Shuster on MSNBC's *Hardball,* Aug. 29, 2007.

Do you worry at all that nonbelievers may feel excluded and diminished
at a time when we're so divided about so much?

—Katie Couric to *The Nativity Story* creators Catherine
Hardwicke and Mike Rich on CBS *Evening News,* Dec. 4, 2006.

This word, "values," "values voters," which is just driving me nuts. This
idea that somehow certain people have a monopoly on values, and that,

you know, if you are not with them on these issues, that you somehow [mock tone of horror] "don't share our values," and you're not just wrong, but you're somehow morally inferior if you're on the other side. And I hope that this election is going to mark the demise of the "values voters," this idea that somehow people who feel so strongly about, you know, these so-called traditional values, that they don't determine the election the way they were seen to have the last time around, and the indications are that they do have less clout this time out.

—*Newsweek* senior editor Jonathan Alter on
MSNBC's *Imus in the Morning*, Oct. 16, 2006.

From Bob Livingston to Newt Gingrich, the hypocrisy of sanctimonious, Bible-thumping, family-values-espousing GOP politicians who get caught with their pants down has become a national joke. Until Republicans abandon their judgmental moralism about all things sexual, their marital peccadilloes will inspire schadenfreude, not sympathy.

—Gary Kamiya, "The Strange Nakedness of
Mark Sanford," Salon.com, June 25, 2009.

Some of the values, depending on your perspective, may be deemed wholesome, but in other ways, I think, people will see this community as eschewing diversity and promoting intolerance. Do you think the tenets of the community might result in de facto segregation as a result of some of the beliefs that are being espoused by the majority of the residents there? You can understand how people would hear some of these things and be like, wow, this is really infringing on civil liberties and freedom of speech and right to privacy and all sorts of basic tenets that this country was founded on. Right?

—NBC's Katie Couric questioning Tom Monaghan and
Paul Marinelli's vision of a Christian community,
on *Today*, NBC, March 3, 2006.

You signed a $13 million book deal, which I understand is bigger than Bill Clinton, Alan Greenspan, and Pope John Paul II, so how do you square your wealth with the tenets of Christianity?

—NBC's Katie Couric to minister Joel Osteen, on *Today*, NBC, May 9, 2006.

Wait just one second. Radical Christianity is just as threatening as radical Islam in a country like America where we have a separation of church and state. We're a democracy.

—Rosie O'Donnell on *The View*, ABC, Sep. 12, 2006.

I wandered through the Wal-Mart, which seemed almost as large as Wasilla, a town that is a soulless strip mall without sidewalks set beside a soulful mountain and lake. I stopped by Sarah's old Pentecostal church, the Wasilla Assembly of God, and perused some books: "The Bait of Satan," "Deliverance from PMS," and "Kissed the Girls and Made Them Cry: Why Women Lose When They Give In." (Author Lisa Bevere advises: "Run to the arms of your prince and enter your dream.")

—Maureen Dowd, "Barbies for War!" *New York Times*, Sep. 16, 2008.

There's a definite sense this morning on the part of the Kerry voters that perhaps this is code, "moral values," is code for something else. It's code for taking a different position about gays in America, an exclusionary position, a code about abortion, code about imposing Christianity over other faiths.

—Diane Sawyer on ABC's *Good Morning America*, Nov. 4, 2004.

I really hope the Catholic Church gets sued until the end of time. Maybe, you know, we can melt down some of the gold toilets in the pope's Vatican and pay off some of the lawsuits because, you know, frankly, the whole tenet of Christianity, of being pious, of living a Christ-like life, has been lost in Catholicism.

—Rosie O'Donnell on MSNBC's *Donahue,* Feb. 24, 2003.

I've always thought the theological, the one theological question I'd like to ask [Pope John Paul II], and it's a serious question, is "What do you think Jesus would think of the way you dress?"

—Diane Sawyer on *Oprah,* Feb. 19, 1997.

It's not just his unfortunate visage that puts people off, or his predilection for the more outré aspects of papal fashion (antique chapeaux and ermine-trimmed capes). . . . It's that Benedict is a Christian believer first and an intellectual second, a man who shows little comfort on the global stage with the messiness of human life and politics.

—Lisa Miller, "Why This Pope Doesn't Connect,"
Newsweek, April 21, 2008.

Does Patrick Henry College actually pose a threat to American values of pluralism, equality and democracy? Certainly, its students are culture warriors in the extreme—committed to breaking down church-state separation and debunking evolution, as well as to overturning Roe and banning gay marriage.

—Lisa Miller, "Campus Crusaders," *Newsweek,* Sep. 3, 2007.